DEFENCE SERVICES

DEFENCE SERVICES

Financial Analysis & Resource Mobilisation

By

SANHITA S. ATHAWALE

ANMOL PUBLICATIONS PVT. LTD.

NEW DELHI - 110 002 (INDIA)

ANMOL PUBLICATIONS PVT. LTD.
4374/4B, Ansari Road, Daryaganj
New Delhi - 110 002
Ph.: 23261597, 23278000
Visit us at: www.anmolpublications.com

Defence Services

First Published, 2004

ISBN 81-261-1773-7

PRINTED IN INDIA

Published by J.L. Kumar for Anmol Publications Pvt. Ltd., New Delhi - 110 002 and Printed at Mehra Offset Press, Delhi.

I Dedicate this Book to my
beloved and dearest Son

Sushrut

Contents

Acknowledgements

I take this opportunity to acknowledge my gratefulness to numerous persons who have rendered valuable guidance and cooperation to me.

First of all, I owe a debt of gratitude to my mentor, Dr. Santosh R. Dastane, University of Pune for encouraging me to work on this topic. This work would not have been possible without his valuable guidance and consistent cooperation and support.

Secondly, I must express my deep sense of gratitude to my mother-in-law, late Prin. Susheela Athawale for her inspiration and valuable suggestions on this topic which were always enjoyable and fruitful.

I am profoundly grateful to Dr. R.S. Deshpande and Dr. S.B. Paranjpe for their cooperation, scholarly and expert guidance and constant encouragement. In spite of their busy schedule they had ample time for discussions with me which brought clarity and preciseness in my research work.

I gratefully acknowledge my thanks to Dr. B.S.R. Rao, Dr. Bhagwan Joshi, Dr. A.M. Deshpande for their co-operation. My thanks are also due to the staff of Gokhale Institute of Politics and Economics Library (Pune), Southern Command Library (Pune), Jayakar Grantthalaya (Pune), IDSA Library (New Delhi) for the kind and quick services rendered to me.

I would like to thank my husband Suhas for helping me in a number of ways and giving me constant encouragement to complete this work. My special thanks to all my family members, my parents, Karkhanis Kaka and Kaku for their moral support.

I would further like to thank management body and staff members at T.J. College, Pune for their cooperation. I am thankful to my friends and all others for their kind co-operation while working on the present study. A special word of gratitude to Mr. Ketan Hirve and Mrs. Rhuta Hirve for their neat and timely typing of the scripts.

Last but not the least, I owe a deep sense of gratitude to M/s Anmol Publications Pvt. Ltd., New Delhi for undertaking the publication of this book.

SANHITA ATHAWALE

CHAPTER 1
Introduction

Defence expenditure constitutes an important part of Government expenditure and needs detailed economic analysis. There are not many studies analysing defence expenditure in India from the economic point of view. The economic issues have gained relative supremacy over all the other issues in the recent past, especially after the end of the cold war era. Therefore, the economic analysis, pattern of allocation of expenditure and determinants of defence budget assume greater importance. This is especially true in the case of developing countries, which have to manage development alongwith stability.

In the present study, an attempt is made to analyse some of the important issues related to defence expenditure through an empirical economic analysis.

In this study, the need for redefinition of defence expenditure has been stressed and attempt has been made to incorporate dual purpose technology areas, paramilitary, internal security, and other related supportive expenditures on defence for a more realistic analysis. While doing this, care is taken to account for methodological discrepancies, data constraints and the limitations of statistical techniques.

Framework for Analysis and Hypotheses

Traditional analysis of defence expenditure has tended to focus almost exclusively on the defence budgets. The United Nations Organisation (UNO) in 1975, tried to give an all pervasive definition of defence expenditure.

This study uses a definition of defence expenditure which includes all operational costs of the three defence wings, all supportive defence expenditure costs, dual purpose technology expenditures, research and development expenditures, paramilitary expenditure and other types of internal security expenditure etc. On similar lines, North Atlantic Treaty Organisation (NATO), International Monetory Fund (IMF) and Stockholm International Peace and Research Institute (SIPRI) have also defined defence expenditure. This broad definition of defence expenditure marks the starting point of this study and we propose to attempt analysis of these areas.

Any study of India's defence expenditure has to include the expenditure incurred on defence budget proper, nuclear, space, electronics, science and technology, ocean development expenditure, paramilitary expenditures, internal security expenditure etc. Our study attempts to test the following hypotheses:

1. In the 1980s, there is a shift in the threat perceptions in India. The threat perceptions are focused more on internal security rather than border wars and external security problems. So correspondingly internal security expenditure i.e. paramilitary and police has as a response to this necessarily increased.
2. The changes in the threat perceptions have also brought about changes in the approaches or strategies to tackle them. Therefore, increased attention is given to the development of dual purpose technology which include areas like nuclear, space, electronics etc., along-with defence modernisation programme for the conventional weapon systems in 1980s.
3. The global changes and economic crisis in the early 1990s, made it necessary for India to resort to economic liberalisation. This called for parallel changes in the defence sector for sustaining modernisation.

Focus of the Study

In this study the defence expenditure for the period 1970-71 to 1994-95 (i.e. 25 years of post-Bangladesh war period) has been analysed. The focus of this study is on 1980s and 1990s. These post war years were crucial for India for several reasons.

In the 1971 war India established its military supremacy in South Asia and it marks watershed in Indian history. From 1970-71 to 1994-95 India enjoyed a comparatively longest peaceful period since independence. In this period, India did not fight any actual war or external aggression. This period is very crucial in the sense that, defence expenditure effort increased not because of any war or external aggression, but due to internal security threats and low intensity conflicts supported by the adversaries. In addition to this, India required adequate defence buildup to project itself as a regional power in the Indian subcontinent.

This period is also marked by the increasing internal security threats and challenges. It is mainly in this period, Indian planners realised that defence and development are not competitive but complementary to each other and India tried to enhance its economic capability. The volatile changes in the international scene and in the world order are also marked in this period. Therefore, an attempt is made to focus this period through this study.

Methodology and Sources of Data

For defence expenditure and other supportive expenditure (dual purpose technology areas) analyses a large number of primary sources pertaining to a number of years have been explored. These include the Union Budget, Demand for Grants of various Ministries and Departments, India Appropriation Accounts: Report of the Comptroller and Auditor General of India, Annual Plans, Five Year Plans of Government of India, India—Annual Year Book of Ministry of Information and Broadcasting etc. The Defence Service Estimates, Annual Reports of Ministry of Defence, Home Affairs, External Affairs, Department of Atomic Energy, Department of Space, Department of Electronics, Department of Science and Technology, Department of Ocean Development etc.

Similarly, Economic Survey, National Income Accounts of India, Reports of Central Statistical Organisation, Statistical Abstract of India, Estimates Committee Reports to Lok Sabha, Public Accounts Committee Reports, Report on Currency and Finance by the Reserve Bank of India etc. pertaining to a number of years have also been referred.

Along with this, Centre for Monitoring Indian Economy (CMIE), Report on Public Finance, June 1996 and India Data Base (A publication of Living Media Publications, New Delhi) have also been referred.

The present study follows the historical-analytical method. The availability of original sources in the form of government documents and statistical data made it possible for us to employ this approach. The theoretical and conceptual data has also been analysed. The numerical data are used for statistical analysis. Various statistical methods including the regression analysis have been used for this purpose.

Conceptual Clarifications about the Data

1. The data about the defence expenditure of India and other defence related items have been collected from Defence Service Estimates of Government of India, Ministry of Defence.
2. The Military Balance and SIPRI Year Book for various years and Institute of Defence and Strategic Analysis (IDSA) New Delhi Publications have been used for collecting comparative statistical data of Defence Expenditure for China, Pakistan, Bangladesh, etc.
3. The data about Gross Domestic Product, other Macro economic indicators, Wholesale Price Index, have been collected from the Economic Survey of India and Reserve Bank of India's Currency and Finance Report for various years.

4. The Data about Police, Nuclear, Space, Electronics, Science and Technology, Ocean Development have been collected from India: Union Budget, Demand for Grants, Comptroller and Auditor General of India Appropriation Account Reports. Economic Survey (1970-1995), Annual Reports of these Ministries/ Departments/Five Year Plans, Annual Plans and various reports of Planning Commission etc.
5. "The Public Finance—India's Central and State Government Expenditure"—A Report of Centre for Monitoring Indian Economy (CMIE) June 1996, India Data Base—Vol. II, India—Annual Reference year Book 1975-1995 (Published by Information and Broadcasting Ministry, Government of India), Data India, National Income Accounting and various publications of Central Statistical Organisation of India, Statistical Abstract of India, Planning Commission Documents have been referred for collection of total government expenditure, total Developmental and Non-Developmental Expenditure, total Central Government Expenditure etc.
6. The actual total expenditure at current prices of these above various Ministries/Departments are Gross Expenditures on it and the recoveries and receipts are not adjusted.
7. The break up of expenditure of each Ministry/ Department is also given. In this break up only important programmes or items are taken into consideration. The expenditure shown in the break ups are Revised Estimates only and they are not actual expenditures. Therefore, it may be noted that the total of item/Programme-wise expenditures do not tally with total actual expenditure of each Ministry or Department. Since the break up of detailed actual expenditure was not available for some years we have taken Revised Estimates which are near approximations of actual expenditures. The details of

actual itemwise expenditure were also difficult to be available for some years due to changes in the structure of demand for grants, presentation of these demands and budget papers, linking or delinking of some of the projects to other Ministries/Departments etc. Hence to avoid inconsistency Revised Estimates are taken into consideration which are almost near (approximate addition or reduction upto 20 per cent) to actual expenditure and it represents the trend and direction of expenditure almost in the similar lines as actual expenditure.

8. For analysis of Defence Expenditure macro indicator of Gross Domestic Product has been deployed. Defence Expenditure has element of foreign trade and Defence Expenditure as per cent of Gross Domestic Product can reflect the share in the economy. It also helps in comparisons of Defence Expenditure with other countries like Pakistan, China etc.
9. Defence Expenditure as per cent of Central Government Expenditure for comparative study of Defence Expenditure of India and Pakistan has also been used. It is not a complete indicator because it neglects state Governments, and local Governments' spending but it can be used for comparisons. In order to get a clear picture of the defence expenditure, burden, the percentage share of the defence expenditure to total gross expenditure has been presented.
10. Methodology used for Interpretation of Data—The tables have been constructed for total expenditure on Defence, Police, Nuclear, Space, Electronics, Science and Technology, Ocean Development (OD) in current and constant prices (1980-81 base). For deflating defence and other expenditures we used Wholesale Price Index with base year 1980-81. This was constructed through the Economic Survey of various years. We have chosen 1980-81 as the base year

because it falls roughly near the middle of our data period under consideration (i.e. 1970-71 to 1994-95) and more importantly just before the speedy inflation growth in the later period.

The Net Defence Expenditure is shown as total Defence Expenditure and it is sum of Net Revenue Defence Expenditure and Net Capital Defence Expenditure. The Net Revenue Defence Expenditure is divided into allocations for Army, Navy, Air Force and Ordnance Factories. Coming to the capital Defence Expenditure account it is divided on Army-Capital, Navy-Capital, Air Force-Capital, Ordnance Factories-capital, Research and Development organisation and Inspection Organisation Capital (In the recent years, Research and Development Organisation and Inspection Organisation's Capital expenditure is given separately).

The Table (27) gives the distribution of defence expenditure into Net Revenue and Net Capital expenditure and indicates what per cent of defence expenditure is accruing towards the revenue account and capital account. The Table (29) gives per cent distribution Net Revenue Expenditure for Army, Navy and Air Force. The Table (30) gives per cent distribution of Capital Expenditure for Army, Navy and Air Force. Here it may be noted that figures for three services reflect Gross Capital Expenditure while Table (27) gives Net Capital Expenditure. Therefore percentages of totals may not add up or tally at certain places.

11. In some tables figures don't tally because in defence expenditure as per convention many expenditure items remain unclassified. The expenditure on operations like—Indian Peace Keeping Force (IPKF) in Sri Lanka etc. are not clearly reflected in the defence budgets of those years.

12. Sometimes totals/percentages don't tally also on account of changes in the basic definitions, budgeting methods, accounting methods in Defence Service Estimates e.g. Ordnance Factories allocations were part of Army allocations till 1st April 1987, then a separate demand for grants for Ordnance Factory was created hence there are some inconsistencies. It is also found that Defence Service Estimates do not clearly mention changes in the basic definitions of items of expenditures.

CHAPTER 2

Review of Literature

Introduction

This chapter presents review of literature. Enlisted here are various issues in resource allocation for defence in India. It also takes into account works done on redefinition of defence expenditure which includes redefinition done by United Nations Organisations. On the basis of these works an attempt is made to redefine India's defence expenditure and therefore, it forms the basis of the central argument in the thesis. This review is by no means exhaustive one but it certainly discusses a few important issues related to defence expenditure.

Review of Literature

Security is one of the prime concerns of a nation state. 'Protection of a nation from external threats and attack' was the traditional definition of national security. The first definition of national security as given by Walter Lipmann took into account only military dimension.[1] But it is essential to widen the scope in the changing political situations. Hence one needs a broader definition of national security today and it should contain economic, political, diplomatic and social dimension in addition to the military dimension.[2]

Kaplan Morton (1957), Arnold Wolfers (1962), Richard Synder H.C. Bruck and Burtons (1962), Garnett John (1970), Frank Traeger and Frank Simonie (1973), K. Subramanyam (1973), A.P. Rana (1976), Jayantanija Bandyopadhyaya (1980), Ravi Nanda (1987), P.V. Kamath (1990) supported this new approach to National security in their studies. Therefore out of the various dimensions military dimension is the most important and as a corollary military expenditure becomes an essential and inevitable part of the Government expenditure.

The subject of defence expenditure is not widely analysd by the academic community in India. This might be due to the feeling that defence is a secret or sensitive subject and data and its confidentiality. There are not many studies related to defence expenditure in India. The Government of India gives substantial information about defence expenditure through budget, reports and other publications to the parliament and public. But, these have not generated similar quantum of analyses.

Defence expenditure is considered as an inevitable expenditure for the survival of a nation-state in the world as well as it is necessary to protect the development of a nation from various kinds of threats. As any nation does not have unlimited resources at hand and it has to allocate resources for defence, the major issues in resource allocation for defence must be taken into account. The important issues in resource allocation for defence in India can be broadly listed as:

A. Are there economic theories related to defence expenditure? And if yes, according to these what are the determinants of defence budget?
B. Is India responding to changes in external and internal security environment and matching its defence expenditure with it?
C. Whether defence policy is consistent over the dynamic situation and rational as regards to inter sectorial policy perspective in India?
D. Has the increase in defence expenditure of India, followed any phases? What constitutes such changing situations and the distribution of defence expenditure among services? Has India achieved self-sufficiency in defence production?

E. What are the effects on defence expenditure on economy—in general and in India in particular? Which are the measures for optimum utilisation of it?

F. What is the role of dual purpose technology areas—impact of nuclear space and other potential capacities on defence capability and defence expenditure in India?

G. Is there a need for widening defence expenditure definition and whether dual purpose technology areas need to be added in Indian defence expenditure?

The present review is by no means an exhaustive one but the literature related to defence expenditure can be divided on the basis of the above issues as follows:

Economic Theories of Defence Expenditure

There are various studies which tried to give strong linkage between economic power and military power. Among these studies economic power is considered as major determinant of military power and military capability of a nation rest on the infrastructure of economic strength. This view is supported by Lincoln George, Stone William and Harway Thomas (1950), Knorr Klaus (1956), Schlessinger James (1960), Hitch Charles and Mackean Ronald (1960), Clark J.J. (1966), Mackean Ronald (1967), Subrahmanyam K. (1973), Thomas Raju G.C. (1978), Brown Herald (1983), Saadet Deger & Robert West (1987), Ball Nicole (1988), Hartley K. & T. Sandler (1999) etc. in their work.

Knorr Klaus has added a few more elements to economic power in order to determine military power of the nations. According to him morale of the people, administrative capacity or management of resources and economic capacity together determine the military power of any nation.[3]

James Schlessinger has also related the problems of defence buildup with economic capabilities. He argues that it is the economic capability of a nation that limits the defence expenditure and that economic capability is a necessary but not a sufficient condition for military capability and suggests harmony in nation's resources with political and military objectives.[4]

'Defence' is treated as an economic problem and inevitable in the nuclear age by Hitch C. and Macken R., Clark J.J. They argue that the limited resources available for defence could be used wisely if economic analysis is used. They recommend the use of programme budgeting, cost and benefit analysis, micro economic analysis can help in better defence planning.[5]

Olvey L, Golden J. and Kelly Robert through their study in (1989) go further to advocate positive use of economics for determining defence and non-defence resource allocation.[6]

Brown Herald (1983) undertook the case study of relationship of economic policies and national security policies in USA for 1970s and analysed how military strength is used for gaining economic advantages.[7]

The subject of economics of defence has been an interesting area since the day of Adam Smith. Adam Smith justified the expenses of defence as a first duty of the government and legitimised the revenue raising methods.[8]

Kennedy Gavin (1975) takes the review of contribution of various economists towards the area of economics of defence. Ricardo, J.S. Mill, Jean Baptise, Malthus, Keynes etc. have contributed in this area. Most of the economists agreed that defence expenditure is an essential expenditure and warned that it should not be very high and provocative because it will affect the ultimate goal of security i.e. peace.[9]

David K. Whyness concluded that ruling elites of less developed countries continue to allocate heavy defence expenditure in order to maintain their political control, to repress internal threats and to acquire regional hegemony inspite of limited economic capability.'[10]

Gavin Kennedy (1979), Ball Nicole (1981), Saadet Deger and Smith (1983) substantiated this conclusion. Kenyes J.M. was of the view that any type of public expenditure including defence expenditure can play demand expanding role in an economy and may contributed to economic growth.[11]

Various issues of economics of defence in the Third World countries (Less Developed Countries—LCD) and their linkages with other systems have remained an interesting area for many academicians all over the world. The notable studies amongst them include Emilie Benoit (1973), K. Subramanyam (1973), Gavin Kennedy (1975), David K. Whyness (1979), Ball Nocile (1981), Robert Looney (1983), Saadet Deger and Smith (1983), Thomas Raju G.C. (1986), Saadet Deger and West Robert (1987), Schmidt C. and Blackbay Frank (1987), Hartley Kith (1991) etc.

For Less Developed Countries (LDCs) specific case studies are also undertaken. For India, K. Subramanyam in his case study of Defence and Development analyses issues related to economics of defence in India. In this he suggested that rapid economic growth rate with social justice can ensure long term security to India.[12]

The effects of defence expenditure on economic growth are analysed by various scholars and their review is taken separately in the later pages.

The concept of 'Public good' is used to analyse and understand the nature of defence expenditure. Adam Smith dealt with the issues related to defence and public economics in his seminal work *Wealth of Nations.*[13]

He gave early statement of public good nature of defence expenditure in which he states that defence was for *common good* and on this basis it was reasonable that the expense of defence should be met by the whole society.[14]

He had given the defence, justice, public work and education as major duties of the sovereign or common-wealth. Out of these, he gave the highest priority to defence and considered it as the predominant branch of public economics.[15]

Smith has categorsed defence as 'pure public good' and discussed the methods of payment of such public good on the ability to pay principle and suggested that poor should be exempted from its payment.[16]

Musgrave and Musgrave (1970), Samuelson (1954), Dalton (1960) Buchanan, Mathew (1973), Kennedy (1975), Collins and Jones (1992) etc. have substantiated defence as a 'pure public good'. A pure public good concept as given in the original formulations of Samuelson is a good which must be consumed in equal amount by all and once it is supplied to one person it can be made available to others at no extra cost. It also has characteristic of non-rival consumption.[17]

The problem of free riders, externalities provided by defence, non-exclusive consumption of defence were analysed by Kennedy Gavin (1975) and Musgrave and Musgrave (1970) in their works.

Further Sandlere (1977), Joff and Tollison (1990) have raised the issue of nature of defence acquired through alliance system and called it as an impure public good.[18]

The public good nature of defence makes the payment provision of defence complex. Musgrave and Musgrave suggested that this good must be provided by the government and paid for through general revenue system or it will not be provided at all. But every nation needs defence for survival in the international environment. The application of market systems fails in pricing of such pure public good. Another difficulty highlighted in this work is that the benefits and costs involved in defence are intangible and their value can be determined by market prices. So the 'political process' is needed to determine the share and resource allocation for defence.[19]

In the same way Schlessinger argued that whether the proposed allocation for defence from government/public expenditure would be tolerable to the public or not, must be taken into account by the decision makers of defence expenditure. It is at this point, economics touches political and social psychology and economic analysis transmits itself into 'Political economy'.[20]

Opinions/Views of Different Economists on Defence Expenditure

Everybody gains from defence and therefore everybody should pay for it. But here Adam Smith held the view that the poor would have to be exempted from the payments even though they gained from the provision of it. This led Smith from the payment according to benefit principle to the ability to pay principle.[21]

One can say that Smith has taken a 'Welfarist' approach in the discussion of defence expenditure. At the time of the Nepolenic Wars between Britain and France David Ricardo worked in the area of defence economics. He observed the financial implications of costly wars at public expense on British economy and therefore concentrated on restraining the government from war expenditure. He has shown that there a large amount of productive capital is wasted in the war and it affects normal commercial life of the people. During this period Ricardo developed the theory of economic rent. This theory is considered as an outcome of his work which studied the influence of war on agriculture.[22]

Ricardo's major contribution in the defence economics lies in the field of war finance. He was a firm believer that governments get involved in unnecessary wars which causes drain on resources. The most important reason for war according to Ricardo was political self-interest and national interest as perceived by the political leaders and therefore he wanted war to be financed in such a way that the political leaders would have to face the outrage of those who pay for the war.[23]

Ricardo stressed the view that war should be financed by taxes and not by loans. This calls for necessary changes in the tax legislations through the Parliament to raise taxes. According to Ricardo it is possible to assess the public opinion on the basis of voting done by representatives of tax payers in the parliament on this issue. Therefore he prefers taxes to finance wars. He has also discussed the effects of war on international trade and has suggested a few measures for the recovery of the British economy disrupted by war. In spite of all this one must remember that there are a number of difficulties in operating the Ricardian anti-war system which arises due to the divergence of private interest from national interest.[24]

Malthus a contemporary of Ricardo regarded war as one of the inevitable checks on population.[25]

He considered war as a moral retribution for economic prosperity, which is turned as a wartime boom, which it brings alongwith it. Such, economic prosperity may lead to population growth therefore he opposed the idea of using war as a means of generating prosperity. Malthus was of the view that the greater the wartime economic gains the more serious would be the distress in the peace that followed.[26]

The value of 'human cost' was introduced by J.B. Say in the discussions of defence economics. He tried to analyse the social cost of human life in the warfare. According to him society invests in its children by providing them basic needs and education. When children reach adulthood and participate in production process the society starts getting the returns of their investment but if a young man dies in the battle then it should be treated as a loss in human investment for a society. The estimation of such loss would not be easy. J.B. Say in his writings also attacked the economic uselessness of war.[27]

Karl Marx did not write specifically about economics of defence but his collaborator, Engels analysed this subject. The changes in the technology have revolutionised some aspects of defence economics and this was the area of study for Engels. He tried to build a relationship between technological changes and military tactics.[28]

Upto the First World War the military/defence matters were studied in isolation. They were considered as the exclusive province of military personnel. The First World War brought out the relevant connection between military power and industrial power: without the latter the former was meaningless. This was the beginning of a new era in the economic analysis of defence expenditure. In the Pre-second World War period several economists turned their attention to the problems and effects of war effects.[29]

In 1911 F.W. Hirst attempted to give three principles of war finance based on British economic studies.

The first principle categorised all the expenses on defence forces as wasteful expenditure. The second principle stated that the defence expenditure although wasteful is necessary until perpetual peace is established. In the third principle it is advised that the level of defence expenditure should be sufficient to maintain an Empire and all the excessive expenditure of defence should be avoided.

He suggested a proportional limitation of armaments. Further he also suggested that there should be a strict financial supervision to make sure that tax-payers get full value for their money.[30]

This shows that F.W. Hirst was against large scale military expenditure. His ideas regarding war prosperity were similar to the classical economists. From the effects of the First World War he concluded that war prosperity gave fictitious stimulus to economic activity. He discussed post war effects on the economy at length in his work and was critical about war debt.

We know that there are some common post-war effects on the economy. Usually it includes cut in the military expenditure along with other public expenditure, increase in unemployment, high rate of inflation and so cut in the consumption and economic activity at all the levels. This leads to cut in new investments, and savings and economy face a critical situation.

Lord Keynes resolved this problem by making theoretical contribution that explained the 'paradox of thrift', in his book 'General Theory' published in 1936.[31]

Keynes (1940) discussed alternative methods of financing war and rejected the Ricardian solution of increased taxes. He suggested that 'deferred income' should be used for financing war.[32]

Government should use the Keynesian type of fiscal and monetary controls. He thought that by this method war prosperity would be followed by greater peace time prosperity.[33] In the later period economists tried to work in the area of efficient management of defence resources and the need to shift the resources to relatively higher valued social activity. All the economists from Adam Smith till Keynes held the common view about the non-developmental nature of defence expenditure. Yet it is found that military expenditures continue to rise in an inexorable fashion in the world.

We all have accepted that defence expenditure is unavoidable and is an essential expenditure. A large number of researchers and economists tried to understand the relationship between defence expenditure and economic growth/development. These studies have come to diverse conclusions.

Therefore it is essential to explore this area. Benoit's study (1979) marks the beginning of analysis of impact of defence expenditure on economic growth. Prior to Benoit, Pryor (1968) studied the nature of substitution between defence expenditure and public investment. Russet (1970) computed opportunity cost of defence. Lotz (1970) tried to analyse the defence budget determinants. Benoits study (1973, 78) shifted the focus of research on the role of defence expenditure and its desirability. Benoit's study covers a large sample of developing economies and has come to a startling conclusion that defence expenditure has a positive relationship with economic growth. Most of the later researches in post-Benoit period tried to work on the hypothesis that defence causes growth.

Many studies disproved this hypothesis and pointed out a negative relationship. The diversity of results variation, specification choices and the time periods are also analysed.[34]

Determinants of Defence Budget

The area of defence budget determination analysed by some of the researchers and experts. The important contributors are Lotz (1970), Olvey, Golden and Kelly (1984), Maizeles Nissanke (1986), Deger and Sen (1988), Hewitt (1991) etc. Lotz's (1970) analysis of the determinants of Military Expenditure was part of his general analysis of each of the main elements of government spending using the data for 37 less developed countries. In this work Lotz concluded that there was a inverse relationship between per capita expenditure and military/defence expenditure of the less developed countries. It has observed that a negative relationship persists between defence spending and per capita income. The determinants of defence include a complete set of domestic, regional and global factors which determine military budget of the developing countries and they vary from country to country. Among economic factors the most important determinant of the defence budget according to them was the share of Central Government budget in GDP and the availability of foreign exchange and foreign capital. A similar view is substantiated by Deger and Sen (1988) and in their work they concluded that the military spending in the developing countries depends upon strategic considerations of threat and security.

Hewitt (1991) conducted a study of 125 countries using data for 1972 to 1987 and concludes that the military expenditure is highly reactive to observable financial constraints and the ratio of military expenditure to GDP is found to rise with GDP in middle and low income countries but remains stable in the high income countries.[35]

Olvey, Golden and Kelly (1984) in their study concluded that it is unlikely to develop any economic model or economic theory that enables decision maker to mechanically determine how to utilise, distribute and allocate resources in defence and non-defence sector. Therefore, positive use of economic analysis can held in indicating consequences of various decisions/alternatives to the decision-makers. They have also discussed the complexity in allocational questions of defence due to usage of value judgements of political actors and decision makers on marginal usefulness of such public goods or services.[36]

Hence, in their further work they have stressed institutional perspective i.e., role of Actors, Institutions and Decision-makers in defence budget determination. This institutional aspect is also substantiated by Kennedy (1975), Thomas Raju (1978), Nicole (1981), Saadet Deger and Smith (1983), Looney (1983) and others. Some other scholars had tried to integrate this aspect with external and internal security factors instead of taking it separately.

An integrated defence budget determination model on the basis of defence budgeting in USA is given by Oley, Golden and Kelly which takes into account foreign policy perspective, domestic policy perspective and institutional perspective.[37]

There are a few studies done in India for the analysis of defence budget determinants. The important one is by Thomas Raju (1978). In this work he threw a light on the factors which decide how much to be allocated for defence in India. According to him it is governed by three essential factors:

1. Indian perception of external and internal threats.
2. Political structure and political decision-making process in India i.e. budgetary process.
3. Economic capacity or economic potential and economic constraints.[38] This work does not take into account internal security threats separately which has been an important determinant. It also did not analyse these threats in depth. It might be due to the reason that this study was undertaken for the time period 1947 to 1974 in which the internal security threats were not as dominant as they are today. Lakshmi (1988) substantiates the above determinants of defence budget in her study. She has stressed the economic capability of a nation and threat perceptions of military and political leaders as important defence budget determinants in India for the period 1962-1986.[39] N.B. Grant in his article (1987) concludes that ultimately foreign policy controls the defence budget. He suggested that it is prudent to plan on the basis of threats, internal economic support and information and analysis for cost effective defence in India. He has advised integration of overall defence efforts for effective use of defence resources in India.[40]

The similar view is expressed by Pendase (1993) in his article.[41]

Paranjape (1990) in his article also had substantiated the same view and the similar or the same defence expenditure determinants.[42]

Naik (1990), Paranjape (1991), have added an element of cost of modernisation programme of armmed forces and development of emerging technology areas/dual technology purpose areas as an additional domestic key factor for deciding defence outlays in the present era through their works.[43]

India's Response to External and Internal Security Environment

This issue is elaborately discussed in the literature. Most of the studies related to Indian defence expenditure show the changes in the external and internal security environment.

In his analysis Thomas Raju (1978) has analysed Indian defence budgets from 1947 to 1974 and showed that changes in India's defence expenditure were the responses to the changes in internal and external security environment. In his analysis he had laid more stress on external security environment changes and only a few internal problems were taken into account. The 1962, 1965 and 1971 external aggressions on India are considered as major causes of changes in defence expenditure by him. On the similar lines Lakshmi (1988) substantiated that changes in external and internal security threats have caused matching changes in Indian defence expenditure during 1962-1986. Both of them have used the basis of changes in internal and external security threats perceptions for explaining the changes in inter service distribution of defence expenditure. The fall in Army's outlays and rise in Naval and Air Force outlays after 1971 war are explained with the changes in security environment and changes in the type of threats to Indian security.[44] Each year Ministry of Defence takes the review of changes in external and internal security environment and on this basis justifies the defence resources allocations. The Annual Report of Ministry of Home Affairs and explanations along with the Demand for Grant of Home Affairs takes a review of paramilitary forces and their expenditure etc. under the demand for gsrant-Police.

Pendse recommended the reforms in defence budgeting process and re-structuring of National Security Council (NSC) are essential for balancing Indian defence budget with external and domestic policy objectives and economic capability.[45]

Smith Chris (1994) has analysed Indian defence expenditure and defence policy pattern from 1947 to 1994 and critcised rise in India's defence expenditure. In the view of Smith, it does not match with external and internal security threats but it is far higher than what is required. India spent more on defence according to Smith and this was done to keep the status of regional power especially after 1971.[46]

The external threat factors have received more attention than internal threat factors. In threat perception analysis one needs to note that these perceptions are perceived or imagined by the ruling elites, political decision-makers and military experts (i.e. Institutions and Actors) and hence, there is a possibility of influences of their own ideology and views in it. These influences can be vividly marked in the periods of Nehru, Indira Gandhi and Rajiv Gandhi. The economic resources at the disposal of the ruling elites has been an important constraint on the decisions about defence budget in India. This aspect is very well substantiated in all the studies related to defence expenditure of India.

Defence Policy in India

Before 1947, India was a part of the British Empire and Indian Leaders and opinion shapers were no longer concerned about external security decisions. Hence, till 1947 Indians did not play any significant role in shaping of the India's Defence Policy. The partition of India created a new concern as well as independence in the defence policy environment of India. In 1954, South East Asian Treaty Organisation (SEATO) and in 1955 Central Treaty Organisation (CENTO) were formed and Pakistan joined these two to become the USA ally in its regional defence network. This type of military alliance between Pakistan and the USA pushed India to consider various defence/security problems in defence policy.[47]

India did not join Eastern or Western Military Alliances and adopted the policy of Non-Alignment. It tried to resolve the disputed issues with its neighbours on the basis of peaceful methods. However, this type of defence policy based on non-aligmment and security through diplomacy failed in 1962. This shows that there was no indepth defence policy study and proper defence policy making till 1962. This view is supported in the works related to India's defence policy and include studies by Kavic (1967), Khera (1968), Subramanyam (1973), Rao (1976), Handa (1976), Thomas Raju (1982), Thomas Raju (1986), Nanda (1991), Subramanyam (1991), Smith (1994) etc. These scholars have explored the area of defence policy making in India in detail. Rao (former defence secretary during 1965 war) held the view that 1962, 1965 and 1971 wars had forced India to understand the importance of an indepth study of defence policy. According to him defence policy in the widest interpretation can encompass practically all activities of modern government.[48] Rao (1976), Thomas Raju (1986) and Nanda (1991) have highlighted organisational lacunae in Indian defence policy making. Rao feels that the decision-making apparatus had been properly institutionalised in India but it lacks co-ordination.[49]

The defence policy has been continuously neglected from the public debate in India and this is the most common point substrantiated by all the studies related to defence policy of India. Smith Chris (1994) disagrees with the view that India sought its security through diplomacy and non-alignment policy in 1947 to 1962. Smith had given the evidences that India continued its weapon procurement and defence buildup at a slow and moderate rate even in this period. India has resorted to confused defence policy but continued the growth of defence build up.[50] Smith Chris considers the period 1962 to 1980 as period for maturing defence policy in India but criticised that there were no clearcut guidelines given to the defence policy even in this period. So the defence policy drifted away from the basic need of acquiring security to the policy of acquiring symbolic weapons for its regional power status after 1971 war.[51]

Handa (1976) substantiated this view and argued that defence policy till to 1971 was built around the weapon acquisition from foreign suppliers and suggested that now India should shift its defence policy to build weapons indigenously to suit own defence needs.[52]

Nanda goes further and remarks that India has failed to evolve coherant defence policy since 1947 to 1991.[53] Kavic, Khera and Rao have concentrated on 1947-1965 time period. The others have taken a review of the whole period till 1990s. The deficiencies in defence policy making and implementation are highlighted in these studies and measures to improve co-ordination and integration are suggested through these studies. The most important recommendation amongst them need to is restructure the National Security Council (NSC) which was set up in 1990 and giving more power and teeth to it. This issue is elaborately discussed by various authors. The work on security policies of developing countries analysed by Thomas Raju (1982) has the impact categorised in three factors:

1. Prime Minister
2. Party politics and parliamentary debate
3. Influence of public opinion on defence policy making in India.

On the other hand Kavic concluded that military experts (Chiefs of Staff Committee) influenced the defence policy making in India than non-military parts of institutional structures and were in minority in defence policy making in 1947-1965.[54]

Smith and Nanda have criticised Indian defence policy in 1980s and 1990s. Smith has concluded that India has over extended its modernisation and weapon procurement programme in 1980s and 1990s due to which since 1988 India is facing serious problems in economic and defence sector. This shows defence policy did not match with resources. In Smith's view India's endeavour in achieving self-sufficiency in technology and programme of indigenisation could not achieve much success and all this has contributed to the military security at the cost of economic security in 1990s.[55] But this criticism is not supported by any data or proof.

It seems that the literature on defence policy has highlighted many inconsistencies and showed that the policy making process has been inefficiently used for various reasons since independence.

Trends in Defence Expenditure

A continuous rise in defence expenditure (defence budget) of India is well supported in all studies related to it. In these studies internal, external threats perceptions, economic capabilities, need of armed forces are used to justify the resources allocations for defence in India. The notable studies for defence expenditure analysis of India include Thomas Raju (1978), Laxmi (1988) etc.

Thomas Raju (1978) has analysed Indian defence budget in three phases

(1) 1947-62, (2) 1962-71, (3) 1971-74

Lakshmi (1988) divided total expenditure period of her study 1962-86 into four phases:

1. War years 1962-63 to 1971-72
2. Post-war years 1971-72 to 1978-79
3. Janata years 1977-79 to 1979-80
4. The return of Indira Gandhi years 1980-89 to 1985-86.

The 1962 and 1971 war were taken as main breaking points for the phases in defence expenditure analysis. The defence expenditure has been continuously rising in India due to changes in security scenario at external and domestic levels since independence. The changes in the Institutions, Actors and Defence Policy, modernisation programmes, arms build up of adversaries, changes in the types and nature of threats, changes in economic capability are used as a basis to explain servicewise distribution pattern of defence expenditure by Thomas Raju and Lakshmi.

After 1971 war, a visible change was noted in the service-wise distribution of defence expenditure that the Army and Air Force started declining their share in defence expenditure and Navy started getting more share than past years. After 1980-81 the Air Force share increased and the share of Army and Navy started declining. This shows that after 1971, Army started getting less share due to changes in the type of threats and changes in technology.[56] This view is also substantiated by Thomas Raju (1978).

In the article by Sreedhar (1990) on India's defence expenditure during the period when Rajiv Gandhi was Prime Minister, an attempt is made to prove that defence expenditure has maximum hike in this period after 1962 war. This argument is well supported by statistical data. The year 1986-87 has maximum allocation for defence during Rajiv Gandhi's regime which was 4.2 per cent of GNP at current prices.[57]

A review taken by Institutes of Defence and Strategic Analysis (IDSA) on Trends in India's defence expenditure substantiate the above empirical analysis.

The analysis done by Lakshmi and Thomas Raju prove that a very large share of Army allocation were absorbed by Pay, Pensions and followed by the Stores. Smith held the view that Army Modernisation Programme continued in India with Soviet or indigenous support which has increased inventory and had minimal drain on foreign exchange reserves.[58]

This view is not supported by others and the issue of foreign exchange usage by the defence sector is overlooked in various studies except in the study by Tehral (1981).

The frequent use of Army in the sensitive areas of internal security is criticised by Jacob and Laskhmi in their works.[59]

The threats from the Indian Ocean Region and super power rivalry in the Indian Ocean, entry of America's USS Enterprise in the Bay of Bangal in 1971 war are taken as important causes for increasing the share of Navy in defence expenditure in 1970s in all the studies. The share of Air Force increased during 1980s on account of modern equipment acquisitions, indigenous production, cost escalations. This view is supported by Lakshmi.

In 1970s, 1980s and 1990s India continued its efforts for self-reliance in defence production, developing own military technology, indigenisation etc. but the success achieved in this direction is in very limited area. These efforts have helped India to develop a strong infrastructure for defence production and it is supported by the studies related to defence production in India by Agarwal (1978), Rao (1984), Mathews (1989).

The role of private sector in defence production and the problems of Defence production sector are different in 1990s. The extended role of private sector in the area of defence in 1990s is supported and discussed by Kumar (1991), Rajiv (1991), Mahapatra (1993), Singh (1993), Khanna and Mehrotra (1993) through their work.

Effects of Defence Expenditure on Economy

The common sense suggests that increased defence expenditure is likely to harm development effort. Economic theory does not provide any clear prediction about the amount and type of net impact on economic growth, development and welfare.

Various studies are conducted to find out the relationship between defence expenditure and economic growth but they have to yeilded common general conclusion. A few empirical studies show positive relationship. Some studies show negative and some studies show neutral relationship between the two. These studies have come to diverse conclusions/ results because each study has chosen different set of countries, different periods of such study, different statistical tools and different related factors and their data. There are many notable researchers worked on this area.[60]

These studies have tried to explore various aspects of relationship of defence expenditure and economic growth. In most of these studies less developed countries sample was chosen and India was included in it.

These studies have tried to analyses the impact of defence expenditure on economic growth. They have generally started with simple economic framework and simple methodology. But in the further period one finds the methodological sophistication and more disaggregated analysis of various variables related to defence expenditure. Benoit (1973), Kennedy (1974), Whynass (1979) have used macro economic parameters like economic growth rate and defence burden (ratio of defence expenditure to GDP/GNP) Deger Saadet (1983, 1986), Hess (1989) have used savings ratio, education expenditure and other social expenditures as other variables. Rothschild (1977) has added an additional variable of export ratio. Looney (1985, 1987) has used various other form of public expenditure as additional variables in his analysis. Dunes and Abell (1990) have used macroeconomic parameters of employment ratio. The details about the parameters used in each analysis are given in the charts on the following pages. These researchers have concluded:

a. There is a positive relationship between defence expenditure and economic growth.
b. There is a negative relationship between defence expenditure and economic growth.
c. There is neutral relationship between defence expenditure and economic growth.

The studies supporting positive relationship can be grouped together. A study in this area was conducted by Emilie Benoit in 1973 for the 44 Less Developed Countries (LDCs) for the time period 1950-65 and also in 1978. The author concluded that "the evidence does not indicate that defence expenditure has any adverse effect on growth in developing countries but they were positively correlated with their economic growth over comparable time periods. The more they spent on defence in relation to the size of their economies, the faster they grew and vice varse."[61]

However, Benoit further found that most of the developing countries spent their non-defence part on consumption and very small part goes to productive investment. Benoit started his study with the hypothesis that increased defence burden/expenditure have both positive and negative impact on economic growth. He has used simple regression analysis to analyse impact of defence burden on the growth rate of civilian GDP and estimated also the negative impact through investment effect, productivity effect income shift effect. The positive impact of defence burden on civilian GDP were measured through, training effect, infrastructure effect, consumption effect and security effect. According to Benoit the positive spin-off effects are far more than negative ones.[62] The main drawback of Benoit's analysis is that he had calculated the negative effects of defence burden statistically but he lacks statistical substantiation for the positive effects on the growth rate.

In spite of various criticisms, Benoit's study marks an important pioneering work in this area because he for the first time tried to analyse whether defence expenditure helps economic growth. This gave a new direction to further research. Benoit has tried to point out both the positive and negative impacts of increased defence burden. It must be noted that the further studies on this topic have generally supported this positive relationship or supported his findings about negative impacts and in this way his results are used as a general basis.

There are many other empirical studies supporting positive relationship the important ones can be summarised as in Chart I on next page.

Name of Researcher	*Period*	*Sample Countries*	*Variables Tested*	*Result/K[illegible] Book*
1	2	3	4	5
Benoit Emilie	1950-65	44 LDCs	1. Mil. exp. as % of GDP 2. Civilian GDP: GDP- Mil. Exp. 3. % growth rate of GDP 4. Govt. to Govt. Economic Aid excluded 5. Gross capital formation as % of GDP.	Strong positive corelation between defence burden and economic growth rate was observed *Defence and Economic Growth in Developing Countries* (Lexington Mass; Lexington (1973)
Whyness David	1972-77	59 LDC + 32 DC	1. Annual Defence Expenditure growth rate 2. Defence Expenditure as % GDP 3. Annual Growth rate of per capita income 4. Per capita income (1977 only)	The economics of Third World military expenditure (London Macmillan, 1979) Higher defence expenditure leads to higher economic growth
Fredrisken & Looney Robert	1950-65	44LDCs as taken by Benoit	1. Defence burden: Mil. Exp. as % of GDp 2. Capital formation as % of GDP 3. Receipts of bilateral aid as % of GDP	Test validity of Benoits finding positive relation for richer LDCs Negative relation for poorer

(contd...)

Chart 1 *(Concld)*

1	2	3	4	5
			4. Real growth of GDP minus Real growth of Def. Exp.	LDCs in defence expenditure and economic growth (Armed Forces and society Summer (1983)
Kennedy G.	1965-72	50LDC	1. Defence burden: Mil. Ex. as % of GDP 2. Investment as % of GDP 3. Industry as % of GDP 4. Growth of exports 5. Growth of capital stock	Positive relation between The Military exp. and the economic growth in the Third World countries (London, Gerald Duckworth & Co. Ltd., 1974)
K. Subrahmanyam	1961-70	8DCs & 8LDCs	1. Def. Exp. as % of GDP 2. Economic Growth Rate	No Clear correlation between the defence burden and growth rate was observed. In case of LDCs positive co-relation especially in India. *Defence and Development* (Calcutta, The Minarva Associates, 1983)

Source: Ball Nicole, *Security and Economy in the Third World,* (Princetone, New Jersey, Princetone University Press, 1988, pp. 405-408) and additions made by Athawale, S.S.

In the case of India, positive relationship between defence expenditure and economic growth is supported in the studies of Subramanyam (1973), Agarwal (1978), Lakshmi (1986), Singh (1991) etc.

Thomas Raju tied to test the relationship between defence expenditure and economic growth in India from 1960-83. His conclusions showed that there exists neutral relationship between two in that period.[63]

There are statistical studies showing negative relationship between defence expenditure and economic growth. Most of the researchers now seem to support the view that defence expenditure retards economic growth. These studies include Smith (1977), Roth Schild (1977), Deger and Smith (1983) and others as listed the Chart 2 on next page.

In the country specific study of India, Teheral (1981), Deger Saadet (1983), Khanna and Mehrotra (1993) concluded negative relationship between Defence Expenditure and Economic Growth.

Ball Nicole (1981), Saadet Deger (1986), Saadet Deger and Smith (1987), Dumas (1982), Taylor (1984), Chand (1985), Chaudhary (1991) had criticised Benoit's findings on methodological and conceptual grounds. In case of India. Tehral (1981), Khanna and Meherotra (1993) and Smith Chris (1994) have established negative relationship in defence expenditure and economic growth. The study by Smith lacks statistical substantiation.

Deger Saadet (1979) used Harrod Domar framework and has shown that there is inverse relationship between military expenditure and economic growth which is also supported by Lim (1983).

a. Deger Saadet (1983, 1985, 1986, 1987) has used econometric models for analysing the impact of defence burden on economic growth and so called 'spin off effect'. Through these studies the econometric

Name of Researcher	*Period*	*Sample Countries*	*Variables Tested*	*Result/Report/Book*
1	*2*	*3*	*4*	*5*
Faini R, Patricia A. & Taylor L.	1952-70	48 LDC + 15DC	1. Growth of GDP 2. Growth of exports 3. Growth of population 4. Growth of Defence burden as % of GDP 5. Growth of Capital inflows 6. Growth of capital stock	Military expenditure has clear negative effect on economic growth *Defence spending, Economic Structure and growth* (Cambridge Mass, MIT, 1980, Mimeograph)
Deger Saadet Smith Ron	1965-73	50 LDC	1. Average annual increase in GDP 2. Savings as % of National Income 3. Military burden, military exp. as % of GDP	Increase in defence spending leads to reduction in investment as proportion in GDP so it has detrimental effect on growth rate via savings *Military Expenditure and growth in less developed countries, the Journal of Conflict Resolution,* (27 June 1983 pp. 335-53).

Lim David	1965-73	54LDC	1. Incremental capital-output ratio 2. Military expenditure as % of GDP 3. Military expenditure % of Central Govt. Exp. 4. Deficit on current account/ gross national saving ratio.	Higher defence expenditure hurt economic growth ("Another look at growth & defence in less developed countries", *Economic Dev. & Cultural Change* 31st Jan. 1983 pp. 377-84)
Raven Hill S. John	1960-73	33LDC from Africa	1. Rate of growth of Mil. Exp. 2. Level of Mil. Exp. as % of GNP 3. Level of GNP 4. Gross Domestic Investment 5. Constant Exports	Significant negative relation between level of development and rate of growth of Mil. Exp. (*Comparing Regime Performance of cross national aggregate analysis, Journal of Modern African Studies,* 18 Jan. 1980 pp. 99-126).
Thomas Raju G.C.	1960-82	India	1. Growth rate of GNP in % 2. Growth rate of savings 3. Growth rate of investments 4. Growth rate of Military Exp. as % of GNP	No positive or negative relationship between defence expenditure and economic growth. Other factors have more influence on GNP growth rate in India *Indian security policy* (Princetone, New Jersey, Princetone University Press, 1986)

(contd...)

1	2	3	4	5
Khanna D.D. Meherotra P.N.	1970-90	India	Deger's simultaneous equation system with suitable amendments for adopting it to India.	Negative influence of defence burden on savings ratio and growth. The positive effects of defence burden on growth rate are not confined as established by Benoit.
			1. Growth and budgetary trade off of model with 26 variables 2. Defence and external economic sector model with 19 variables 3. Defence budget and inter-sectoral economic interaction with 43 variables	*Defence versus Development: A Case Study of India,* Indus Publishing Co. New Delhi, (1993)

Source: Ball Nicole, *Security and Economy in the Third World,* Princeton, New Jersey, Princeton University Press, 1988, pp. 405-408) and additions made by Athawale Sanhita S.

models were used to test a direct effects of defence burden through resource mobilisation.

b. Indirect effect of defence burden through its effect on savings.

c. Externality or Exogeneity of military expenditure

Deger has shown that the military expenditure has substantial negative effects on economic growth through adverse impact on capital formation, savings ratio and inflow of foreign resources.

Fredericksen and Looney (1983) in their study tried to group their sample into resource rich and resource constrained countries and they have found that in resource rich countries in defence expenditure and economic growth are positively correlated and in resource contained countries they are negatively correlated. Robert Looney (1982, 1987) has used factor analysis of seven variables and divided his sample into resource rich and resource constrained countries. Hewitt (1991) tried to analyse various trade-offs between defence expenditure and other forms of government expenditure and found positive correlation.

Cambridge Journal of Economics (Vol. 14, No. 4, December, 1990) had taken out a special issue consisting of a symposium on the political economy of military expenditure. The focus of the symposiums's was on the developed world and in particular the USA and UK and had discussed various effects on employment, investment, economic growth, international trade, human resources of military expenditure in developed countries/capitalist countries. The attempt was made in this symposium in some country specific studies to understand the relationship of military sector with the industrial sector and vice versa. The experts have stressed the need of more disaggregate analysis and clear framework formation than simple macro economic studies in this area.[64] Chan (1985) had taken an exhaustive review of available literature on this subject and concluded that there is no consensues about the actual impact of military expenditure on economic growth. Neuman (1979), Jung and Marshall (1985) Biswas and Ram (1986), Joerding (1986) have questioned the basis of defence expenditure and economic growth debate. They point out that it is quite possible that there is no causal relationship between defence expenditure and economic growth and it might be possible that economic growth may be the cause of high defence expenditure but the later is not confirmed in the studies. There are some studies like McKinley and Cohen (1976) in which they have tried to analyse the impact of defence expenditure on economic growth in terms of non-economic parameter.

Role of Dual Purpose Technology Areas

India's Nuclear, Space, Electronics and other programmes are in civil sector. India has always reiterated its peaceful intentions in developing these programmes. These capabilities have inherent military use potential and so the developments in these areas are often referred in the security related studies.

Subramanyam (1973), Cohen (1982), Rao (1984), Geoffrey (1984), Thomas Raju (1986), Mohan (1986), Tinbergen and Fisher (1987), Mathews (1989), Nanda (1991), Subrahmanyam (1991), Pendse (1991), Paranjape (1993), Smith (1994) etc. have taken into account the impact of nuclear and space developments in security threat analysis and defence policy analysis in India. These studies have considered dual purpose technology areas as a modern factor contributing defence capability of India since 1970s.

But these studies lack indepth analysis of expenditures done by India on these dual purpose areas. India has not yet signed Nuclear Non-Proliferation Treaty (1968) and has kept its nuclear weapon option open. The issue of India going towards nuclear weapon option for reducing the cost of defence had been highlighted in a few studies but it is inadequately analysed issue. There is no change in the government policy in this direction.

Towards Redefining Defence Expenditure

Defence expenditure determinants, effects of defence expenditure on economic growth, role of military in development and in technological progress have remained controversial for various reasons. It is necessary to explore this area and so research in this area will call for re-definition and clarification of some of the concepts. The most important one is redefinition of military or defence expenditure. The first difficulty in this area is of conceptual nature: that of determining what is covered in the present era by 'Military Expenditure'. The concept of National Security has widened and there has been growing interweaving of internal and international conflicts. Therefore there is a need to extend the concept of military or defence expenditure. Defence expenditure should include all or part of resources employed by the state to maintain internal security and public order along with external security.[65]

Ball Nicole (1983), Deger (1986), International Monetary Fund: A manual on Government Finance Statistics, (1986), Sen (1992), Herrera (1994) etc. have tried to review the conceptual, methodological problems and sources in collecting the statistics on military expenditure in developing countries. The definition of military/defence expenditure vary considerably from one country to another due to differences in classification, accounting and in the way in which the state budget is drawn up. For this reason the defence budget is not necessarily full-fledged indication of a country's real military/defence efforts. In some countries, the ministry of Defence assumes the functions of civilian nature and conversely there may be public expenditure from the budgets of civilian ministries which is primarily for military/defence purposes. The research efforts in the nuclear and space fields may also lead to applications of a military nature, even though these programmes may be financed by the civilian sector. There is difficulty in distinguishing between strictly military/defence functions and civilian functions of the state in such dual purpose areas.[66]

The Organisation for Economic Cooperation and Development (OECD) document by Herrera Remy (1994) has elaborately discussed the conceptual, methodological and sources difficulties in assessing military expenditure in less developed countries. As per this study there are three basic definitions of defence expenditure, serving as standards for the different international institutions that published data on defence expenditure: that of the NATO (North Atlantic Treaty Organisation), IMF (International Monetary Fund), UNO (United Nations Organisation). The definition of military expenditure/defence expenditure given by NATO includes:

(a) All current and capital expenditure of Armed Forces, Defence Departments, Government Agencies, Space projects.
(b) The cost of paramilitary forces and police.
(c) Military R&D, pensions of military personnel and civilian employees for military.
(d) Military aid is included in the expenditure of the donor countries.[67]

The definition given by IMF is fairly close to NATO and according to this, the defence budget or military expenditure includes:

(a) All expenditures by defence and non-defence department for maintenance of military forces.
(b) Military construction, training, recruiting, feeding, clothing, housing, medical, military schools R&D and other costs for military services.
(c) All expenditures related to paramilitary organisations including civil defence and war time emergency agencies.
(d) Expenditure for foreign military aid and contributions to international military organisations and aliances.[68]

There is substantial difference between IMF and NATO definition in the financing of military pensions, inclusion of military aid and weighing the status of security forces.

But still as per Organisation for Economic Cooperation and Development (OECD) Document (1994). Definition of NATO and IMF are very close.

Stockholm International Peace and Research Institute (SIPRI) has also given its definition of military expenditure. According to SIPRI documents military expenditure of a country includes:

(a) Pay and allowances of military forces
(b) Pay and allowances of civilians supporting defence
(c) Operational and maintenance cost
(d) Procurement cost and construction costs
(e) Research and development costs
(f) Military Pensions
(g) Military aid
(h) Civil defence, para military expenditure
(i) Military aspects of atomic energy, space etc.[69]

In 1975 United Nation's Organisation (UNO) tried to give all pervasive definition of military expenditure. This definition of military expenditure includes:

A. Operating costs

1. Personnel:
   a. Conscripts
   b. Other military
   c. Civilian
2. Operations and maintenance:
   a. Current-use material
   b. Maintenance and repairs
   c. Purchased services
   d. Rent

B. Procurement and construction

1. Procurement:
   a. Aircraft and Engines
   b. Missiles, including conventional warheads

c. Nuclear warheads and bombs
d. Ships and boats
e. Armored vehicles
f. Artillery
g. Other ordnance and ground force arms
h. Ammunition
i. Electronics and communications
j. Non-armored vehicles

2. Construction:
a. Airbases
b. Missile sites
c. Naval bases
d. Electronics
e. Personnel
f. Medical
g. Training
h. Warehouses and depots
i. Command administration
j. Fortifications
k. Shelters

C. Research and Development

1. Basic and applied to development testing and evaluation.[70]

On the basis of above constituents India's defence expenditure should include paramilitary force expenditure, nuclear, space and other dual purpose technology expenditures in it. It is very difficult to get the detailed expenditures of some of the items of operating costs and procurement and construction costs supporting to defence. Hence, on the basis of available data an attempt would be made here to analyse military/defence expenditure in wider sense.

The issue of determinants of defence budget is not adequately analysed in Indian context. The changes in the security environment, economic environment and technological environment calls for re-definition of defence expenditure for realistic analysis. The traditional definition of defence expenditure seems to be insufficient and hence, an attempt is made through this study to redefine defence expenditure, determinants of defence budget for India and analyse them for the period 1970-71 to 1994-95. This work is just the beginning in this direction.

NOTES AND REFERENCES

1. Bekonwitz M. and Bock P.Q., "National Security", *International Encyclopedia of Social Sciences,* Vol. XI, (New York: The Mac Millan Company and Free Press, 1968), pp. 39-40.

2. Collins John M., *How to Analyse National Security: Conceptual Framework in US Defence Planning—A Critique* (New York: West View Press, 1982), p. 5.

3. Knorr Klaus, *The War Potentials of Nations* (New Jersey: Princeton University Press, 1956), p. 40.

4. Schlessinger James R., *The Political Economy of National Security* (London: Atlantic Books Stevens and Sons Ltd., 1960), p. 73.

5. Hitch Charls and Mackean Ronald, *The Economics of Defence in the Nuclear Age* (Cambridge: Harward University Press, 1960), pp. 17-19.

#. Clark J.J., *New Economics of National Defence* (New York: Random House, 1966), pp. 220-21.

6. Olvey L., Golden J. and Kelly Robert, *The Economics of National Security: Weighting the Costs of Defence* (New Jersey: Avery Publishing Group Inc., 1984), p. 11.

7. Brown Herald, *Thinking About National Security* (Colorado: West View Press, 1983), p. 120.

8. Smith Adam, *An Inquiry into the Nature and causes of the Wealth of Nations* (Oxford, Clarendon, Campbell and Skinner (eds.), vol. II, 1976) pp. 686-688 as quoted in Schmidt C. and Blackbay Frank (eds.), New York: St. Martin's Press, 1989), p. 24.

9. Kennedy Gavin, *Economics of Defence* (London: Faber and Faber, 1975), pp. 24-40.

10. Whynes K., David, *The Economics of Third World Military Expenditure* (London: The MacMillan Press, 1979), pp. 20-25.
11. Kennedy Gavin, *op. cit.,* p. 37.
12. Subramanyam K., *Defence and Development* (Calcutta: The Minerva Associates, 1973), p. 67.
13. Schmidt C. and Blackbay Frank (eds.), *Peace and War Economics in Retrospect, Peace Defence and Economic Analysis* (New York: St. Martin's Press, 1987), p. 23.
14. Kennedy Gavin, *op. cit.,* p. 41.
15. Schmidt C. and Blackbay Frank (eds.), *Ibid.* p. 24.
16. Kennedy Gavin, *Economics of Defence* (London: Faber and Faber, 1975), p. 26.
17. Samuelson P.A., "The Pure Theory of Public Expenditure," *The Review of Economics and Statistics,* Vol. 36, No. 4, Nov. 1954, p. 387.
18. John Cullins and Philip Jones, *Public Finance and Public Choice: Analytical Perspectives* (London: McGraw Hill Book Company, 1992), p. 65-66.
19. Musgrave, R. and Musgrave P., *Public Finance in Theory and Practice* (5th edition) (Singapore: McGrawHill Book Company, 1989), pp. 164-165.
20. Schelessinger James; R., *The Political Economy of National Security* (London: Atlantic Books, Steavens and Sons Ltd., 1960), p. 23.
21. Kennedy, Gavin, *op. cit.,* p. 26.
22. Kennedy, Gavin, *op. cit.,* p. 27.
23. Kennedy, Gavin, *op. cit.,* p. 29.
24. Kennedy, Gavin, *op. cit.,* pp. 29-30.
25. Kennedy, Gavin, *op. cit.,* p. 30.
26. Kennedy, Gavin, *op. cit.,* p. 31
27. Kennedy, Gavin, *op. cit.,* p. 32.
28. Kennedy, Gavin, *op. cit.,* p. 33
29. Kennedy, Gavin, *op. cit.,* p. 34.
30. Kennedy, Gavin, *op. cit.,* p. 35.

31. Kennedy, Gavin, *op. cit.,* p. 37.

32. Keynes J.M., *How to pay for War* (New York: Har Court Brace, 1940), pp. 120-5.

33. Keynes J.M., *Ibid.,* pp. 30-31.

34. Biswas B. and Ram Rati, Military Expenditure and Economic Growth—An Augmented Model for Future Evidence, *Economic Development and Cultural changes,* Vol. 34, No. 2, University of Chicago Press, Jan. 1985., p. 362-64.

35. Hewitt Daniel, "Military Expenditure in the Developing World", *Finance and Development,* New York: September 1991).

36. Olvey L. Golden James and Robert Kelly, Op. cit., p. 11.

37. Olvey L. and others, *op. cit.,* p. 47.

38. Thomas Raju G.C., *Defence of India: A Budgetory Perspective of Strategy and Politics* (Meerut: The McMillan Company of India Ltd. 1978), p. 7.

39. Y. Lakshmi, *op. cit.,* pp. 10-12.

40. Grant N.B., "Military Budgetting and National Security" in *Indian Defence Review,* Vol. II (New Delhi: Lancer Publication, 1 January 1987)(, p. 101.

41. Pendse K.S., "India's Defence and Development", *Indian Journal of Strategic Studies,* Vol. XVIII (Allahabad: University of Allahabad, 1993), pp. 21-34.

42. Paranjape H.K., "How much defence expenditure can India afford", *Mainstream* Vol. XXVIII, No. 28 (New Delhi, 5th May 1999), pp. 6-9.

43. Nailk M.B., "The Defence Budget" *Janata,* Vol. 45, No. 13 (Bombay, May 13, 1999), p. 13.

$ Paranjape S.B., "Defence Expenditure in India: Some explorations in the context of changing perceptions about security", *Mainstream,* Vol. XXIX, No. 51 (New Delhi, October, 12, 1991), p. 7.

44. Thomas Raju G.C., *op. cit.,* pp. 142-219.

Y. Lakshmi, *op. cit.,* pp. 93-113.

45. Pendase K.S., "India's Defence Budget — A case for better planning", *Indian Defence Review,* Vol. XV, No. 6 (New Delhi: Lancer International Publication, July 1989), p. 167.

46. Smith Chris, *India's Ad-Hoc Arsenal—Direction or Drift in Defence Policy?*, SIPRI Study (Oxford: Oxford University Press, 1994), p. 219.

47. Smith Chris, *Ibid.,* p. 14.

48. Rao P.V.R., *India's Defence Policy and Organisation Since Independence,* USI National Security Lectures (New Delhi: USI—United Service Institution of India Publication, 1976), pp. 6-8.

49. Rao P.V.R., *Ibid.,* p. 24.

50. Smith Chris, *op. cit.,* p. 72-73.

51. Smith Chris, *op. cit.,* p. 103.

52. Handa Rohit, *Policy for India's Defence* (New Delhi: Chetana Publications, 1976), p. 77.

53. Ravi Nanda, *National Security—Perspective, Policy and Planning* (New Delhi: Lancer Books, 1991), p. 7.

54. Kavic L. *India's Quest for Security: Defence Policies 1947-1965* (California: University of California Press, 1967), p. 217.

55. Smith Chris, *op. cit.,* p. 131.

56. Y. Lakshmi, *Trends in India's Defence Expenditure* (New Delhi: ABC Publishing House, 1988), pp. 123–127.

57. Sreedhar, "Defence Expenditure during Rajiv Gandhi's Years", *Strategic Analysis,* Vol. XIII, No. 2 (New Delhi: IDSA Publication, June 1990), p. 224.

58. Smith Chris, *op. cit.,* p. 115.

59. Jacob G., "India's Army", *Asian Defence Journal,* No. 9 (New York, Sept. 1985), p. 4.

60. They are Pryor (1968), Russet (1970), Lotz (1970), Emilie Benoit (1973), K. Subrahmanyam (1973), Navin Kenedy (1974), Agarwal Rajesh Kumar (1978), Emilie Benoit (1978), Smith Ron (1978), Deger Saadet (1979, 1983), David K. Whynes (1979), Ricardo F. and Taylor L. (1980), Tehral P. (1981), Ball Nicole (1981), L. Dumas (1982), Lim G. (1982), Robert Looney (1983)), Chan (1985), Thomas Raju G.C. (1986), Joeding (1986), Y. Lakshmi (1986), Saadet Deger and Smith Ron (1987), Rothschild (1989), Abell (1990), Dunes (1990), Jasjit Singh (1991), Chaudhari (1991), Khanna D.D. and Mehrotra (1993) etc.

61. Benoit Emilie, *Defence and Economic Growth in Developing Countries* (London: Lexington Books, 1973), p. xix.

62. Benoit Emlie, *Ibid.,* p. xx.

63. Thomas Raju G.C., *Indian Security Policy* (New Jersey: Princetone University Press, 1986), pp. 214-17.

64. Dunne P., "The Political Economy of Military Expenditure", *Cambride Journal of Economics* Vol. 14, No. 4, December 1990, p. 402.

65. Herrera Remy, *Statistics on Military Expenditure in Developing Countries: Concepts, Methodological Problems and Sources,* OECD (Organisation for Economic Co-operation and Development), document, Paris, 1994, p. 13.

66. Herrera Remy, *Ibid.,* p. 14.

67. Somnath Sen, *Military Expenditure Data for Developing Countries: Methods and Measurement* in Lamb G. (ed.), "*Military Expenditure and Economic Development*": A Symposium on Research Issues, The World Bank Discussion Papers, The World Bank Washington, D.C., 1992, p. 3.

68. Sen Somnath and Deger S., *Military Expenditure in the Third World Countries: The Economic Effects* (London, Routledge and Kegan Paul, 1986), pp. 37-58.

69. Becker Abraham, *Military Expenditure Limitations for Arms Control: Problems and Prospects* (Cambridge Massachusetts: Ballinger Publishing Company, 1978), p. 19.

79. Herrera Remy, *op. cit.,* p. 17.

CHAPTER 3

Concept of National Security

Introduction

This chapter attempts to elaborate modern concept of National Security and National Security Policy. The idea is to analyse the rationale and inevitability of defence expenditure in terms of its relations to the concept of National Security. In this context, this chapter discusses the concept of 'public good', one of the primary concepts that deals with military expenditure or defence expenditure Finally this chapter seeks to present the main determinants of defence expenditure in the broad perspective.

National Security Concept

The term National Security is widely used and it is an ambiguous one. Different authorities interpret it differently. The term "National Security" has always been used by leaders of the country and politicians in quite a dramatic manner and for military objectives.

'Protection of a nation against external threats and attacks' was the traditional definition of National Security. But it is a very narrow view and it primarily takes into account only military defences against military threats.

In the traditional definition of "National security", the military leaders used this term to describe only military objectives. Here National Security becomes a function of the military power. However, the concept that nations seeking security rely completely on the military power, is inadequate.

It is also experienced that increase in military power alone cannot ensure security and one requires to take a much broader perspective of National Security. It should include economic, political, diplomatic, social objectives, along with military dimension.[1]

Walter Lipmann explicitly defined National Security. According to him, 'A nation has security when it does not have to sacrifice its legitimate interests to avoid war and is able, if challenged, to preserve them by war'.[2]

The internal core-values of a nation determine the national interests and it is the attempt of every nation to legitimise and protect them. The values themselves are subjective in nature and therefore Arnold Wolfers suggests that, 'National Security in the subjective sense is the absence of fear that such values will be attacked by others' but in an objective sense it measures the absence of threat to the acquired values.[3]

The analysis of various definitions of National Security lead us to the following points:

(1) National Security is directly related to values but it is not value in its own right. It is only the condition which allows a nation to maintain its acquired values.

(2) It is extremely difficult to measure security in any objective fashion because it is a relative condition. It is an evaluation based on the perceptions of a nation.

(3) It is very important to note that National Security is not a static condition that exists in a vacuum. But it is a dynamic concept determined in the context of continuously changing domestic and international environment.[4] Therefore broadly speaking National Security is the nation's plan to protect its important core values in the continuously changing environment. The core values or national values are generally territorial integrity, freedom, sovereignty and survival of the state and National Security is attainment and maintenance of these values.

The origins of the concept of National Security, at least in the USA can be traced to the different formulations of national interest. The concept of national security emerged due to dissatisfaction with the concept of national interest. The early definitions of National Security were not well framed and the concepts of national interest were not stressed.

Walter Lipmann, Arnold Wolfers and others tried to introduce clarity and exactness in this concept. Morton Kaplan's work (1957) in this area suggests that all aspects and sub systems of social behaviour constitute the behaviour system and therefore national interest and the national security interest should be considered as single important aspects in the problem of system maintenance.[5]

This type of system analysis also leads to the confirmation that national security system is interlinked with many other subsystems.

In this direction efforts were made for the integration of domestic, foreign and military policies relating to National Security. The classic example of this can be seen in the USA. In 1947 the US Congress passed the National Security Act which led to the establishment of National Security Council (NSC) to advise the President to take on integrated approach towards the matters of National Security. During that period, academicians were invited to present their views and make suggestions, in the form of papers or studies, about specific aspects of National Security. And hereafter, National Security came to be a subject of academic interest in the United States of America.[6]

Initially it was observed that military problems formed the focus of many studies on National Security. Gradually people began to understand the interlink age between political and economic scenarios and military problems. This result emanated due to the impact of the two world wars. After these world wars it became clear that industrial growth and economic resources are indicative of a nation's potential for war. Thus national security experts started studying the subject from economic angles too.

As a result an attempt has been made to assess and define, as accurately as possible, all elements that sum up to indicate a nation's economic potential for war. Many economists all over the world have devoted their time in studying and ensuring that national resources are allocated appropriately between military and non-military sectors of the economy. The studies focused on finding the answer to what proportion of resources is needed to protect internal values from the external threat. When we talk of internal values, it is also the social, economic and political aspects. They also need to be given due importance.

The field of National Security has many common links with international relations and external policy. There is a growing realisation that the security of a nation cannot be studied in isolation and therefore National Security focuses on integration of the internal (domestic policy) and external (foreign policy) activities of the state which gives the total and final shape to the behaviour of the nation.[7]

Therefore, today we accept a broader definition of National Security which includes economics, diplomatic, political, social and foreign policy dimensions in addition to the military dimension at domestic and international environment level.

National Security Policy; Values, Power and National Interests

Concern for the security of a nation is an ancient one and each nation tries to optimise its national security. The policy designed to achieve it, in simpler terms can be called as National Security Policy. Like national Security the concept of national security policy is quite difficult to define. Frank Trager and Frank Simone have described it as "It is that part of government policies having its objective as the creation of national and international political conditions favourable to the protection and extension of national values against existing and potential adversaries."[8] On the basis of this definition we can identify some of the important elements which should be analysed in order to understand the process of national security policy formulations. These key elements are values, national interests, governments, the domestic and the international environment. The essence of National Security policy is to protect and if possible extend national values.[9]

National Values

National values can be different for different nations and they depend on national goals. But there are certain common and universally important values which can be termed as core values. Most of the times the basic values tend to be vague and abstract.

It is also difficult to measure the relative importance of the specific value because of their competitive nature. Generally Freedom, Survival and Prosperity are considered as the core values of the nation-state. The most fundamental national value out of these is survival.[10]

Every national security policy is planned to ensure survival of the nation. The national value survival includes territorial integrity, sovereignty, and protection of the population. These values are generally assumed to be as the collective will of the people.[11]

By and large national values are determined by the ruling group (the Government) and the policy makers. Therefore they tend to be highly subjective but the core values remain universal and therefore they are the most fundamental values. In real policy making these national values are related to specific situations to make them less abstract. National security policy makers relate these values to the domestic and international environment in which a nation has to survive. This relationship builds the foundation and gives concrete shape to the national interest.[12]

National Interests

National interests in simpler terms can be explained as the conditions that the nation is attempting to attain in both domestic and international environments at any cost. They are the links between values and policies.[13]

National interests like values can be many and conflicting with each other at various stages and environments therefore it is necessary to reconcile them as per the priority. Sometimes the nation may have to make acceptable compromises without giving up vital national interests.[14]

International environment is an important factor influencing the national security policy. This is due to the fact that any security policy is a response to perceive threats from external powers. No nation can precisely measure the level of threat, but on the basis of the capabilities and intentions of potential enemies a nation determines its response by adopting a different National Security Policy.

The primary focus of national security policy aims at the countering of military threats but this aspect is not sufficient in the present day context. All potential threats do not take the military form and they can be in any other form like economic threats, ideological challenges, and political and social challenges.

There are various challenges even at the domestic level which might turn into an internal security threat. These threats may be on the economic, political, social, religious or any other grounds causing great dissatisfaction.

National security policy must be designed in such a way that it provides the ability to the nation to counter all these internal and external threats.

Concept of National Security in India

In the early periods India adopted the term National Security in a narrow sense and only focused on military component but now we accept a much broader view.

According to K. Subramanyam. "National Security does not mean safeguarding territorial integrity. It also means ensuring that the country (India) is industrialised rapidly and has a developed cohesive, egalitarian and technologically advanced society. Anything which comes in the way of these developments internally or externally is a threat to India's National Security."[16]

Thus in India we interpret the National Security as the permanent and continuing guarantee provided by the state to ensure the safety of its subjects and their values, national unity against an attack or any potential danger of attack externally or internally.

National Security policy making and its implementation is fast emerging as a new area of work. The first known work in this area in the broad sense appeared when Richard C. Scyder, H.C. Bruck and Butron, completed their study in 1954 which was published as Foreign Policy Decision-Making in 1962.[17]

Earlier India's national security policy was mainly determined by Jawaharlal Nehru in consultation with a few individuals. There did not exist any well laid down mechanism for national security policy making. In that period all the relevant inputs were not taken into account for integrated national security policy.

The only contribution to National Security policy was the publication of policy related speeches of policy makers in 1950s and 1960s. Even after this Indian contribution in this area is limited to very few works like Dr. A.P. Rana's work on Nehru's Foreign Policy in 1976. In 1970s and 1980s an important contribution was made by Jayantanuja Bandopadhya and Shashi Tharoor and other retired military experts. They analysed the processes, institutions, personalities and basic determinants of foreign and national security policy making.[18]

During this period K. Subramanyam advocated the need to create a systematic mechanism and a single body to plan and coordinate all the aspects of national security. He recommended the creation of a National Security secretariat.

During the same period Bandopadhya proposed creation of national security planning council analogous to the planning commission. This period also witnessed the beginning of the analysis of decision making processes in national security area in India. The Institute for Defence Studies and Analyses (IDSA), New Delhi was established during this period which contributed to some extent to the new trend. There are a few studies which aim at examining the role of the parliament, political pressure groups in the training of national security in India.

In the late 1980s National Security Council (NSC) was proposed to be established for the proper national security policy making which came into existence only in 1990. But still it is not playing a very effective role. Therefore, we have to go a long way in the making of a National Security Policy and to chalk out its implementation.

Rationale for Defence Spending—Need and Inevitability of Defence Spending

We have seen that National Security is a comprehensive term that entails the defending of the values the people cherish in the nation-state from internal and external threats. Today we understand the term National Security (N.S.) in the broader sense but still military power remains the most important ingredient of National Security.

'Survival' is the most fundamental national value and therefore the ultimate focus of any National Security policy should be to preserve this value. Mere physical survival by itself is not enough but it includes protection of the population, territorial integrity and sovereignty.

Military power is essential for the survival of a nation because it provides the capability of protecting the value called 'survival'. In reality, it is the defence expenditure which generates the military power of a nation.

It is the primary duty of any government to protect the people it governs. Adam Smith was one of the first economists who justified the expense on defence as the first duty of the government. 'Smith's view that defence expenditure is a necessity and should be done efficiently is probably still the mainstream one'.[19]

Therefore, we see that 'defence' is one of the most important single items of expenditure in all the countries of the world. Defence expenditure ensures national freedom and other advantages.

Military power is created by defence expenditure. Any power is a form of influence and it has several dimensions. Military power is ultimately the power to destroy and kill or to occupy and control and hence to coerce people. The important ingredient of military power is military force. Military force and military power are often confused, in fact equated.[20]

Here one must understand that regiments, weapons systems, naval vessels, nuclear weapons etc. are only instruments of generating military power. Infact military power like any other power and influence is relational and it exists only in relation to other nations.

The present world order is conflicting in nature and every nation-state in the system is determined either in conserving its core values or extending national goals. There is a possibility that while pursuing these goals other nation-states are likely to be affected and due to this the danger of war has not as yet vanished from this world.

Because of this danger of war and a threat to the territorial integrity, sovereignty and survival, all the countries of the world are spending large amount of money and resources on their national defence. It is also important to note that almost all regimes believe that military expenses create and sustain a power which is indispensable for the pursuit of key foreign policy goals and for the maintenance of national security against both external and internal threats. No country in the world is completely secure and safe from threats to its integrity and therefore defence spending has become essential and inevitable from times immemorial.

The rationale of defence spending can be summarised as follows—

(a) The 'survival' is the most fundamental national value. It includes protection of territorial integrity, sovereignty, freedom, protection of population and protection of other important national values. The defence spending provides the power to the government/ruling elite to protect this value of the nation state.

(b) Defence spending helps in preserving the process of development—The term 'threat' has only connotations of external aggression or attack. But there are many threats which are indirect in nature and they may be in the forms of unfavourable trade terms, increasing public debt, political blackmail, technological impediments etc.

(c) Defence spending generate military power and it is used for guarding economic assets of a country. In a war or in subversive acts like terrorist activities economic assets are often attacked which cripple the economy. Military power can be used to project the process of economic development against such attacks.

(d) Defence spending can be used in the actual process of development. There are spin-off effects of defence R&D. It expands mass communication, employment, education facilities, construction activities, nuclear, space and other advanced technological areas. In short civil-military relations are effectively employed in the economic development of a country.

(e) Defence spending provides security to the life and property of the people. It also ensure trade and prosperity of the nation.
(f) The armed forces of a nation-state provide sanctity to the government authority.
(g) Military power helps the nation–state in projecting it as a powerful entity in domestic and external security environment.[21]

'Defence' as a Pure Public Good

Adam Smith can be very rightly called as the father of Defence economics. The summary given by Smith in his introduction and repeated at the end of Book IV of 'An Inquiry into the Nature and Causes of the Wealth of Nations, 1776' appears to be a complete research programme on public economy.

In this section he has clearly stated that the necessary expenses of the sovereign or common wealth are directly induced from three major duties (i) defence (ii) Justice (iii) Public works and Education.[22]

Adam Smith has considered Defence as a predominant branch of public economy. As a priority among other public economy, defence is not treated by Smith Adam as a by product but as an economic matter in itself.[23]

Adam Smith also has pointed out the difference between defence and other public goods i.e. justice, education and public works. According to him defence is a 'pure' public good and defence expenses must be entirely contributed by the whole society on the principle of contribution in proportion to their abilities.[24]

The Concept of Public Good

A public good is a commodity or service which if supplied to one person can be made available to others at no extra cost. A public good is said to exhibit non-rival consumptions of the good i.e. one person's consumption of the good does not reduce its availability to any one else.[25]

The main point of distinction between public good and private good is that in case of private good one person's consumption precludes the consumption of the same unit by another person and this is not the case in public good. Defence is considered as a pure public good.[26]

The concept of pure public good in the original formulations of Samuelson P. and Musgrave R. is a good which must be consumed in equal amount by all and no one can be excluded from enjoying it.[27]

The important characteristics of public good can be enumerated as below—

(1) *The principle of non-exclusion*—This means if a public good has been made available it can be consumed by everybody and anybody without limiting a supply of it to a few people. It is impossible to ensure that only those individuals who paid for the good could obtain it because there is no such device by which any one can be excluded from its consumption.
Since this good could be obtained without payment then no one will be willing to pay for it and there is a tendency of 'free-rider' (Those enjoying benefits of public good without paying for it).

(2) *Failure of market mechanism*–people do not reveal their preference for public good as in case of private good. In the case of private good those consumers who pay the price have an exclusive right to enjoy what they have paid for but it is not possible in the case of public good.[28]

(3) *Non-rival consumption*—In the case of private good one individual's consumption of the good deprives the other from consuming it, on the other hand the public good is equally consumed by all. Samuelson

P.A. introduced a strong case between private and public good in 1955 in his theory of public expenditure. He explains as follows—

"A private consumption good like bread is one whose total quantity can be parcelled among two or more persons with one man having a loaf less if another gets a loaf more. Let us assume that X_1 is the total bread loaves. There are two persons Man 1 and Man 2 and X^1_1 and X^1_2 were their respective private good consumptions. Since it is a private good we can say that consumption $X_1 = X^1_1 + X^2_1$.

There is also public good provided in the society and its total consumption is X_2. Each person can consume or enjoy according to his/her taste and it is related to total X_2 good by a condition of equality due to non-rival consumption i.e, consumption of public good X_2 and Man1 and Man2 are equal. Their respective consumptions of public good X_2 are X^1_2 and X^2_2 and it is related to total quantity X_2 in this way $X_2 = X^1_2$ $X2 = X^2_2$.

It means the consumption of public good by Man1 does not affect or reduce the commodity of the same good by another one i.e. Man2. So both of them can equally enjoy the public good in same quantity.[29]

(4) *Consumption externality*—This term refers to the economic effects which flow from the production or use of goods to other parties or economic units. These effects are often found in case of public goods. It can be called as spill over, neighbourhood or third party effects. Such externality may be economic gain or loss. Thee benefits are externalized rather than internalised in cases of public goods because nobody can be prevented from enjoying it.

(5) *Marginal cost is zero or near zero*—It means an additional member of a society can be benefited by the use of public good without appreciably adding to the total cost. It means the marginal cost is zero or near zero.

(6) *Non-divisibility*—A pure public good is enjoyed rather than consumed and it is not possible to divide it into pieces/units.[30]

All such characteristics show that pure public good and pure private goods are two extreme poles. In reality pure public good is a rare phenomenon and what we commonly experience is a mixed or impure public good.

'Defence' is often regarded as pure public good. The supportive argument is that once defence capability is established every citizen benefits from it equally. Once public good such as defence is produced it does not matter whether an individual wants to consume it or not, the consumption of defence cannot be exclusive.[31]

The externalities are also found in case of defence. It means benefits are available to others as a result of its production. These benefits are externalised due to non-excludability.[32]

Public good such as defence can be obtained without payment and therefore marginal cost of it is near zero. Like private good price cannot be determined for public good and there arises a need to find out the method to collect the resources for provision of such public good.

Individuals have an interest in concealing their marginal benefits from the provision of a public good and as far as possible try to avoid to pay the contributions. One must remember that it is very difficult to assess individual contributions towards providing public good.

Different consumers can put varying amount of value on the marginal benefits received to them from public good. Adam Smith is of the view that the cost of public good (defence) should be met by contributions from the citizens on the basis of the benefits principle. But it is found that benefit principle would prove to be unworkable because of the unwillingness of the citizens to contribute to such defence expenditure and liability of the community to search that individuals were declaring their true interests or reveal their real economic preferences.[33]

Therefore one can say that the economic concept of a pure public good helps in understanding the nature of defence expenditure but it shows some limitations when we analyse the matter in greater depths. Adam Smith's views on the provision of defence expenditure on the basis of benefits to individuals are analytically sound but they fail when applied in practical application.

We know that in reality provision of public good such as defence is a matter of collective choice. Generally we find that such public good is provided by the government and paid for through compulsory taxation so economics of defence has become important part of pubic finance. The relation between public good and public expenditure is thus a straight forward matter and the principle of 'marketing mode' can not be applied here.[34]

Defence Spending or Security Determinants—External and Internal Factors

The above mentioned points strengthen the argument that defence spending is unavoidable expenditure. This is because it gives security to the people it governs.

Security is often described either as a freedom from insecurity or simply a state of mind. It is essentially a subjective phenomenon and essential for the 'survival' of a nation in the world.[35]

The security in its totality is derived from factors both at the internal and external levels. It is also compounded of economic, diplomatic, political, social and cultural, technical and military attributes at national (internal) and international (external) levels. The military attribute has remained the dominant one. Military power is generated from the level of defence spending. Military power gives the capacity to use violence or any other method for the protection, enforcement or extension of national interest. It remains as the most important instrument with which no nation-state has yet found it completely to dispense with.

The military power of a nation depends on three factors. One is military power potential i.e. resources base which can be mobilised for establishing military force. The second is 'value' placed on military power by a nation which determines actual proportion of potential resource transformed into military strength. The third factor is 'skill' with which resources are used political as well as militarily.[36]

Three Basic Determinants of Defence Spending at General Level

This means allocation of resources for defence/Military is not purely economic process but it is also a part of the political bargaining process. These resource allocation decisions for defence/military/security are taken by evaluating the following factors—

(a) External environment around the country–Foreign policy objectives of subregional, regional, global levels.
(b) Domestic environment in the country—Political, economic, social, technological and military factors and goals to be achieved.
(c) Economic capability or available resources with the country, Institutions, Actors and processes deciding the allocation patterns and their threat perceptions.

In this way the level of defence spending is determined at the focal point of influences from both international and domestic sources. The changes in national and international scenarios, threat perceptions, institutions (taking decisions) economic capability can bring about changes in defence spending levels.

NOTES AND REFERENCES

1. Bekonwitz Morton and Bock P.G., 'National Security', *in International Encyclopedia of Social Sciences,* Vol. XI, (New York: The MacMillan Company and Free Press, 1968), pp. 39-40.

2. Lipmaan Walter, *U.S. Foreign Policy Schield of the Republic,* (Boston Little, 1943), p. 5.
3. Wolfers Arnold, *Discord and Collaboration: Essays on International Politics* (Baltimore N.D., 1962), p. 150.
4. Collins John M., *How to Analyse National Security: Conceptual Framework of US Defence Planning: A Critique,* (New York: Westview Press, 1982), p. 4.
5. Kaplan Morton, *System and Process in International Politics,* (New York, 1957), p. 149.
6. Beckonwitz Mortan and Bock P.G., *op. cit.,* p. 41.
7. Beckonwitz Morton and Bock P.G., *op. cit.,* pp. 41-42.
8. Frank Trager and Frank Simonie, 'An Introduction to the study of National Security' in Frank N. Trager and P.S. Konnenberg (eds.), in *National Security and American Society* (Manhatten: 1973) p. 6.
9. Frank Trager and Frank Simonie, *Ibid.,* p. 7.
10. Collins John M., *op. cit.,* p. 5.
11. Collins John M., *op. cit.,* p. 6.
12. Collins John M., *op. cit.,* p. 6.
13. Collins John M., *op. cit.,* p. 7.
14. Collins John M., *op. cit.,* p. 6.
15. Collins John M., *op. cit.,* p. 7.
16. Subramanyam K., *'Our National Security',* (New Delhi: Minerva Associates, 1972), p. 7.
17. Kamath P.V., "Trends: The study of National Security Policy", *Strategic Analysis,* Vol. XIV, No. 4, New Delhi, July 1991, p. 432.
18. Kamath P.V., *Ibid.,* p. 432.
19. Kennedy Gavin, *The Economies of Defence'* (London: Faber & Faber, 1974), p. 38.
20. Knorr Klaus, "International purposes of military power", in Garnett John (ed.) *Theories of Peace and Security: A Reading in Contemporary Strategic Thought* (London: Macmillan and St. Martin's Press, 1970), pp. 50-52.

21. Y. Lakshmi, *Trends in India's Defence Expenditure,* (New Delhi: ABC Publishing House, 1988), pp. 11-16.
22. Smith A., *An Inquiry into the nature and causes of the Wealth of Nations,* as cited in Schmidt C. and Blackbay Frank (eds.), *Peace, Defence and Economic Analysis* (New York: St. Martin's Press, 1987), pp. 24-25.
23. Schmidt C., *Peace and War Economics in Retrospect* in Schmidt C. and Black Bay Frank (eds.) *op. cit.,* p. 24.
24. Schmidt and Black Bay Frank (eds.), *op. cit.,* p. 27.
25. High Dalton, *Principles of Public Finance,* London, p. 59.
26. Samuelson P.A., The Pure "Theory of Public Expenditure", in the *Review of Economics and Statistics,* Vol. 36, No. 4, Nov. 1954, p. 387.
27. Musgrave R. and Musgrave P., *Public Finance in Theory and Practice* (5th edition), (Singapore: McGraw Hill Book Company, 1989), pp. 42-45.
28. Mathew T., *The Economics of Public Expenditure,* (Bombay: Vora and Company Publishers Pvt. Ltd., 1972), pp. 123-126.
29. Samuelson P.A., "Diagramatic Exposition of a Theory of Public Expenditure", *The Review of Economics and Statistics,* Vol. 37, No. 4, Nov. 1995, p. 350.
30. Olvey L.D. and others, *The Economics of National Security: Weighting the Cost of Defence* (New Jersey: Avery Publishing Group Inc., 1984), p. 9.
31. Kennedy Gavin, *op. cit.,* p. 40.
32. Kennedy Gavin, *op. cit.,* p. 41.
33. Kennedy Gavin, *op. cit.,* p. 48.
34. Musgrave P. and Musgrave R. *op. cit.,* p. 164.
35. Wolfers Arold, *Discord and Collaboration: Essays on International Politics,* Baltimore, 1962, p. 150.
36. Garnett John (ed.), *Theories of Peace and Security: A Reader in Contemporary Strategic Thought* (London: Macmillan and St. Martin's Press, 1970), p. 51.

CHAPTER 4

Theoretical Model of Defence Budget in India—An Attempt for Redefinition

Introduction

In the previous chapter the general determinants of defence expenditure were analysed and it also made a survey of the theories and the concepts which constitute the rationale for defence expenditure for a country, keeping in mind National Security considerations. Given this overview, now an attempt is made to present an integrated model for defence expenditure determination in India. This model seeks to spell out the role of economic capability, internal security factors and external security factors and in the context of these two, the way in which defence expenditure can be analysed or perceived. An attempt here is being to redefine the approach to defence expenditure. In fact, this model broadens the traditional definition of defence expenditure that restricts defence expenditure only to the military spending *per se*.

This broad definition of defence expenditure on the basis of U.N.O's work and other works is already discussed in chapter 2 of this book. There is a need to accept this broader defence expenditure for realistic analysis. Hence, this chapter also analyses defence expenditure of India for the period 1970-71 to 1994-95 on the basis of this broader definition. This broad definition of defence expenditure now includes expenditure in the areas of dual purpose technology, paramilitary, police and other internal security expenditures and other supportive defence expenditures. This chapter also evaluates the exponential growth rates of these various constituents of defence expenditure for the period of 1970-71 to 1994-95.

Factors Determining the Size of Defence Budget

We know that national security is a multidimensional concept. It covers various factors of national endeavours and assumptions which lead to national existence. The Military factor is the most important component of national security. Security concerns have compelled the diversion of a part of valuable national resources for the purpose of defence. The quantum of resources that a country diverts for its defence purposes is shown by its defence budget.

The size of defence budget is primarily determined by—

1. External and Internal security threat perceptions of a nation and
2. The resources available to meet these threats i.e. economic capability and hence it is an act of balancing in these two factors.

Defence budget determination is a complex process not a simple one as it seems to be. This is because it involves the following aspects (i) analysis of geo-strategic environment, (ii) geopolitical compulsions (iii) geo-economic compulsions around the country, in the light of (iv) national values, (v) national objectives (vi) national interests. This kind of analysis gives a clear picture of the requirements of essential security of a nation. National priorities will give shape and size of defence budget.

Every nation will try to be closer to its national objectives taking into account its resources. The resources are limited and needs are unlimited therefore a nation tries to harmonize the needs and resources in such a way that the prevailing national objectives and preferences are satisfied. Here economics play a crucial role in the decision-making of national security.

At the normative level economics helps in understanding the fundamental issues of (i) what national objectives should be in the present strategic environment. It also goes beyond issue of technical efficiency and tells us which of (ii) the feasible outputs to be produced and (iii) how to distribute the same to individuals. No economic model will enable a decision-maker to mechanically determine the division of resources in defence and non-defence areas or among different types of goods within the allocated resources for defence. This is primarily due to public good ensuing from defence.

Parties to Decide Defence Expenditure

In case of public goods the allocation of resources is determined by political arena and it involves decision-maker i.e. (institutions and actors) employing subjective value judgements on marginal usefulness of particular good or service related to social costs of procuring it. It is also not easy to reconstruct the preference system of decision-maker easily. Therefore economics has a great impact on national security decision-making process by developing alternatives concerning national security.[1]

Role of Nation/State

Once the state policy objectives and national security policy are chosen by a nation it helps in deciding the level of defence spending and is explicitly given in the defence budget. Defence spending is predominately a public good and its macroeconomic effects are inextricably connected with government spending. Defence expenditure like any other form of macroeconomic expenditure is based on the benefits it provides as well as the cost it entails. For most of the defence spending output cannot be evaluated in rupee terms.

This lack of commensurability between cost and benefits create a special analysis. But there is a basic agreement that although the cost of defence is high its output is very vital for every nation, in spite of the fact that it cannot be measured. One should agree that defence utilises scarce and valuable resources yet it cannot be subjected to the same type of scrutiny as used for any other type of public expenditure because of its vital importance to the country. Due to the pure public good nature of defence, a political process of budget determination is needed to seek efficient provision of it. In principle the resources may be allotted liberally, but how far the burden will be borne by the public willingly has to be considered. It is here that economics touches political and social psychology and imposes a limit on public expenditure. Economic capability and a set of priorities also play a vital part in the decision-making about public expenditure. The government machinery, decision-makers and the process of decision have an impact of defence spending determination. The setting for defence budgeting and planning vary from nation to nation but the economic issues are similar everywhere.

Pre-requisites for Resource Allocation

The allocation of productive resources or 'inputs' involves the choice of various outputs, and the object of choosing is to maximise the satisfaction of goals and preferences effective in the nation.[2]

The allocation process involves ranking of various alternative combinations of output and choosing them in such a way that no other combination would better satisfy prevailing goals of National Security and preferences. It means allocation of resources, reconciling expanding needs with shrinking resources.

Implication Resource Allocation

It must be remembered that every resource has an alternative usage so each usage is at the expense of using it for something else. It means more of one product less of others so the most efficient combination of products is required to hormonise demand on the basis of preferences. The optimum allocation of resources can be attained when it makes a proper balance in total output. The limited resources/inputes impose restrictions on the output that can be attained and therefore selection of or a choice is necessarily a part of the problem of allocating resources. Economics is concerned with the utilisation of scarce resources and it helps in finding out the method of rational allocation of resources. The principle of marginalism helps it.[3]

The decision of resource allocations for defence and non-defence sector are always interdependent and nothing should be decided in isolation. Allocation problems arising in the defence sector concern the division of inputs between immediate production of military goods and long-term investment, the choice between better quality and larger quantity of military goods, choice of different types of weapon models, interservice allocations of military goods etc. The allocated resources for defence can be misused due to lack of co-ordination, misdirection or misinformation and may lead to wastage of productive resources. Therefore it must be carefully handled.[4]

Basis for Defence Budget Model, and an Integrated Model for India

The resource allocation for defence or size of defence budget in India is determined by economic capability, external security threat perceptions and internal or domestic security environment. It is the role of Institutions, Actors, and process to evaluate the three perspectives and give shape and size of defence budget on the basis of available resources and objectives. In India government institutions, the Parliament, Cabinet Committee for Political Affairs (CCPA), National Security Council (NSC), Defence Minister and his advisers, Finance Minister, Minister for External Affairs, Minister for Home Affairs, The Three Service Chiefs, Joint Intelligence Committee etc. are the main institutions and actors in the process of defence budgetting. This process of defence budget determination work is done in an integrated manner.

Taking into account these three parameters of defence budget and National Security Concept one can build an integrated model for better understanding of the subject. The outlined integrated model is admittedly a great simplification of very complex process of defence budget determination in India. In this model a broader definition of Defence Expenditure is used which included actual defence expenditure, paramilitary and other internal security expenditures, dual purpose technology expenditures and other defence supportive expenditures (for detailed discussion refer to in further Paras). In the light of this framework an attempt is being made to analyse Indian defence budgets since 1971.

Explanation of the Model

In this integrated model arrows are shown to indicate general sequence of events under normal conditions. Each of the steps shows the process of matching national values with budget allocation. It must be noted that decisions necessarily do not always flow from national values downward, but rather resource constraints affect state policy objectives and defence policy objectives and even in some cases national values.[5] This model is based on "requirement approach" in which output requirements are first determined and supporting budget is developed to meet these requirements. However, it is clear that national objectives and rational values are constrained by the availability of resources.[6]

This may call for modification in objectives/policy of State. The changes in international and domestic environment can produce changes in defence spending. It also can produce changes in state policy objectives and vice-versa. So the two sided arrow is shown. In the same way changes in institutions, actors and the processes can change international and domestic threat perceptions and state policy objectives.

Chart 3

An Integrated Model of Defence Budget Determinants in India

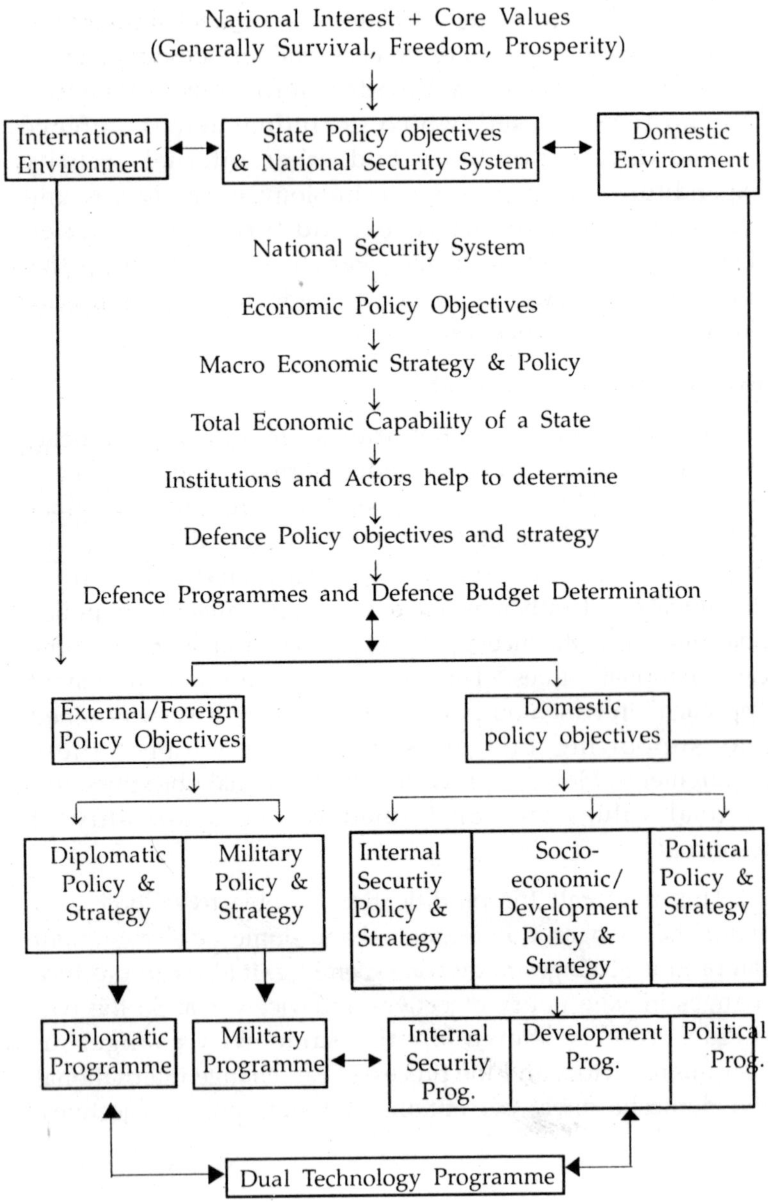

National Values and Goals

In the integrated model of defence budget, national values are the starting points. National values as defined by Traeger and Simonie are the most fundamental principles on which the social, political and physical existence of state are based.[7]

National goals and National interests determine national values. Every state tries to keep its national values intact and one of the basic and important national values is its (i) 'Survival' and it dominates other values. The other important national values can be generalised as (ii) maintenance of territorial integrity, (iii) autonomy, (iv) stability, (v) homogeneity of social existence, (vi) balanced economic development etc. It is very difficult to give precise definitions and ranking order to the national values in a democratic nation.

These national values become the basis of foreign policy objectives of a nation because attainment or promotion of national values may require interactions with other nation-states.

The concept of national values is broad and not precise concept and therefore one has to narrow it down and give a concrete and specific shape for its operational purposes. The objectives are defined to suitable form of values and they enable a nation to devise a plan of action of strategy for attaining the same. It determines State policy and National Security policy objectives. The strategy is backed by the specific programme and expenditure on it to realise the objectives.

National Values in the Indian Context

The fundamental national values to the Indian nation state revolve around democratic norms, of a secular society, a federal polity, moral and ethical values, equal human rights, the integrity and cohesion of the pluralistic society, national strength and economic power. When these core values adopted by us are closely scrutinized in relation to the core values adopted by states in our vicinity one finds many contrasting elements and contradictions which has been leading to dissonance and friction in our security environment since independence."[8] It has also caused changes in our foreign policy.

External Security Environment

The external environment is the international environment in which a nation-state pursue its national interests and national values, it includes all those events and conditions originating beyond the political boundaries (and/or control) of state that presumably affect its military and other policies. Therefore international environment encompasses the global security environment, relations of super power and big powers, the security threats from neighbours (both at the regional and sub-regional levels), their military potential and spelling out their possible pattern and aims of relations with the concerned nation. The historical experience with other nations also affect the international environment of that nation. It is in such international environment that a nation has to promote its national values and objectives and the foreign policy is devised for this purpose. The external security environment can be analysed at three different levels (1) the global (2) the regional (3) contiguous or neighbours. The geostrategic location, geo-political and geo-economic environments are important determinants here.

External Security Factors for India

India's strategic position bears heavily on its external security. India faces an extensive defence and security perimeter today. Over 16500 km of land border, including nearly 7000 k.m. of borders with states with which significant territorial disputes still persist, a 7600 km. long coast line and 2.5 million sq. km. of Exclusive Economic Zone (EEZ) to protect besides over 500 islands most of them separated from the mainland; increasing shares in off shore resources and trade across the seas, presence of extra regional military forces in the Indian Ocean, power rivalries competition and tensions stemming from various sources including nuclear issue in the region and different types of terrain with internal security threats add to the difficulties.[9]

(i) The vastness of the country, (ii) its weak economy, (iii) its long coastline and (iv) its unsatisfactory frontiers with some of its neighbours objectives make India more vulnerable. She is exposed to security threats from all levels. (v) There are external threats from various directions such as nuclear China, hostile Pakistan, unstable Bangladesh, Afghanistan, Nepal, Volatile Sri Lanka, Myanmar, South East Asian Countries, Indian Ocean region countries and Superpower i.e. U.S.A and disintegrated USSR.

Domestic Environment and Economic Capability in India

The domestic environment includes socio-economic and political system in the nation. It includes all those factors and systems that are necessary for the preservation and perpetuation of national values or core values. In the domestic environment broad national values give only orientation to national policy and they need to be defined to concrete and specific objectives for formulation of strategic, policies and programmes. These national objectives which are derived from national values can be further classified into economic and non-economic objectives. Non-economic objectives do not entail resource expenditure but they bring about changes in the orientation of the domestic policy. On the other hand economic objectives require expenditure of resources to attain those objectives. These economic objectives are of two types-

(1) Those which limit aggregate public expenditure and affect total resource allocation between public and private sectors in India.
(2) Those economic objectives which compete for specific amounts of available public funds. This includes the competition for available resources in defence and non-defence sectors.

The government, the politicians and the decision-making authorities in India take into account international and domestic environment and formulate state policy objectives and national security of India. Here the interaction is two way and accordingly modifications are made to achieve various objectives.

Working of an Integrated Model in India

The state policy objectives shape broader economic policy objectives in India. This serves as the basis of Macro Economic Policy and Macro Economic Strategy in India. The main objectives of macroeconomic policy in India are maintenance of high levels of employment. Satisfactory increase in growth of productive capacity of economy, price stability, reducing income inequalities etc. The resources at the hand are always limited and hence according to Greenwald Doughlas, "Each state takes considerable efforts to determine its macro economic objectives and tries to accept the feasible objectives.[10]

The Macro economic strategy is generally a specific method adopted by the state of achieve macro economic objectives. The principal tools of macro economic strategy are monetary and fiscal policies. The most important vehicle of fiscal policy is the government budget. It is planned annually in India, reviewed and if required improved and modified by the Parliament. The success of macro economic strategy depends upon the co-ordination of monetary and fiscal policies. In this way macro economic objectives and strategy finally give shape and size to the total economic capability of a nation.

Authorities/Institutions Deciding Defence Budget in India

The government institutions, the Parliament, ruling party leaders, perceptions of CCPA, the three Service Chiefs, National Security Council, the Prime Minister, Defence, Finance, Home, and the External Affairs Ministers, Intelligence Bureau Information, Advisors to the Prime

Minister and the Defence Minister play very significant role in the determination of the defence policy objective and defence budget in India. They use three determinants: (a) Economic capability (b) External security threat perceptions and environment (c) Domestic Security threat perception and environment.

In India external security rests with the Ministry of Defence and the internal security rests with the Ministry of Home Affairs except in some exceptional situation both work together but there is a continuous linkage between internal and external security management programmes for overall security/defence of the country. Hence in the integrated model it is shown by a dotted double arrow. In the dotted part dual purpose programmes are shown because they have both military and developmental/civil uses. This dual purpose technology areas include programmes like nuclear, space, Ocean development, electronics etc. which are well developed in India.

In the model two sided arrow is shown from foreign policy objectives and domestic policy objectives to defence budget because these both can influence each other. Some foreign policy objective in India are achieved by diplomatic method which includes political and economic diplomacy. The other are military policy objectives achieved by defence programme.

The domestic policy is divided broadly into internal security strategy; socio-economic/development strategy and political strategy and programmes in India. These strategies direct the policy and specific programmes in these areas.

Internal security programme and defence programme are linked together for a coherent defence policy of a state. The dual purpose technology area contribute as a modern factor supporting defence capability. The dual purpose area is also called as hidden defence expenditure area. Dual purpose area contributes to the defence as well as development programmes therefore a link is shown to both the directions from this area. The political strategy aims at developing the political stability programmes which was necessary for the successful implementation of various policies and for the security of the country.

Institutional perspective of defence budget determination is important because it exerts pressures, shows institutional interests and their relative importance in terms of influence in defence budget determination.

The National Security objectives are variable and they change according to challenges and threats. External threats are met by evolution of foreign policy and defence strategy. Threats to internal security whether from within or outside support have to be met by formulation of a sound internal security policy. The resources India has and is likely to have at each stage have to be assessed.

Under the existing systems in India there are no statutory structures for evaluation of threats to the security or to define the decision-making process for the evaluation of security policy separately. In India's existing political systems, the Prime Minister with his cabinet is responsible for national security. The other important institutions include Parliament, Ministry of Defence, Ministry of Finance, Ministry of External Affairs, National Security Council (NSC), Chiefs-of staff committee, Army, Navy, Airforce headquarters.

The important key persons are President, Prime Minister, Defence Minister, three service chiefs, Defence secretary, Fiance Minister, Scientific and other advisers to Prime Minister and Defence Minister and a number of interrelated persons and media.

As in the British system, the supremacy of Parliament in all matters is the corner stone of the Indian political system. It is the Parliament where decisions regarding defence expenditure are taken. There is a fusion of executive and legislative power, the former being part of the latter and overriding power is given to the executive as long as they command majority in the Parliament.[11]

The chart 4 gives a very rough idea of the institutional perspective. The arrows show that these institutions and Actors try to play a role in defence budget determination and their brief details are as below-

Chart 4
Institutional Perspective of Defence Budget in India

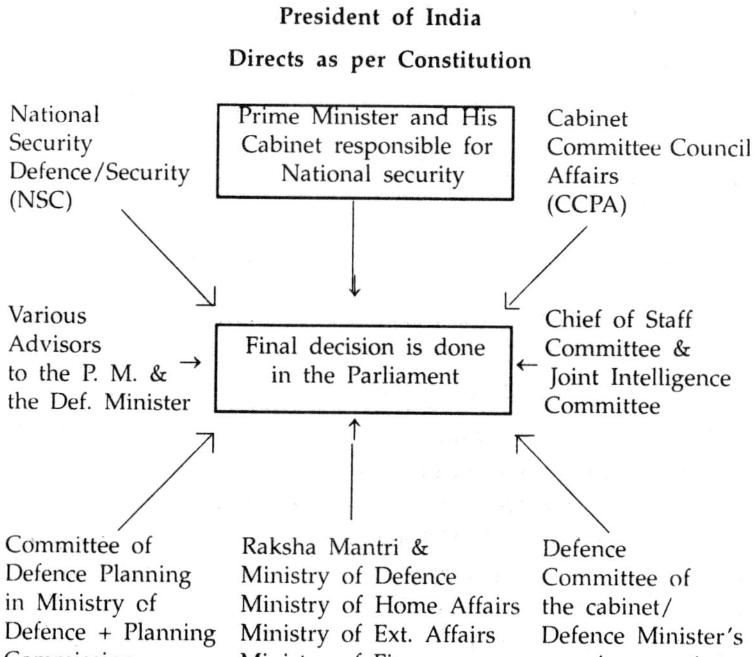

Cabinet Committee on Political Affairs (CCPA)

In a parliamentary democracy the Prime Minister is the head of the government. He and his cabinet is finally responsible for national defence and are supposed to take final political decisions. Since the cabinet is too large a body a much smaller body the Cabinet Committe on Political

Affairs (CCPA) was created. The CCPA is designed to analyse and evaluate the internai and external situations, and provide direction and policy to the government to run the country. In addition to this there is a Defence Committee of the cabinet (DCC). It was designed to take care of political higher control of defence but is failed miserably in the 1962 Sino-Indian war. Therefore it was converted into the Emergency committee of the cabinet. This ECC lasted till 1967 and thereafter functions of this committee were added to the CCPA and in this way the CCPA widened its scope.[12]

The CCPA is chaired by the Prime Minister. Its members are the Home Minister, the Minister for External Affairs and Minister for Defence. In May 1986 the Minister for Human Resources Development and the Minister for Finance were also made the members of the CCPA. Any expert who was required by the committee could be asked to attend. The composition of the CCPA is not statutory and it can be as effective as the Prime Minister wants it to be.

Defence Minister's Committee

There is a Defence Minister's Committee with the Defence Minister in the chair and three Service Chiefs, the Defence Secretary and the Financial Adviser as members. At present there are also Chiefs of the staff committee which includes the Army, Navy and Airforce chiefs. The Chief and staff having the maximum length of service in the Committee is made the chairman of the Committee. The chiefs of staff of the three services are responsible for the war worthiness of their respective service and act as advisers to the Defence Minister. They are also advisers to the Prime Minister functioning through Chiefs of Staff Committee.

Since 1963 the Defence Minister's committee was gradually replaced by the Defence Ministers morning meetings. By 1974 the Defence Minister's committee went into suspended animation. The last occasion this committee met was in May 1974 and it has not met since then.[13]

Committee for Defence Planning

In 1978 a committee of Defence planing was set up under the chairmanship of the Cabinet Secretary. The three service chiefs, Secretary to the Prime Minister, the Defence Secretary, the Secretary Defence Production, the Foreign Secretary, the Finance Secretary and the Secretary Planning Commission are the members of this committee.

In 1986 a Policy Advisory Committee was set up under the Chairmanship of Mr. G. Parthsarathy to take a view of long term options of foreign policy and national security but it proved to be a non-starter and it was soon wound up.

National Security Council

In August 1990 the National Security Council (NSC) was set up by the Government of India. The Prime Minister is the chairman of the NSC and the Ministers of Defence, Finance, Home Affairs and External Affairs are the other members of it. The NSC as necessary request other Union Ministers and any Chief Minister of state to attend meeting of the council. The council may also invite experts and specialists to attend the meetings if found necessary. At present the Chairman of Joint Intelligence Committee serves as the secretary to NSC. The NSC was set up in order to get integrated and coordinated view of national security by considering economic, political, military and social aspects at international and domestic levels. The NSC will provide long term assessment and shape the Government policy.

The NSC will ensure the implementation of its recommendations by constant monitoring process and review. In this way efforts are made to restructure and strengthen institutions related to defence budget determination.

The Structure of Ministry of Defence

Chart 5 whihc is given below will help in understanding the linkages and relationship of various institutions and actors in the process of budget determination for defence.

Chart 5
Structure of Ministry of Defence

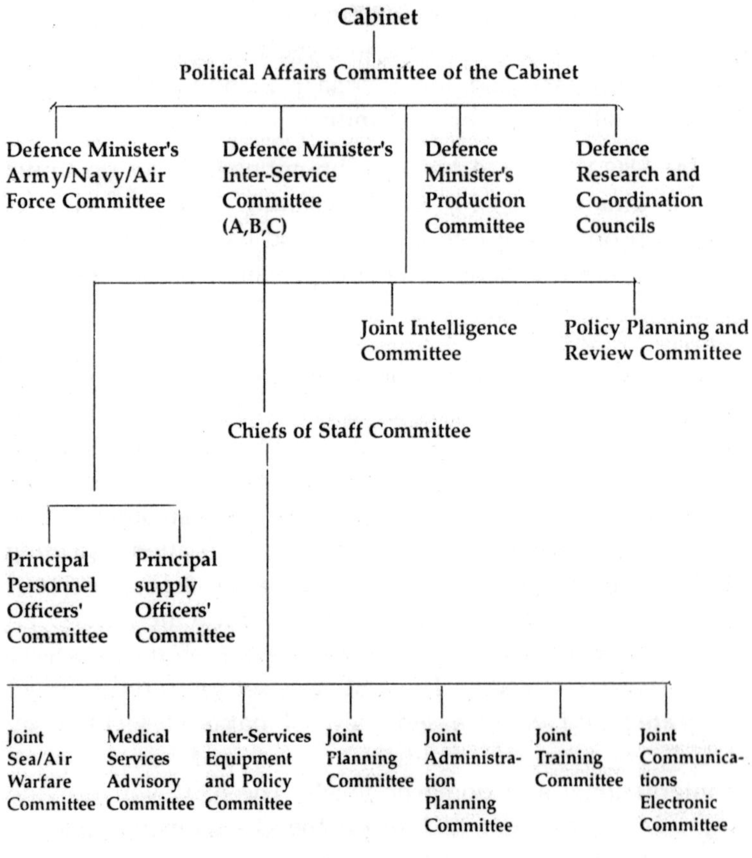

Source: Venkateshwaran, A.L., *Defence Organisation in India: A study of Major Developments in Organisation and Administration since Independence.* (Ministry of Information and Broadcasting: Delhi Jan. 1967)

On the basis of an integrated model given and on an institutional perspective one can analyse India's resource allocation for defence. In this analysis a broad definition of defence expenditure is used and therefore it would be appropriate to take a review of India's defence/security strategy and policy for detailed understanding of the subject.

India's Security Strategy

A nation's security environment comprises the entire gamut of prevailing issues that may directly or indirectly internally or externally underline or reinforce her political, economic and military well being. Therefore India's security perspective like most other countries must be shaped by geo strategic, economic and geopolitical environment in which it has to operate.

The security of a vast country like India has many dimensions – sociological, economic, political environmental, ethnic, internal as well as external. We have already taken a review of external and internal threats to the security of India. Like any other country India has also tried to preserve and perpetuate its core values with the help of national security strategy. The National security of a country can be termed as the art and science of employing a nation's intellectual economic, political, technological and military resources, to achieve its national objectives both in peace and war. It is essentially in evolutionary process.

It requires analysis of security environment vital national interests, assessment of available resources and formulation of meaningful and comprehensive policy to tackle the threats. The sense of preparedness against external aggression is of fundamental importance in national security strategy. The problems of development, poverty alleviation, social welfare, technological developments etc., take priority over security issues. It is not easy to formulate policies and strategies that will meet national security objectives of a nation as it requires huge investment and a long gestation period. India's security strategy is evolved on the basis of its political structure, strategic environment, social and economic goals and levels of technology. When the review India's national security strategy is taken following one finds things which are expressed in the chart 6 on next page.

In the initial years of independence the defence/security was looked through the framework of nonalignment. In the

Period	*International Environment*	*Regional Environment*	*Domestic debate*	*Security Policy/Strategy*
1	2	3	4	5
1947-1961/62	1. Cold war in Europe and emergence of alliances	1. Emergent consciousness about regionalism in Asia & Africa	Defence vs. Development Nehru model of development Security through Self-reliance	Defence through diplomacy Security is a Political function.
	2. Cold war enters Asia Korean system of alliances.	2. Decline of regionalism in wake of alliances		
		3. Emergence of non alignment.		
1962-1970/71	1. Cold war in post-Cuba phase-implications of deterrence and brinkmanship and attempts made by the US and USSR to reduce tensions	1. India-China war and its effect. 2. Indo-Pakistan conflict	Collapse of earlier framework. Shift in priority-defence industry and defence buildup gets priority	Security linked to military capability Consequent narrowing of focus to South Asia.
1971-1980	1. Detenter area of application is Europe and bilateral arms control	1. Impact of Brezhnev Plan for collective security and Nixon's Guam Doctrine (Both 1969)	Consolidation of the earlier shift. Rationale given is the new power Position in South Asia (Consolidation includes	Consolidation of position in South Asia on basis of military capability.

	2. Afro-Asia remains out of the scope of detente	2. Indo-Pak war of 1971 and the emergence of India as a major power in South Asia 3. Indian PNE of 1974 4. Consolidation of Indo-Soviet relations through 1971 Treaty	forays into nuclear technology, space & other areas)	
1980/81 to 1990	1. 1980s Post-post war world US and USSR as powers on the withdrawal.	1. Emergence of SAARC	1.Shift in economic Policies. Beginning of liberalisation. Recognition given to concept of dual purpose techonology especially in frontier areas (Space, Nuclear) R&D expenditure in defence increases	1. Change in perceptions about security, emergence of a cogent internal security crisis shift from exclusive use of military capability to diplomacy (Politico military approach) Area focus is Asia Pacific.
	2. Emergence of economic factors as key determinants	2. Shift in Indian policies towards Pakistan and China, Rajiv Gandhi's visits	2. New response to changes in world order	2. Emergence of Indo-US strategic under standing.
	3. Gorbachev changes-changes in USSR and Eastern Europe	3. Responses to Gorbachev policies		

(contd...)

1	2	3	4	5
	4. disintegration of Soviet Union	4. Responses to chnages in regional balance of power		
1990 to date	Disintegration of Soviet Union World going towards Market Economy. Formation of World trade organisation	SAPTA - Normalisation With China, Bangla Desh, ASKAN Dialogue partner instability, shift of	Limits of economic Policy of liberalisation, political drift and economic capability. power postures	Development of defence, dual technology areas and

Source: Dr. Paranjape S. B., "India's Defence Policy: New perspectives", Journal of Strategic Studies, Vol. XVII, University of Allahabd, Allahabad, pp. 15-17) 1991

And additions made by Mrs. Athawale Sanhita S.

period 1947-62 the focus was on the use of diplomacy for tackling security problems. Nehru gave higher priorities to development expenditure than defence expenditure. It kept India away from power politics of groups during the Nehru years. This period can be termed as policy of defence through diplomacy. It can be said that during the period Indian security policy rested on Nehruvian model of development and policy of defence through development.

It was the 1962 China–India war that brought a change in perceptions about defence security expenditure and defence preparedness. Defence expenditure after 1962 debacle (Sino-Indian war) showed a marked increase. India realised the importance of defence preparedness and began continuous/serious rearmament programme which lasted for almost a decade. This was primarily aimed at acquisition of new defence systems, laying down foundations of larger defence industries improving border area logistics. By 1970 India emerged as a major conventional military and economic power in the region. Attention was given for developing self sufficiency in military equipment manufacture and maintenance. India was able to realise its new potential. The 1970 Bangladesh war translated the potential into reality. The creation of Bangla Desh and the emergence of India as a regional power in South Asia is the most significant event in the history of South Asia. The 1971 Indo-Soviet treaty further confirmed Soviet help to India. The ansuing political and security stability in the region raised the question about allocation of expenditure for defence and demanded reduction in defence expenditure. In this decade the complementary nature of defence and development expenditure became slowly acceptable to India and serious efforts were made to further develop military capability through non-conventional means and development of dual purpose programmes like nuclear and space research. India channelled a large portion of its defence expenditure to modernisation and R&D programmes. In 1974 India demonstrated nuclear capacity by Peaceful Nuclear Explosion

(PNE) and developed space technology. Simultaneously at a political level deliberate efforts were made to shift away from an almost exclusive dependence on the USSR for defence equipment. In 1980 the opening up of Indian economy through the liberalisation process was started by Mrs. Indira Gandhi to consolidate India's economic power required for its regional supremacy.

The 1980s saw new scenarios developing in the security and other fronts that had direct relevance to the Indian security strategy and defence expenditure allocations. Internal security threats are becoming more dominant and therefore demanding more resources for such low intensity warfares in terms of sub-version, insurgency, terrorism etc. Changes in technology are taking place at a very fast pace and continuous advances in equipment/weapon systems are making the old systems/weapons obsolete. Therefore, sophisticated technological capability has become a crucial factor in the international sphere. Dual purpose areas like nuclear science, space programmes, electronics, information technology provide a key to changing perceptions about defence policy. India has made remarkable progress in these areas.

The years 1989-91 brought dramatic changes in the world environment. The end of the cold war between the two super powers, disintegration of the USSR, reunification of Germany the US victory in the Gulfwar, international debt crisis and supremacy of economic affairs over other affairs can be termed as important events. Similarly emergence of a military and economically strong China and its increasing influence in South-East Asia and Pacific region together with the economic clout of Japan and its latent military potential are developments of extreme strategic concern. At the same time nuclear Pakistan along with other neighbours continue to pose external threats to India in 1990s. There is also rise in internal security threats to India coupled with grave economic crisis in 1990s.

The end of the cold war and the disintegration of USSR have made India lose friendly veto in the security council, reduced the Rupees Rouble trade made acquisition of spare parts and high technology weapon system from former Soviet Union very difficult.[14] This can be observed in recent incidence in which the sanctions imposed by the US on the Indian Space Research Organisation (ISRO) and Russian Space Agency Glavkosmos for sale of rocket engines to India is under inviolation of Missile Technology Control Regime (MTCR) guidelines. This had brought into public focus one of the global structures controlling transfers of advanced technology to developing nation. In 1990s technology has emerged as the supreme arbiter in international affairs. Therefore India needs to concentrate on its R&D programmes in military and non-military fields. India continued to consolidate its technological base by DRDO and dual purpose R&D programmes. Developed countries are squeezing less developing countries in a variety of ways. Some of their ways are NPT, missile control regime, intellectual property right, condition of reduction of military expenditure for getting economic aid from international institutes like World Bank IMF etc,. India is likely to find it quite difficult to catch up with the world in sophisticated military technology for quite some time with its own resources. Therefore India is welcoming the technological transfer by open and liberal economic policies. This can help India to build technology information. The world economic order is also changing during the 1990s. There is slow emergence of multicentred world with Japan and the European community taking more or less equal place with the US in economic terms. The attempts are made to build regional trading organisations like NAFTA, EC ASEAN SAPTA and these blocks will have important economic ramifications. Nations in 1990s are highly interdependent particularly in the area of economy and security and this is manifested through new military equations and economic policies and economic reorganisations.

India also had modified its strategy to meet new challenges in the 1980s and 1990s. It is a mix of defence capability and dual purpose capability and economic openness. So one needs to redefine defence expenditure and accept this new definition of it.

Redefinition of Defence Expenditure / Broad Definition of Defence Expenditure in India

In the Chapter - 2 of literature review an attempt is made to throw light on this area. The theoretical model given on page 110 for defence budget determination in India uses the broad definition of defence expenditure based on a U.N. Document of 1975 in this area. Here, one has tried to incorporate dual purpose technology areas, paramilitary, other internal security and other related supportive expenditures with defence expenditure for a more realistic analysis. In most of the studies on the defence expenditure of India have taken a narrow definition of defence expenditure and so only actual expenditure on defence services were analysed. In this broad definition which is used in this study the actual defence expenditure becomes the most important constituent along with other supportive expenditures. In Chapter - 4 of this book an attempt would be made to analyse this actual defence expenditure. In Chapters 7 and 8 internal security expenditures and dual purpose technology expenditures for the period 1970-71 to 1994-95 are analysed. This can give holistic approach to the analysis of defence expenditure.

We believe that the traditional definition of defence expenditure is inadequate and therefore one needs to take up the broader definition of defence expenditure which incorporates paramilitary, police, other internal security expenditures, dual purpose technology expenditures and other supportive areas. Now on this basis, defence expenditure of India for the period 1970-71 to 1994-95 looks as given in the Table 1 at current prices and in Table 2 at (1980-81) constant prices.

Table 1
Defence Expenditure of India on the Basis of Broader Definition
Actual Expenditure (Current Prices Rs. Crores.)

Year	*Def.*	*Police*	*Nuclear*	*Space*	*Elec*	*Scie-tech*	*OD*
1	*2*	*3*	*4*	*5*	*6*	*7*	*8*
70-71	1199.00	345.00	70.02				
71-72	1525.00	389.00	103.11		3.63	29.88	
72-73	1652.00	424.00	118.08		1.11	36.15	
73-74	1681.00	470.00	116.25	18.99	1.58	36.34	
74-75	2112.00	557.00	154.06	30.73	5.07	51.40	
75-76	2472.00	654.00	193.50	36.84	4.78	64.86	
76-77	2563.00	696.00	215.51	39.19	6.48	76.97	
77-78	2634.00	764.00	241.44	37.37	9.39	86.58	
78-79	2868.00	834.00	250.82	51.45	15.41	89.61	
79-80	3356.00	955.00	260.23	57.00	13.94	97.04	
80-81	3867.00	1163.00	291.80	82.11	14.78	108.37	
81-82	4652.00	1376.00	358.00	109.07	21.25	141.26	
82-83	5408.00	1634.00	447.63	94.89	47.25	213.79	49.28
83-84	6309.00	1894.00	759.56	163.37	37.55	171.21	19.08
84-85	6661.00	2165.00	849.35	181.61	98.70	208.10	18.27
85-86	7988.00	2544.00	963.00	229.10	110.91	294.56	14.12
86-87	10477.00	2955.00	1102.70	309.99	104.88	328.01	16.29
87-88	11968.00	3535.00	1110.09	347.09	127.61	337.81	16.24
88-89	11341.00	4086.00	1347.63	422.24	151.98	444.10	25.09
89-90	14416.00	4833.00	1178.13	398.56	104.91	497.79	31.21
90-91	15427.00	5657.00	1095.20	391.11	109.12	500.00	39.58
91-92	16347.00	6563.00	1209.12	482.60	121.44	537.00	41.37
92-93	17582.00	7815.00	1399.10	490.92	87.12	640.68	45.53
93-94	21844.00	8789.00	1505.33	718.60	178.00	770.00	56.41
94-95	23245.00	9848.00	1223.50	774.99	156.80	853.16	59.00

DEF = Defence Expenditure
POLICE = Police Expenditure
NUCLEAR = Nuclear Expenditure
SPACE = Space Expenditure
ELEC = Electronics Expenditure
SCIEN-TECH = Science & Technology Expenditure
OD = Ocean Development Expenditure.

For Sources–Refer to Table 2.

TABLE 2. Actual Expenditure in Constant Prices (1980-81 Base)

Year	Def.	Police	Nuclear	Space	Elec	Scie-tech	OD	Deflator (W.P.I.)
1	2	3	4	5	6	7	8	9
70-71	3072.78	884.16	179.45					39.02
71-72	3699.66	943.72	250.15		8.80	72.49		41.22
72-73	3643.58	935.16	260.43		2.45	79.73		45.32
73-74	3083.27	862.06	213.23	34.83	2.90	66.65		54.52
74-75	3094.05	816.00	225.70	45.01	7.43	75.30		68.26
75-76	3660.59	968.46	286.54	54.55	7.08	96.05		67.53
76-77	3718.26	1009.72	312.65	56.85	9.40	111.66		68.93
77-78	3632.10	1053.15	332.93	51.53	12.95	119.39		72.52
78-79	3954.77	1150.02	345.86	70.95	21.25	123.57		72.52
79-80	3951.49	1124.46	306.41	67.12	16.42	114.26		84.93
80-81	3867.00	1163.00	291.80	82.11	14.78	108.37		100.00
81-82	4236.79	1253.19	326.04	99.33	19.35	128.65		109.80
82-83	4694.85	1418.53	388.60	82.38	41.01	185.60	42.78	115.19
83-84	5093.65	1529.14	613.00	131.90	30.32	134.23	15.41	123.86
84-85	5051.19	1641.77	644.08	137.72	74.85	157.81	13.86	131.87

(contd...)

1	2	3	4	5	6	7	8	9
85-86	5820.03	1853.55	701.68	166.92	80.28	151.62	10.29	137.25
86-87	7190.30	2028.00	756.78	212.74	71.98	255.11	11.18	145.71
87-88	7590.30	2241.88	704.00	220.12	80.93	214.23	10.30	157.68
88-89	6693.62	2411.62	795.39	267.80	89.70	216.11	14.81	169.43
89-90	7923.49	2656.37	647.53	249.23	57.56	273.60	17.15	181.94
90-91	7690.04	2819.90	545.94	219.06	54.39	249.23	19.73	200.61
91-92	7164.39	2876.36	529.92	211.50	53.22	235.35	18.13	228.17
92-93	7001.43	3112.05	557.14	195.50	34.70	255.50	18.13	251.12
93-94	8028.22	3230.18	553.24	264.10	65.42	282.99	20.73	272.09
94-95	7811.60	3309.47	411.17	260.43	52.72	286.70	19.82	297.57

DEF = Defence Expenditure
POLICE = Police Expenditure
NUCLEAR = Nuclear Expenditure
SPACE = Space Expenditure
ELEC = Electronics Expenditure
SCIEN-TECH = Science & Technology Expenditure
Od = Ocean Development Expenditure

Sources for Table Nos. 1 & 2

1) *Sources*: For Defence Expenditure Government of India, Defence Service Estimates for various years (1970-1995), Ministry of Defence, New Delhi.
2) Governments of India, India Budget (Expenditure Budget Part Vol-II) for various years, Ministry of Finance, New Delhi.
   Source: For Police/Internal Security, Nuclear, Space, Electronic, Science & Technology, Ocean Development Expenditure.
3) Government of India, *India Budget,* (Expenditure Budget & Demand for Grants) for various years (1970-95) Ministry of Finance, New Delhi.
4) Government of India, Comptroller & Auditor General of India Report: India Appropriation Account, for various years (1971-95) Ministry of Finance, New Delhi.
5) Government of India, Ministry of Defence, Home Affairs, Department of Atomic Energy, Department of Space, Department of Electronics, Department of Science & Technology, Department of Ocean Development their *Annual Reports* for various years.

Sources: For Deflator

6. Government of India, *Economic Survey* for various years (1970-95) Ministry of Finance, New Delhi.

The glance of these above tables of defence expenditure for the period (1970-71 to 1994-95) on the basis of a broder definition of defence expenditure in current and constant prices can help us in understanding defence expenditure in a better way. One can see from these tables that especially, in 1980s actual defence expenditure increased and at the same time police i.e. internal security expenditure, para military expenditure and dual technology purpose expenditures i.e. nuclear, space, electronics, science and technology etc. also have increased at current and constant prices. All the constituents of defence expenditure certainly show increasing trend but each one of them has different growth rate.

Hence in the following pages an attempt is made to evaluate the growth rate of these expenditures for an overall period of the study (1970-71 to 1994-95) for each constituent for detailed analyses.

Evaluation of Growth Rate of Constituents of Defence Expenditure on the Basis of Broad Definition of Defence Expenditure (with the help of Regression Analysis)

A Linear trend was assumed for total defence expenditure (1970-71 to 1994-95). In the same way a linear trend was also assumed for total police (i.e. internal security expenditure) and nuclear expenditure for the period of (1970-71 to 1994-95). The regression results are summarised in Table 3 of Exponential growth rate in percentage per annum.

It shows that the defence expenditure has 13.31 percent of exponential growth rate per annum at current prices and 4.56 per cent of exponential growth rate per annum at (1980-81) prices. The police expenditure (which includes internal security expenditure) grew at the rate of 15.53 per cent per annum and at 6.57 per cent per annum at (1980-81) prices. The total nuclear expenditure in this period grew at 13.90 per cent per annum and 5.07 per cent per annum at (1980-81) prices.

It shows that Internal Security expenditure grew at higher rate than the external security expenditure in this period. (defence expenditure had exponential growth rate of 4.56 per cent per annum and police expenditure had exponential growth rate of 6.57 per cent per annum at 1980-81 prices).

The Nuclear, Space, Electronics, Science and Technology, Ocean Development are taken as important dual purpose areas and a linear trend for them was assumed and their results are also given in Table 3. A linear trend for total space expenditure during (1973-74 to 1994-95) was assumed and from it we get the result that space expenditure in this period grew exponential at 19.00 per cent per annum at current prices and at 10.39 per cent per annum at (1980-81) prices.

A linear trend for total electronics expenditure was assumed for the period (1971-72 to 1994-95). The electronics expenditure in this period had exponential growth rate 23.96 per cent per annum at current prices and at 13.96 per cent per annum at (1980-81) prices.

A linear trend was assumed for total science and technology expenditure for the period (1971-72 to 1994-95). From its results it is found that Science and Technology expenditure had exponential growth rate of 15.67 per cent per annum at current prices and 6.60 percent per annum at (1980-81) prices.

A linear trend was assumed for total Ocean Development expenditure for the period (1983-84 to 1994-95). The Ocean Development Expenditure grew exponentially at the rate of 14.22 per cent per annum at current prices and 5.32 per cent per annum at (1980-81) prices. It is found from the results that the expenditure on Electronics grew at the higher rate than Science and Technology expenditure. It is also found that in the dual purpose expenditures the Electronics expenditures has the highest exponential growth rate i.e. 23.36 per cent per annum at current prices and 13.96 per cent per annum at (1980-81) prices. The space expenditure is second highest from the point of view of exponential growth rates. It grew at the rate of 19 per cent per annum at current prices and 10.39 per cent per annum at (1980-81) prices during (1973-74 to 1994-95).

TABLE 3. Exponential Growth Rate in Percentage Per Annum

Name of the Ministry/Dept. and time period	*Current Prices*			*(1980-81) Prices*		
	Growth Rate % p.a.	*Std. Error*	R^2	*Growth Rate % p.a.*	*Std. Error*	R^2
Total Defence Expenditure (1970-71 to 1994-95)	13.31	0.002	0.9928	4.56	0.0030	0.9039
Total Police/Int. Sec. Expenditure (1970-71 to 1994-95)	15.53	0.0020	0.9955	6.57	0.0028	0.9565
Total Nuclear Expenditure (1970-71 to 1994-95)	13.90	0.0068	0.9406	5.07	0.0072	0.6725
Total Space Expenditure (1973-74 to 1994-95)	19.00	0.0061	0.9756	10.39	0.0067	0.9149
Total Electronics Expenditure (1971-72 to 1994-95)	23.26	0.0162	0.8849	13.96	0.0165	0.7406
Total Science & Expenditure (1971-72 to 1994-95)	15.67	0.0033	0.9884	6.60	0.0036	0.9331
Total Ocean Development Expenditure (1983-84 to 1994-95)	14.22	0.0167	0.8650	5.32	0.152	0.5386

This result underlines the importance of electronic technology and Space technology in the modern nuclear era. This gives more realistic picture of India's defence expenditure.

In later chapters an attempt is made to analyse three basic determinants of defence budget in India which are given by an integrated model given in this chapter.

NOTES AND REFERENCES

1. Olvey L.D., Golden James R., Kelly Robert C., *The Economics of National Security: Weighing the Cost of Defence,* (New Jersey: Avery Publishing Group Inc.., 1984), pp. 10-12.
2. Klaus Knorr, *The War Potentials of Nations;* (New Jersey: Princetone University Press, 1956), p. 120.
3. Schelesinger James R., *The Political Economy of National Security,* (London: Atlantic Books Stevens & Sons Ltd., 1960), p. 8.
4. Deger Saadet, *Military Expenditure in the Third World Countries: The Economic Effects* (London: Routledge & Kegan Paul, 1986), p. 18.
5. Olvey Golden and Kelly, *op. cit.*, pp. 47-48.
6. Olvey Golden and Kelly, *op. cit.*, p. 48
7. Olvey Golden and Kelly, *op. cit.*, p. 38.
8. Singh Jasjit, "India's Strategic and Security Perspectives," *Strategic Analysis,* Vol. XIII No. 5, (New Delhi, August 1990, p. 475-476.
9. Singh Jasjit, *op. cit.*, p. 481.
10. Dougles Greenwald (ed.), *Encyclopedia of Economics,* New York 1982, pp. 619-20.
11. Thomas Raju, *Defence of India: A Budgetary Perspective of Strategy and Politics,* (Meerut: Macmillan Publishers of India, 1978), pp. 66-78.
12. Sinha, "Higher Defence Organisation" *U.S.L. Journal.* Vol. CXXI, No. 503, (Pub by Authority of the Council of U.S.I., New Delhi), Jan.-March 1991, p. 6-7.
13. Sinha, *Ibid.,* p. 13.
14. K.S. Pendse, "India's Defence and Development," *Indian Journal of Strategic Studies,* Vol. xviii, (Allahabad: Department of Defence and Strategic Studies, University of Allahabad) 11 May 1992, p. 22.

CHAPTER 5

Economic Capability Factor and Defence Industrial Base in India

An integrated model of defence expenditure determination for India given in the earlier chapter considers economic capability as the most important determinant of defence expenditure. In the light of this an attempt is made here to take review of India's economic capability for the period 1970-71 to 1994-95. This chapter presents statistical relationship and analysis of Defence Expenditure with other macro economic variables.

This chapter covers many issues related to defence expenditure. It discusses defence and development issues, civil-military relations, defence industrial base of India, defence planning, defence production, modernisation programme etc. It also tries to throw light on the role of private sector in the defence production in the economic liberalisation era and the role of defence research and development programme in the changing economic scenario. This chapter also discusses the institutional setup for defence planning and defence production in India.

Economic Capability of India

'Economic capability in an important determinant of defence budget in India. An integrated model of Defence Expenditure determination for India given in the earlier chapter elaborately discusses this point. Hence, while analysing India's Defence Expenditure we have to analyse India's economic capability for the study period of 1970-71 to 1994-95. An economic capability of a nation in the real sense provides resources for the defence sector. One can get clear picture of India's economic capability during this period with the help of macro economic indicators. The important macro economic indicators of Indian economy are given in the following Tables.

Table 4
Macro Economic Indicators-I

Year	*GDP AT Market Current Price in Rs. Crores*	*GDP AT 1980-81 Prices In Rs. Crores*	*Annual Rate of Increase In GDP % 1980-81 Prices*	*A.R. of Gross Domestic Savings as % of GDP*	*A.R. of Gross Domestic Capital Promotion As % of GDP*	*Index of Agri. Prod. (80-81) Base*	*Index of Ind. Prod. (80-81 Base)*
1970-71	43163	101362	5.1	15.7	16.6	82.4	65.3
1971-72	46253	103203	1.0	16.2	17.3	82.2	69.1
1972-73	51005	102566	-0.3	15.4	15.9	75.5	71.8
1973-74	62007	105556	4.6	18.4	19.1	83.1	72.4
1974-75	73235	106885	1.2	17.4	18.3	80.3	74.7
1975-76	78761	116675	9.0	19.4	18.8	92.5	79.6
1976-77	84894	118748	1.2	21.2	19.7	86.0	87.3
1977-78	96067	127293	7.5	21.1	19.5	98.2	90.6
1978-79	104190	134638	5.5	23.2	23.3	102.0	97.5
1979-80	114356	127572	-5.2	21.6	22.1	86.5	96.2
1980-81	136013	136013	7.2	21.2	22.7	100.0	100.0
1981-82	159760	144900	6.1	21.1	22.8	105.6	109.0
1982-83	178132	150379	3.1	19.5	21.0	101.6	112.8
1983-84	207589	161547	8.2	19.9	21.1	115.6	120.4
1984-85	231343	167525	3.9	19.6	21.0	114.3	130.7
1985-86	262243	176682	4.1	21.0	23.4	117.0	142.1
1986-87	292949	184690	4.3	21.6	23.4	112.8	155.1
1987-88	333201	193804	4.3	20.2	22.1	*115.3	166.4
1988-89	395782	212640	10.6	21.4	24.5	140.0	180.9
1989-90	456821	227367	6.9	22.2	25.6	143.0	196.4
1990-91	535534	240238	5.4	23.6	27.0	148.4	212.6
1991-92	616799	241255	0.8	22.8	23.4	145.5	213.9
1992-93	705328	253979	5.1	21.2	23.1	151.5P	218.9
1993-94	801032	263871	5.0	21.4	21.6	156.9P	232.0
1994-95	945615	280502	6.3	24.4	25.2	164.1P	251.9

* denotes starting of 81-82 base

p = Provisional estimate
A.R. = Annual Rate
GDP = Gross Domestic Product
AGRI. = Agriculture
IND. = Industrial

Table 5
Macro Economic Indicators-II

(In Rupees Crores)

Year	*Total Exports*	*Total Imports*	*BOP Deficit*	*Total External Debt*	*Ext+Int Debt Interest*	*Money Supply M3 Rs. Crores*	*Foreign Exchange Reserves + (Gold + SDR)*
1970-71	1535	1634	907.3	6485	747	11019	975
1971-72	1608	1825	1256.9	6831	832	11692	1194
1972-73	1971	1867	723.8	7124	864	15013	1219
1973-74	2523	2955	908.7	5869	1005	17624	1325
1974-75	3329	4519	1641.0	6421	1168	19550	1379
1975-76	4036	5265	1035.0	7489	1461	22480	2172
1976-77	5142	5074	178.1	8611	1949	27781	3747
1977-78	5408	6020	200.5	8985	1742	32906	5824
1978-79	5726	6811	356.3	9373	2190	40112	7268
1979-80	6418	9143	1250.7	9964	2665	47226	7361
1980-81	6711	12549	3147.9	11298	2957	55774	6823
1981-82	7806	13608	4067.4	11790	3745	62752	4390
1982-83	8803	14293	3428.6	13144	4637	72868	4896
1983-84	9771	15831	2887.4	15120	5524	86089	5649
1984-85	1744	17134	1243.9	16637	6863	102357	7243
1985-86	0895	19658	3187.7	18153	8006	118679	7820
1986-87	2452	20096	3788.4	20299	10591	140720	8151
1987-88	5674	22244	5410.1	23223	12991	163142	7687
1988-89	0232	28235	6308.9	25746	16447	193493	4802
1989-90	7658	35328	6230.0	28342	20501	230950	6251
1990-91	2553	43198	2529.0	31525	25006	265828	5834
1991-92	4041	47851	9845.0	36948	30994	317481	9220
1992-93	3688	63375	2563.0	42269	35864	366825	9832
1993-94	9751	73101	27819.0	45892	42553	434407	19254
1994-95	2338	88705			51985	530802	19386

Sources: Economic Survey, Government of India of relevant years
India – A reference annual, Ministry of Informational Broadcasting Government of India
RBI – Current and Financi Report – various years India – Union Budget (1970-95) National Income Accounting and other publications of Central Statistical Organisation.

The glance at these tables show that India's economic capability during the study period has certainly increased except few problems. This is reflected in the GDP figures of the table. It is found that the fundamentals of Indian economy are very strong. The 1980s saw the average GDP growth rates of 5.5 per cent while the economy had grown only by 3.5 per cent year in the previous thirty years. During this period the annual rate of gross domestic savings as proportion of GDP average around 20 per cent in India since mid 1970s. The 1990-91 it was 23.6 per cent which declined about 2 per cent points to 21.4 per cent in 1993-94 and increase to 24.4 per cent in 1994-95. The annual rate of gross domestic capital formation as proportion of GDP averaged around 23 per cent during the study period which is not very unsatisfactory. One knows that it is lower than the expected investment rate but it is likely to improve in near future. During this period money market and capital market in the Indian economy have been widening and deepening. India is rated highly in International Investment Markets. Index of Agricultural production and Index industrial production (at 1980-81 base) given in the tables indicate increasing/upward trend which reflects that India's economic potential is increasing during this period.

One major criticism of this growth process of 1980s was that it was unsustainable as it put pressure on inflation and Balance of Payments (BOP). The BOP deficit as shown in the macro economic indicator Table 5. It continued to increase in this period. In addition to this the expansionary fiscal policy followed by the government and other several factors led to the economic crisis of 1990-91. In mid 1991 some stabilisation measures and structural reforms were adopted to put Indian economy on the higher growth part on a sustainable basis. One finds that external sector has been suffering continuously in India and therefore it was at the centre stage of economic reforms. The burden of external depth, interest payments continues to be major problems as seen in the tables.

The changes are taking place in the external sector and they are reflected not only by huge flow of foreign capital and reserve built up recently, but also by the increasing importance of imports and exports in the economy. These reforms have certainly helped India to recover from foreign exchange reserve problem as shown in the table.

In spite of a few problems, one can say that in the period (1970-95) India's economic capability increased. This has helped in allocating more resources for defence sector in India. This has also helped in allocating more resources for dual purpose technology areas.

The linkage in the average GDP growth rate and average defence expenditure/GDP ratio can show this and it is given in the following Table.

Table 6
Average GDP Growth Rate and Defence Burden Relations

Year	*Average Annual GDP Growth rate (1980-81 prices) in %*	*DEF. EXP./ GDP RATIO*
1970-74	2.52	2.93
1975-79	3.86	3.01
1980-84	6.10	2.98
1985-89	6.11	3.35
1990-94	4.82	2.62
1995-96	6.80	2.35

Source: Economic Survey for various years. Defence Service Estimates for various years.

This Table indicates the five year block's average GDP growth rate and Defence/GDP ratio. From 1970 to 1989 the average GDP growth rate is increasing. It dropped for 1990-94 five year block. The increase in defence expenditure seems to have coincided with higher GDP growth rates. In the period 1985-89 the average growth rate at GDP was highest i.e. 61.11% and defence expenditure as proportion of GDP was also highest i.e. 3.35 per cent. Both the average GDP growth rate and Defence Expenditure/GDP ratio dropped in the period 1990-94. So possibly it could be argued that in India defence spending level up to the order of 2.75 to 3.50% of the GDP has in fact stimulated economic growth. Even higher level of defence pending can be sustained without notable negative impact on economic growth as reflected in the GDP growth rates.[1]

Defence Expenditure is an important part of Central Government Expenditure (CGE) in India. Therefore, for better understanding of defence expenditure one can study the relationship of defence expenditure with CGE and GDP. This can be studied from the table 7 on next page.

This table gives India's defence expenditure at current and constant prices for (1970-95). It has also given defence expenditure as percentage of GDP defence expenditure as percentage of Central Government Expenditure (CGE).

India spent an average of 1.6 per cent of its GDP on defence over the fifteen years since 1947. Defence expenditure higher than this level was considered to be an excessive burden on national economy and its growth.

It was the 1962 Sino-Indian war which brought a realistic approach to defence expenditure and caused increase in it which averaged at 3.08 per cent of the GDP for over next twenty five years. It is inclusive of the two Indo-Pakistani wars in 1965 and 1971.[2] In the period 1963 to 1970 India carried out considerable expansion of defence capability.

When one examines the GDP growth rate (1980-81 prices) data one finds that in 1972-73 and in 1979-80 GDP growth rates had slumped to negative figures – 0.3 per cent and – 5.2 per cent respectively. Otherwise GDP growth rate is positive. The GDP growth rates seems to have been significantly higher in the 1980s when defence expenditure was also rising continuously. The years 1986-87, 87-88 marks the highest ratio of defence expenditure as percentage of GDP in the whole period.

Table 7
India's Defence Expenditure and its Relationship with GDP and CGE

Year	*Population (Mns.)*	*Def. Forces (000S)*	*Def. Exp. Rs. CRS. in Current Prices*	*Def. Exp. at 1980-81 Prices*	*GDP. Growth Rate (%) (80-81 Base)*	*Def. Exp. As (%) of GDP*	*Def. Exp. As (%) of CGE*
1970-71	554.0	930	1119.28	3072.78	5.1	2.78	21.51
1971-72	566.0	980	1525.34	3699.66	1.0	3.30	22.73
1972-73	579.0	960	1652.23	3643.58	-0.3	3.24	21.05
1973-74	591.0	948	1680.89	3083.27	4.6	2.71	20.67
1974-75	604.0	956	2112.27	3094.05	1.2	2.88	21.59
1975-76	617.0	956	2472.29	3660.59	9.0	3.14	20.54
1976-77	630.0	1055	2562.53	3718.26	1.2	3.02	19.49
1977-78	643.0	1096	2633.64	3632.10	7.5	2.97	18.77
1978-79	661.0	1096	2867.63	3954.77	5.5	2.94	17.27
1979-80	674.0	1096	3355.63	3951.49	-5.2	3.10	19.18
1980-81	689.0	1104	3866.77	3866.77	7.2	3.01	18.19
1981-82	704.0	1104	4651.80	4236.79	6.1	2.91	18.31
1982-83	720.0	1120	5408.30	4694.85	3.1	3.04	17.74
1983-84	736.0	1150	6309.17	5093.65	8.2	3.04	17.53
1984-85	752.0	1380	6660.51	5051.19	3.9	2.88	15.18
1985-86	768.0	1515	7987.00	5820.03	4.1	3.05	15.04
1986-87	784.0	1492	10477.00	7190.30	4.3	3.58	16.37
1987-88	800.0	1362	11967.49	7590.05	4.3	3.59	17.02
1988-89	807.0	1260	11341.02	6693.62	10.6	3.37	16.39
1989-90	817.0	1200	14516.15	7923.49	6.9	3.17	15.26
1990-91	843.0	1200	15426.48	7690.04	5.4	2.88	14.69
1991-92	854.0	1150	16347.04	7164.39	0.8	2.65	14.50
1992-93	858.0	1100	17581.79	7001.43	5.1	2.49	13.76
1993-94	892.0	1100	21844.00	8028.22	5.0	2.68	15.58
1994-95	910.0	1100	23245.23	7811.60	6.3	2.43	15.15

Sources: For Defence Expenditure Data – Defence Service Estimates, Military Balance (IISS, London) various years
Economic Survey, Government of India of relevant years.
India – A reference annual, Ministry of Information, Broadcasting Government of India
RBI – Report on Currency and Finance Report for various years.

India's net defence spending since 1970-71 is outlined in this table. It shows that after 1971 the defence expenditure was kept for a decade at an average of 2.99% of the GDP. India's defence expenditure has continuously risen in the 1980s. India's defence expenditure in current prices started rising at a faster rate from 1982-83 onwards and the highest rate of growth was in 1986-87.

The year 1986-87 marks a record 31.11 per cent growth than the previous year. The defence expenditure at constant (1980-81) prices shows slightly different picture. From 1973-74 to 1987-88 it is indicating continuous increase and after that it has been fluctuating and remained stagnant on a declining vector. The rise in defence expenditure has been attributed to modernisaiton of equipment by India rising outlays on defence in Pakistan, China's military modernisation drive and super power rivalry in the Indian Ocean etc. Since 1987-88 the defence expenditure has maintained a reaching trend and it came down to 2.43 per cent of GDP in 1994-95.

The decrease in defence expenditure indicates the impact of economic crisis on it which India is facing specially since late 1980s and early 1990s. The modernisation programme of armed forces could not be sustained in 1990s. So how to manage the security with decreasing resources/decreasing outlays and increasing need of armed forces is dilemma Indian planners are facing today. The share of defence expenditure as a proportion of the central government expenditure (CGE) has been coming down from 22.73 in 1971-72 to 15.04 in 1985-86. In 1986-87 and 1987-88 it slightly rose to 16.37 per cent and 17.02 per cent respectively. Again it declined till 1992-93 and indicated marginal increase in 1993-94 and 1994-95. It is about 15.15 per cent in 1994-95.

Defence expenditure as percentage of Total Government Expenditure (TGE). i.e. including centre, and states and UTs. It can provide clear and unambiguous indication of actual defence burden on the economy. Almost all countries

International organisations and various studies use these indicators of GCE & TGE for assessing defence expenditure burden. Of course, one needs to bear in mind that there are various criticisms in using these indicators. The defence expenditure as a percentage of total government expenditure is suggested as better indicator. Here, defence expenditure as a percentage of Central Government Expenditure has been presented because in India's expenditure on defence forms the part of central Government expenditure list. But now even states are also making large amount of expenditures on internal security and so the TGE is indicator is also used. The following sample table for short period 87-88 to 94-95 can throw some light on this area.

Table 8
Defence Expenditure as Percentage of TGE

Year	*Def. Exp. As % of TGE*
1987-88	10.66
1988-89	10.25
1989-90	9.17
1990-91	8.73
1991-92	8.19
1992-93	7.79
1993-94	8.23
1994-95	8.89

TGE = Total Government Expenditure

Sources: For Defence Expenditure Data – Defence Service Estimates of Military Balance (IISS, London) various years Economic Survey, Government of India of relevant years. RBI – Report on Currency and Finance Report – various years For TGE – *Asian Strategic Review* 1994-95 (New Delhi: IDSA)

The Defence Expenditure as a percentage of Total Government Expenditure (TGE) have been assessed at between the minimum and maximum of 8 and 11 for India for the period 1970-95.

The budget provides an annual outlay for defence. Budgetary data has been used for the analysis. Usually the budgetary expenditure is divided in to developmental and non-developmental expenditure. Developmental expenditure consists of two categories: economic services and community and social services. The non-developmental expenditure consists of mainly defence expenditure interest payments, subsidies and other administrative expenses etc.

This table gives details of development/non-development expenditure, their ratio to total budget expenditure and budget deficit.

Table 9

Combined Developmental and Non-Developmental Expenditure

(In Rupees Crores)

Year	*Combined Rev. & Cap Exp. (Centre + State+Uts)*	*Combined Dev. Exp.*	*Combined Non Dev. Exp.*	*Budgetary Deficit*	*Dev. Bud. Exp./Bud. Exp. (5)*	*Non Dev. Bud. Exp./ Bud. Exp. (%)*
1	2	3	4	5	6	7
1970-71	8067	3537	3513	383	43.84	43.54
1971-72	9726	4327	4241	797	44.49	43.60
1972-73	10840	4847	4536	892	44.71	41.85
1973-74	11908	5306	5052	459	44.56	42.43
1974-75	14790	6680	5756	751	45.17	38.92
1975-76	18115	8182	6985	350	45.17	38.56
1976-77	20357	9253	7746	790	45.45	38.05
1977-78	22341	10797	7857	1016	48.33	35.17
1978-79	25905	12513	9186	6307	48.30	35.46
1979-80	29166	14545	10515	2655	49.87	36.05
1980-81	35380	17716	12709	3451	50.07	35.92
1981-82	40547	20292	14463	2519	50.04	35.67
1982-83	48015	23795	17659	2346	50.93	36.78
1983-84	55694	39274	21555	2135	70.52	38.70
1984-85	66734	48085	24740	5106	72.05	37.07
1985-86	76416	53397	30564	3439	69.68	39.99

1986-87	91581	63778	37012	9150	69.64	40.41
1987-88	103243	68801	43369	7663	66.63	42.00
1988-89	112611	79548	50500	8356	70.63	44.84
1989-90	158107	98501	59606	10613	62.30	37.69
1990-91	176548	105922	70626	1486	60.00	40.00
1991-92	119370	118715	80655	7081	99.45	01.03
1992-93	224688	134020	90668	12540	59.65	46.35
1993-94	258459	150162	108297	12477	58.10	41.90
1994-95	304335	172827	131508	6065	56.78	43.22

Sources: Economic Survey, Government of India of relevant years.
India – A reference annual, Ministry of Information, Broadcasting Government of India
RBI – *Currency and Finance Report* – various years
India – Union Budget (1970-95)
National Income Accounting and other publications of Central Statistical Organisation.

The ratio of developmental and non-developmental expenditure in India has only marginal changes during the 25 years under study. The share of developmental expenditure by and large remained 57.05 per cent with exception of few years since mid 1970s. The share of non-developmental expenditure in the total budget expenditure remained around 38.22 per cent.

In the non-development expenditure, defence expenditure and interest payments are two major items.

The table 10 gives defences expenditure and total interest payment for the period 1970-95. It clearly indicates that interest payments has gone up continuously and constitute the largest item of non-developmental expenditure. Interest payments has overtaken defence expenditure from the year 1984-85. Since 92-93 the interest payments are almost the double the amount of defence expenditure. These two together account for more than 23 per cent of total budgetary

Table 10
Defence Expenditure and Interest Payment Expenditure

Year	*Def. Exp. Rs. crores (Net)*	*Ext+Int Debt Interest payment Rs. crores*
1970-71	1119.28	747.00
1971-72	1525.34	832.00
1972-73	1652.23	864.00
1973-74	1680.89	1005.00
1974-75	2112.27	1168.00
1975-76	2472.29	1461.00
1976-77	2562.53	1949.00
1977-78	2633.64	1742.00
1978-79	2867.63	2190.00
1979-80	3355.63	2665.00
1980-81	3866.77	2957.00
1981-82	4651.80	3745.00
1982-83	5408.30	4637.00
1983-84	6309.17	5524.00
1984-85	6660.51	6863.00
1985-86	7987.00	8006.00
1986-87	10477.00	10591.00
1987-88	11967.49	12991.00
1988-89	11341.02	16447.00
1989-90	14516.15	20501.00
1990-91	15426.48	25006.00
1991-92	16347.04	30994.00
1992-93	17581.79	35864.00
1993-94	21844.00	42553.00
1994-95	23245.23	51985.00

Source: For defence expenditure – Defence Service Estimates for various years
For interest payments – Economic Survey for various years.

expenditure. One finds that defence expenditure as a percentage of total budget expenditure was highest in 1973-74 (i.e. 13.73 per cent). After that it declined and hovered around 11 per cent of total budgetary expenditure. The share of interest payment expenditure as a percentage of total budget expenditure remained 7 to 8 per cent till 1982-83. But it has continuously gone up since than.[3] Hence major cause of concern in India in interest payments and not defence expenditure in the non-development expenditure part of budget. One knows that economic capability can act as limiting factor for defence budget therefore, there is a need to integrated defence and development efforts. In the later pages an attempt would be made to throw a light on India's Defence Industrial base.

Defence and Development Issues

A general overview of global resources use would show that a considerable amount of world's resources is taken up by defence. Defence expenditure is often considered as unproductive, since the days of Adam Smith because the armed forces per se did not add value to national wealth, in a way that a factory or firm did. They are thus held not useful from the point of view of the functional mechanism of the economy.[4]

The rising defence expenditure causes suppression of development expenditure. For the developing countries the economic effect of defence expenditure is considerable as it involves the use of real resources such as raw material, machinery, productive resources and manpower all of which have alternative uses. It is often argued that these resources could be devoted to the development programmes like reducing poverty, hunger, disease mortality, unemployment, illiteracy, technical backwardness, social inequalities etc. for substantial human development which really merits top most priority. This is the defence and development debate in the world. In less developed countries defence and development expenditures are often considered to be competing forces for scare resources.[5]

This, of course, does not mean that a country can or should unilaterally disarm for the sake of economic development. For there are a number of political reasons, national values and goals to show as to why this cannot be done. The security threats at the domestic and global levels confronting a country do not permit to do so. Therefore, every county is compelled to divert a part of its resources to defence.[6]

A distinction is required to made in the concept of development and the concept of economic growth. The former has a broader meaning which includes the political economic and socio-cultural dimensions of human life. A high economic growth rate does not necessarily imply corresponding rates of economic development. The economic growth refers to increase introduction of goods and services and it cannot be an end in itself. The consumption and distribution of this increasing output in the economy for the mass of the people is most important consideration while understanding the concept of economic development. There is a possibility that benefits of economic growth are availed by a narrow group of people and the masses might be deprived of it.

Many of the experts tend to lose the sight of this distinction and use these terms as synonymous to one another. It must be noted that a large number of pre–Benoit and post–Benoit experts and researchers have tested the relationship between defence expenditure and economic growth. They have conducted a study of various countries, as also group of countries for different periods employing different statistical methods and this has given them diverse results. Over the years one finds that in the area of defence and development the models of study have been turned to simultaneous equations from a single equation system, with more sophistication in the methodology, use of better disagregated data and specific macro economic parameters. This has certainly helped in understanding interaction between two in depth.[7]

The important defence and development issues emerged from these works are (a) whether defence efforts divert developmental resources?, (b) what are the effects of defence expenditure on the development process? (c), if defence is to be reduced then which part of defence effort should be reduced?, (d) how to integrate defence and development effort to get optimum utilisation of resources in LDCs. etc.

These studies have been using the demand side effects and supply side effects of any government expenditure to explain the defence and development issues.

What are Demand and Supply side effects?

The thinking that government expenditure including defence expenditure has impact on the level of aggregate demand has a beneficial effect on employment, capacity utilization, production and income distribution. The changes in the level of defence expenditure may affect the price level (monetary demand) and it has been well recognised by the IMF studies. Defence expenditure is viewed as an exogenous source of demand by some researchers.

There are direct and indirect effects which are collectively known as 'Spin-off' effects. The direct effects of military expenditure on the supply side are negative in nature and are clearly defined. The indirect effects are highly controversial and they are in the form of training effects, infrastructure effects, consumable effects and security effects.[8]

The post–Benoit researchers concluded that negative influence of spin-offs are powerful enough so that defence burden has negative influence on economic growth. This idea has dominated the thinking of development planners and international agencies including the World Bank, IMF, United Nations and so on.

The idea has a positive effect that defence expenditure has positive effect on economic growth is supported by some studies. Emile Benoit in 1973, 1978 conducted a study on the relationship between defence expenditure and economic growth by taking a sample of 44 LDCs. He established a positive correlation between defence expenditure and the growth rate over the comparable time period, i.e. "the more the defence expenditure in relation to the size of their economies, less is the growth rate and the vice-versa. This basic correlation was strong enough so that there was a less than one chance in a thousand that it could have occurred by accident.

He has further explained the positive effects of military expenditure in the development process of an economy. According to him defence expenditure helps in skill enhancement, development of infrastructure facilities, and for promotion of the utilisation of the existing productive capacity. He noted that "at first sight the conclusion that defence expenditure did not impede a growth appears highly implausible if not paradoxical.[9]

Indian economists and strategists also tried to analyse defence and development relations in the Indian context. K. Subramanyam (1973) concluded from his studies that there is no correlation between defence burden and the growth rate. He has denied such compartmentalisation like defence and development expenditure and suggested mutual-exclusivity' view of these two.[10] He favoured integration of the political, social and economic policies. This would enhance and safeguard the security of the nation. (Detalils about other studies are given in the issue E of the literature review).

Since the Keynesian era it has generally been accepted that when economic growth is constrained by deficiency of demand, then any activity including absolutely unproductive ones which create demand may spur investments and hence economic growth also. Defence expenditure also can be used in such cases to increase demand in the economy and may spur investments and economic growth. But the extent to which defence expenditure will increase demand depends on several factors including the method of financing expenditure. So it is difficult to assess the magnitude and type of effect on the economy.

It is also argued that during the period of demand deficiency the government should resort to productive activities rather than unproductive activities, such as military expenditure. The productive activities would also benefit the masses immediately in such situations.

A situation where the economy is already operating at full capacity output (full employment level) then any demand increasing activity including military expenditure will lead to inflation. There are various possible negative effects of defence expenditure on the economy.

Amartya Sen, an eminent economist highlights the wastefulness of defence expenditure. According to him, "defence spending diverts resources from more useful activities and reduces the productive potential of commodities which are vital for human well-being. In the demand deficiency situations also the demand expanding role of defence expenditure can be taken over by other more fruitful forms of public spending."[11]

Saadet Deger disagreed with Benoit's conclusions and tried to show that there exists negative relationship in defence spending and growth in developing countries, when all the interrelated factors are taken into account. Her studies show that the military expenditure has detrimental effect on the development in the sample of fifty less developed countries.[12]

We can say from a review of some above important studies that there are diverse conclusions between defence and development/economic growth relations. Hence one need not isolate defence efforts from development efforts because they are interlinked.

Civil-Military Relations in India

India had left behind the defence and development dichotomy in 1960s and since then tried to realise their complementary nature by integrating their efforts together.

India is the world's largest and most populous democracy, the largest developing country and has fully established civilian control over Indian military since independence. Veena Kukreja feels that, "It is remarkable that the appalying problems of low economic development, inflation, income inequalities, mass poverty, over population, illiteracy, ethnic antagonism, absence of any linguistic unity, cultural fragmentation, social diversities and a complex class and religious system do not seem to hinder civilian control of the Indian Military.[13]

The political disorder, economic disruption, use of violence, corrupt social disorder, debasement of values are often considered as classic sources of disintegration and can cause internal threats to security. It is found that in 1980s and in 1990s such internal security threats are becoming more dominant in India and they are supported by adversaries in the neighbourhood. Therefore many times army or defence forces are deployed/called to aid the civilian authorities in recent years. There are five different tasks connected with aid to the civil authority and they are counter-insurgency operations, restoration of law and order, maintenance of essential services, assistance during natural calamities and development tasks.

However, restoration of law and order, has become the most common type of aid that army provides to civil administration in internal security problems in recent years. e.g. Jammu and Kashmir, Assam–Bodoland, West Bengal–Gorakhaland etc. The military's frequent involvement in these tasks and for a long period of time may be a forerunner of propel the military to enter into political area or may the military's influence in such areas. Today the Indian army stands away from politics but this type of frequent use of military should be avoided. It also badly affects the efficiency and morale of military forces. India needs to seriously consider this issue to maintain stable pattern of civilian control over military in future too. The facilities required for manufacturing military hardware and civil engineering goods are almost identical and due to this, it is possible to integrate the functioning of civil industrial structure with defence manufacturing structure. However, in India, this strong commonness has not been fully exploited.

Military–Industrial Complex (MIC) is another aspect of civil military relations. The military industrial complex has been an integral element in the fabric of industrial society for close to two centuries. The coining of this expression is entirely a recent phenomenon. This term was used and popularised by U.S. President Eisenhower.[14]

In simple terms there are groups of private companies/ industries producing military equipments with a profit motive. They can be state-monopoly complexes, private-state complexes or only private military industries.

Military industrial complexes are governed by twin objectives: Manufacture of superior quality of weapon system and increasing profitability. This type of merging of weapon systems and increasing profitability. This type of merging of military interests and Industrial interest has led to the development and expansion of MIC and this has been influencing the economic and political life of capitalist countries.

Such type of a military industrial complex does not exist in India. All important industries, including defence were placed under the purview of the public or state sector by the 1948 and 1956 Industrial Policy Resolutions. Therefore, it does not involve the type of relationship that exists between arms producing private companies and armed forces in the U.S.A.

Due to such a policy private sector and civil sector played insignificant role in India in the initial years of independence.

Hence, their potential has not been fully exploited for defence production. Professor Kennedy argues that defence sector is associated with and integrated into the metal and engineering sector and there appears to be some positive association between these two sectors in India. He believes that certain capital goods and intermediate industries underprin arms production. Their scope spans the spectrum of engineering and metal producing activities. The strategic industries relevant to both civil and defence production include: Iron and steel, Non-ferrous metals, Metal products, Non-electrical machinery, Metallurgical Industry, Electrical Machinery, Ship building and repairs, Electronics, Transport equipments and all the other types of advanced technology industries.

These industries represent what Kennedy terms as 'Potential defence capacity'. In India, potential defence capacity grew sizeably in the 1970s.[15] India supported development of machine tools production, electrical machinery industry, electronics machinery industry, computer technology, information and communication system development through expansion of its public sector in this area. India has also increased its capability in frontier technologies like electronics, space, satellite communications, nuclear energy industries which have duality in application. In 1980s Indian science and technology policy increasingly focused in the fields of telecommunication, computerisation and other areas of emerging technologies. All this built supportive civil base necessary for the development of defence industries.

In 1980s a shift is seen in the civil-military relations in India. A sizeable proportion of defence public sector undertakings is channeled to civil customers like Railways, Meteorological labs, Communication systems etc. In 1980 a policy decision was taken by the government of India that in modernisation and indigenous production programme the domestic civilian sector will participate in order to attain self-sufficiency in defence sector. This encouraged closer and continuous interaction between civil industry and military industry sector. In early 1980s the phased programme of off-loading of low technology items to the civil sectors has been undertaken. This increased the interaction between the small scale industry and the defence industry.

This was followed by setting up of an apex body for Defence production and supplies Department. This Apex body deals with major policy matters such as off loading of items from defence sector to civil sector, financing the projects, helping civil industries in developing and production of proto type. This type of interaction has developed between civil small scale industries and defence industry. It has helped in the development of industrially backward areas of some states e.g. Orissa and Andhra Pradesh. But K. Subramanyam has pointed out that, "spin-offs from civil to defence is more real and reverse is difficult and mythical in India."[16] The increasing interaction in civil military areas are working as catalysts for industrial development and consolidating defence potential base. It also helps in improving infrastructure, accelerating the process of indigenisation and leading towards the goal of self-sufficiency. I feel that the strong and co-ordinated civil-military relations can relieve the government of some of the expenditure on defence production and on Defence Research and Development. It will be in fact mutually beneficial for both the sectors to integrate and benefit by reverse spin-offs and linkages.

Defence Planning and Efforts to Integrate Civil-Military Sectors in India

Defence planning is the process of determining the national security objectives of a nation and formation of policies and strategies that will govern the allocation of funds acquisition, use and disposition of resources to achieve these objectives.[17]

Defence planning tries to harmonise the activities of various units of an organisation and endeavours to achieve predetermined objectives. In defence planning a nation does not have to create harmony and co-ordination only in various units of an orgnisation but also in political and administrative set up within the country. This makes defence planning complex and it is subjected to natural, institutional, technological time and resources limitations. The resource limitation is the most important constraints in defence planning and therefore defence planning process has become an attempt to match likely resources with the desired defence capability to achieve the objectives. In a developing country like India the core of defence planning involves two major elements, one is the quantum of resources to be allocated to the defence sector as against other competing non-defence sectors and secondly how to distribute the resources in order to achieve maximum defence capability.

The need for defence planning in India can be summarized as follows:

(a) Due to continuous shifts in charge in strategic event in and around country there are charges insecurity threats.

(b) To carry out judicious allocation of resources and to ensure cost effective utilisation.

(c) Rapid advances in technology results in defence equipment of weaponry becoming obsolete and calls for redirecting weapon acquisition programmes.

(d) Long term gestation period of defence industry

(e) To bring about co-ordination among defence, economic, science and technology, industrial activities and also among the armed forces.

(f) Reduced reaction time to fight a war and for changes in strategies, tactics and nature of war.[18]

In the light of above when a review of Indian defence planning is attempted. Till 1962 there was hardly any system or institutionalised effort in this direction and defence planning was done on an ad hoc and reactive basis.

After the defeat we realised its importance and endeavoured to make conscious efforts in the field of defence planning. The need to assess availability of financial resources is obvious. We need to cover assessments of 3-Ms (Money, Manpower, Machines and weapon systems) for effective defence planning. Our present system of planning national resources for developmental planning by the Planning Commission does not apparently take into account the factor of resource requirement and availability for national security. It is due to this fact that national security expenditure (defence expenditure) is treated as "nonplan expenditure".

Jasjit Singh has rightly pointed out that, "There also appears to be a time gap between the formulation of the national plans and corresponding defence plans. This disjunction needs to be removed if planning is to be made efficient and relevent."[19]

The First Five Year defence plan was prepared for the period 1964-65 to 1969-70. This was a need based plan because the debate after the 1962 debacle stressed the need for expansion and modernisation of army and air force, Navy. This also brought a realisation to the Indian Government that it needs to develop its own defence production base for developing adequate defence capability and for reducing external dependence. "While this plan was under way the government recognised the urgency for synchronising defence with development instead of planning each item on a separate basis and therefore the National Development Council authorised the Chairman of the Planning Commission to review the needs of both defence and development. This led the way for establishment of a planning cell in MOD in Nov. 1965. In this way an attempt was made to integrate defence efforts with over all developmental efforts.[20]

Taking into consideration all these requirements and defence consciousness the first plan outlined as below:

1. Expansion and modernisation of the Army

2. Modernisation of the Air-force.
3. Creation of an adequate production base
4. Improvement and expansion in the means of communication and transport
5. Replacement of over age ships of the Navy and making a balance force.

The detailed objectives of 1964-65 to 1969-70 defence plan were as below:

a. The building up and maintenance of a well-equipped army with a strength of 8,25,000 men.
b. Maintenance of a 45 squadron Air force including programmes of re-equipment and replacement of the older aircraft like Vampires, Typhoons by more modern aircraft and improvement of the air defence radar and communication facilities.
c. a phased programme for replacement of overage ship of the Navy.
d. Improvement of Road communication in the border areas.
e. Strengthening the defence production base to eventually meet the requirement of arms and ammunition of our armed forces and
f. Improving the organisational arrangements in the fields of provisioning and procurement, storage, training, etc. to ensure the most economical utilisation of funds allotted for Defence.[21]

The experiences of the first five year defence planning brought to the forefront the issue of long–term planning for defence. The cycle of weapon development and equipment requires long gestation period and huge investments which necessities long–term planning. In order to mitigate the drawbacks in defence planning, the second financial year defence plan (1969-79) was formulated on a roll on basis. This plan was a resource base plan. After one year was completed an additional year was tagged at the other end so that defence services should always have before them a revised and up dated five years plan. It was expected that this would help in re-orienting the programmes, shifting in the emphasis bringing latest concepts into the system within the resources. This type of roll on planning was also expected to facilitate the planning of projects which require more than 5 years and those projects which depend on foreign exchange situation. This plan took into account the changes in strategic needs, technical conception and ten year forecast of requirements.

Due to 1971 Bangladesh war it was not possible to adhere to the discipline and the pattern of roll on plan. In 1971-72, the Annual Report of Ministry of Defence (MOD) items acknowledged that the planning cell in the MOD was an insufficient and unsatisfactory one in meeting the economic crisis produced by the Military crisis or vice versa. To mitigate this drawback steady and long-term defence perspective planning was adopted. The third defence plan (1974-79) was made co-terminus with the national plan in order to integrate defence sector with overall economic planning. Modernisation and self-reliance were the main objectives and the need for civil & military integrated efforts to achieve these aims was also taken into account. The three service chiefs worked out board military aims and strategy which was coordinated in by the chiefs of the staff committee and got approved by the Defence Department. Each service thereafter planned its own force laid, choice of weapons equipment and buildings & infrastructure. Planning units were also established in the Department of Defence Production and Supplies and in defence R&D. This process of defence planning revealed that each service headquarters prepared its own plan and then compiled it into the defence plan. This lacked coordination between service and department plans. Therefore, a planning and coordination cell was created in the MOD to coordinate and compile the various plans into a well balanced 'Defence Plan'. Then it was approved by the Defence Minister and the Cabinet Committee for Political Affairs (CCPA). In 1977 the government formed a committee for defence planning

(CDP) to undertake regular assessments relevant to defence planning in the light of all factors affecting National Security and Defence.

This Committee for Defence Planning (CDP) includes the cabinet secretary, three service chiefs, secretaries of defence, & planning commission, secretaries finance, external affairs, defence production as members. The CDP reviews and assesses geo-strategic development and recommends allocation of resources. It is responsible for hormonising, economic, technological, foreign and defence policy. It also recommends distribution of resources based on programmes projected by each service and other defence departments. At the implementation level coordination for purchases or production is done by the Ministry of Defence. This clearly shows that defence planning in India has a vertical character and defence plan is essentially a sum total of services of department wise programmes.

There is a dire need to integrate and coordinate these efforts and defence plans need to be worked out jointly by defence planning staff. The most important drawback is that the Ministry of Defence does not have contain any professional military officers. Jasjit Singh is critical about this and states that, "We are today the only democratic country in the world where the higher military professional staff is not an integral part of the governmental frame work which undertakes planning for future forces and capabilities.[23]

The 1980-85 was the period of the Fourth Defence Plan. Due to changes in security, economic and political environment this plan stressed self reliance as its chief objective most of weapon system and equipments had become obsolete by this time and therefore there was a need for replacing these equipments and a need to modernise the three services. This plan was directed towards a rapid modernisation programme and in this process the optimum integration of civil-military technology was sought. Indigenisation was also the chief aspect of this plan.

The Fifth Defence Plan (1985-90) had accelerated modernisation, sought the replacement of the old weapon system, indigenisation for self-reliance and growth of modern R&D set up. The Sixth Defence plan (1992-97) aims at achieving minimum seventy per cent self-reliance in defence equipment production. In order to achieve to these objectives restructuring was done in defence planning mechanism and an attempt was made to integrate and coordinate various defence and non-defence organisations. As a first step a cabinet committee of national security established in 1984.

1984-89 was a period of the regime of Rajiv Gandhi's Prime Ministership in which some significant alterations were made in defence budget accounting and defence planning. It was the first time since independence that defence expenditure was taken into account by the Planning Commission at the formulation stage of the Seventh Five Year Plan and in the real sense Defence Planning was integrated with national planning. Some structural changes were brought in defence budgeting, for instance Defence Pensions were deleted from defence service estimates. Defence service estimate started giving detailed breakup of capital expenditure accounts and planning about new weapon acquisition programmes. During this period long-term planning was done for speedy modernization programme of defence forces to match with international advance technology level.

The supportive institutional structure was created in 1986 in the form of nucleus defence planning staff (DPS) for the Chiefs of Staff Committee. The main functions of DPS were to formulate clear miliary aims and objective, undertake threat perception analysis and devise clear cut defence policy.

In order to examine and review India's defence expenditure and defence budgeting a Committee on Defence Expenditure (CDE) was set up in 1990 under the chairmanship of Arun Singh. The CDE went into the whole gamut of defence planning and its report has already been submitted to the Ministry of Defence.[24]

It is reported that the CDE has advocated specific and time bound national security objectives and a 15 year long-term perspective planning divided into 5 year plans.

It is expected that each service will be drawing its own 15 year long term plan and submit it to the Joint Chief of Committee and then it will be integrated with Department of Defence Production and will be submitted to scrutiny by the Finance Ministry and the Cabinet Committees on Political affairs. This integrated approach is expected to help in the areas like availability of foreign exchange, proper defence production policy, integrated R&D efforts and rationalisation of Defence Expenditure.[25]

All these efforts show the desire to integrate defence planning machinery. But despite evidence of the existence of sophisticated machinery designed for defence planning and defence policy making in India one finds that the system does work well in the realm of defence.

Jasjit Singh has referred in his article to the 19th Estimates Committee report presented to the Lok Sabha on 20th August 1992 which expressed dismay over the fact that sudden emergence situation like Gulf War (1990-91) should have thrown the country's defence planning into disarray and shown that our country does not have a clearly articulated defence policy and planning.[26]

Therefore now it seems that the National Security Council can be a comprehensive coordinating body for defence planning in India in future.

National Security Council (NSC)

All these years there has been no dependable mechanism in India to integrate all aspects of National Security and defence planning. Therefore the decision to establish the NSC has fulfilled a long felt need to adopt rational approach to National Security. In 1990 V.P. Singh's National Front Government provided an institutional response in the form of NSC to resolve ever increasing problems of National Security.

The NSC was set up by government in August 1990. The constitution of NSC is as follows:

Prime Minister	-	Chairman
Minister of Defence	-	Member
Minister of Finance	-	Member
Minister of Home Affairs	-	Member
Minister of External Affairs	-	Member

The council may as deemed necessary request other Ministers and any Chief Minister of State to attend the meeting of NSC. It may invite experts and specialists to attend the meeting as necessary. Currently Chairman JIC works as the Secretary of NSC. The NSC was set up in order to consider aspects of N.S. Military and non-military threats

The NSC is expected to apply itself to the formulation of medium and long-term assessment which would give crystal clear directions for shaping Indian Defence policy and planning. The present structure of NSC seems to be inadequate and it requires many changes for its effective working.

The NSC will require support of many governmental and non-governmental agencies. There is also a need for having a broad based National Security Advisory Board and the creation of a task force on crisis management and policy implementation at the lend of secretariat level to support the NSC. Since the threats to National Security are not just purely military in nature they have to be met with a perspective defence and therefore the strategy and planning for defence must be in totality.

Defence Industry and Defence Production in India

The Union Cabinet of India dealing with defence matters under the guidance of a Cabinet Committee discharges its responsibility regarding defence policy and planning as well as Armed Forces regulation of India under the guidance of the Defence Minister. There are three separate services with a separate head for each: Army, Navy and Airforce. There is a Committee – "Defence Committee" – which takes up the responsibility of planning programmes and executing the policy under the Prime - Minister's approval through the Defence Minister. Thus the role of the Defence Ministry is to make an efficient defence preparedness and much importance is attached to the organisational component of various branches with their specific functions. There are four Defence Departments within the Ministry of Defence:

1. Department of Defence.
2. Department of Defence Production.
3. Department of Defence Supplies.
4. Department of Defence Research and Development.

Among these four, the "Department of Defence" is mainly responsible for chalking out the line of Armed Forces development, policy and planning. The overall policy is derived from this department. The responsible government authorities who help in making the policy are the three services, the Defence Minister, the Defence Secretary, and bodies like the Planning Commission etc. In this system India has to spend a long period of time to formulate a plan or policy. Under this system India enjoys a close co-operation among the three services and civilian bodies which make sure of a successful operation in different environments.[28]

Other heads have their specific and separate functions under the policy programme of Defence Department.

Department of Defence Production deals with the manufacturing of the Defence Services' requirement, controls the production centres of various items like weapons, ammunition, technical equipment, general stores, heavy vehicles, meat factory etc. It is under this Department that Defence Public Sector factories and ordnance factories function. The responsibility of this department covers the two sectors of inspection and standardisation. It functions in cooperation with the defence supplies department which deals with defence stores, and implementing the schemes of indigenous production. On the other hand the efforts of the DRDO are utilized by the Indian Defence Industry. The basic function of research and development is to increase items. It covers modification, improvement, indigenous production of weapons and equipment. It helps to speed up self-reliance and self-sufficiency.

Defence production is an important component of National Industrial Production. It provides the equipments needed by the country's armed forces and it helps to save valuable foreign exchange which reduces dependence on external sources for security. The possession of domestic arms production capacity enables the country to create a powerful influence among the Third World countries and therefore local military production is of great value. Mathew Ron is of the view that, "In terms of technical status, the military equipment produced by the less-developed countries is still virtually on the 'starting blocks' compared with the advanced nations, Indian is an important exception to this."[29]

The origin of arms production in India goes back to 1801, when the East India Company established the Gun Carriage Agency near Calcutta.[30]

Defence Production Policy in India

India has inherited a nucleus of defence production base at the time of independence with 16 ordnance factories. The Indian leaders accorded low priority to defence industrialisation for two reasons: one was that it would absorb scarce investment resources and secondly it was through as non–productive expenditure which would make no impact on economic growth. Defence was seen as nonproductive and taxing expenditure.

In short it was Guns versus Butter dilemma. Therefore Indian defence spending from 1947 to 1960 was low and the annual average defence budget was below 2 per cent of GNP.

At the same time India tried to ensure its security through Diplomacy i.e. policy of 'Non-alignmet'. The notion of Indian neutralism was on the lines of the Gandhian ideal of peaceful coexistence and it seemed eminently sensible for a poor country like ours to enter the expensive regional arms race at that time. It was one way of keeping India out of the arms race, super power rivalry and regional conflicts. This helped India in concentrating and promoting her efforts towards building a strong base for industrialisation. The Industrial policy Resolutions of 1948 and 1956 formalised India's classification of industries and placed key sectors such as machine tools, iron and steel, defence industry, atomic energy, railways in public sector. In this way defence industry and even non critical and fringe military products are reserved exclusively for public sector or state agencies in India. In the initial years of post-independence period India tried to manufacture simple weapon system small arms, ammunition, artillery pieces and only those items that are strategically critical and cost effective. The more expensive and complex weapon systems were purchased from abroad as and when required. This naturally lead to imposition of limitations on the growth of Defence Industrial Base (DIB) in India.

In the aftermath of 1962 Sino-Indian conflicts, India experienced the dangers and pressures of outright purchase of major weapons system from external sources and decided not to depend on these sources.

The arms supply was used as in instrument by which a arms supplying nations may submerg. Therefore a self-reliant defence industry was seen as the only means of escaping pressure from the world's arms supplying nations.

In this process India shifted to domestic armament production. The indigenous arms production was viewed as an essential and necessary capability to counter the pressures of major arms suppliers and to reduce vulnerability to political and economic and military crisis situations. The major arms supplying countries to India included the USA, the Soviet Union, Britain, West Germany, France, Canada and Yugoslavia and Sweden, during the 1962 Sino-Indian war the Western Block countries took the position that, "arms would be given to India on the condition that it moved closer to Pakistan's policy stance over the Kashmir dispute and that non-alignment should be diluted in favour of west."[31]

In 1965 and 1971 wars with Pakistan India also suffered because of the 'Spare parts Diplomacy' (denial of spare parts in the crisis situation) by the traditional suppliers of military equipment i.e. Western Countries. These experiences brought the realisation that India's dependence on foreign countries for supply of arms and stores was not desirable. It became clear that indigenous base of defence production would have to be created.

This type of linkages and preassures from the West created some disturbance in India's relation with the West and India had to move towards Soviet Union for defence Industialisation.

As a consequence of this the Soviet Union provided the main helping hand in India's post-1962 defence industrialisation and modernisation programme. India adopted/launched modernisation of defence forces and self-reliance as twin objectives of defence production in 1970s.

The close and enduring military Industrial relationship with the Soviet Union continued in the 1970s and 1980s. One must keep in mind that there are many flaws, limitations operational and financial deficiencies in such cooperative ventures. India deliberately encouraged licensed production in defence sector in 1970s and 1980s and developed as a regional military power after 1971 Bangla Desh war and slowly moved towards indigenisation and self-sufficiency. India has recognised the need of establishing local science and technical base for defence collaborations programmes and developed and consolidated DRDO and other R&D networks since 1958. India has also developed dual technology areas like nuclear, space etc. In 1980s it has been found that India has developed defence technology and other capabilities to a level where increasingly high technological weapon systems and equipment programmes can be acltivated successfully.

Roy Chowdhary in his article gives valuable information that, "The Indian government recently approved a major ten year self-reliance plan aimed at making the country significantly independent of foreign technology in critical spheres of defence by the year 2005."[32]

1980s and Role of Private Sector in Defence Production

The private sector tended to play an insignificant role in defence production in India till 1980s. The government policy and public sector monopoly sidelined the role of private sector in Defence Industrial Base (DIB). However some scattered attempts were made to involve the private sector in small/medium/major defence projects e.g. at one stage Kirloskars were involved in the development of an indigenous engine for the Arjun Main Battle Tank. It has also been found that private sector has been involved in the ancillary and small scale level to support defence productions to some extent. Many of the smaller items characterised by dual civil-military items continued to be supplied by the private sector e.g. items of general stores, clothing, tentage, nets, paints, electronic irons a small sub parts, chemicals etc. The economic, political and security environment changes in the 1980s brought closer and continuing interaction between the defence public sector and private sector in India. In 1980 Indira Gandhi regained political power and began an era of liberalisation of Indian economy. The eighties was an era of resource constraints, zero budgeting and cost effective decision-making in Government. India's security strategy in 1980s was to consolidate and modernise defence capability along with dual purpose technology capability. The internal threats to security were becoming far more serious and resulted in terrorism in Assam and Punjab. Therefore, Indira

Gandhi's regime stressed more on modernisation of technology, replacement of obsolete military equipment and handing over of low technology items like boots, blankets, tentage etc. with the private cooperation and small sector. This shift in policy and private sector participation gave a boost to defence production. The modernisation of defence forces in 1980s include programme of self-reliance in defence requirement and indigenisation to replace imported defence equipments. The private sector can play a complementary role in achieving these objectives. In 1984 Dec. the Dept. of Defence production and Dept. of Defence supplies (Set up in 1965) were merged and functions as suppliers. It is entrusted with the following functions:

(a) Indigenisation of imported defence store and equipment through the civil/private sector.
(b) Production in the civil sector industry of new stores and equipments developed by Defence R&D.
(c) Purchase of all items required exclusively for Defence for the civil sector industry including those off loaded by the ordnance factories. The Department is assisted by technical committees and the year responsible for identifying equipment and stores for indigenisation, selection of civil sector sources providing assistance in developing prototype manufacture, technical cum user evaluation and bulk production.

Major Steps for Increasing Role of Private Sector in Defence Production

The government decided to have more meaningful involvement of private sector (civil sector) in defence production and to facilitate this in 1985 a two tier mechanism was created and this comprises an Apex body chaired by the Secretary (Def, Production and supplies) and three disciplinewise functional groups chaired by Joint Secretary (supplies). There functional groups include representatives of major federations and associations of industry.[33]

This Apex Body can help the government in indicting specific areas in which private (civil) sector can play a role and can guide in building cooperation and help in the appreciation of mutual problems in a better way. The apex body has been helping the government in exploiting the Infrastructure and capability of private sector for manufacture of defence items. The Government sources report that, "In 1986-87 the contribution of this sector accounted for 35% of the total production."[34]

The Annual Report of Ministry of Defence (1988-89) spells out the National Policy on Defence Production and it states that defence production aims at the modernisation of arms and equipment and achievement of maximum degrees of self-reliance, increase of indigenous base for design and production. Presently indigenous base includes:

(a) 35 OFs which are departmental undertakings - Ordnance Factories (OF)
(b) DPs undertakings – Defence Public Sector Undertakings (DPSU)
(c) Civil sector industry comprising public and private sector. It has been government policy to exploit available capacity in the civil sector to maximum extent possible.

The above policy shows that it has been decided by the government to build a strong domestic defence Industrial base. Consistent with this approach for the first time, according to Annual Report Ministry of Defence for 1988-89 about 50% of the systems sub systems required for manufacture of new combat vehicles in OFs have been earmarked for development and production by civil industry both public and private.

Simultaneously more ambitious programmes of dual technological development system were planned in nuclear, space, electronics communication and other areas in 1980s in the civil sector. Major missions were planned and executed to completion. The most striking area was in the field of missiles with NAG, AKASH, PRITHVI and AGNI having been tested, proved and commissioned into production. The government also took a few other steps to encourage private and civil sector participation in defence preparedness and to consolidate modernisation and infrastructure. For the first time a Defence exhibition named DEFEX 88 was organised at Khadki in Pune on 5th October 1988. It was part of an effort to indigenise, to obtain private sector participation in the manufacture and supply of spares and weapon components and to develop our own weapon designs. Since the mid-eighties DPSUS tried to diversify its production and they not only continued supply to the military establishments but also supplied their products to civil sector like Railways, communication, meteorological establishments.

Shift in Defence Export Policy

In the mid-eighties India started showing her interest in export of arms. Until 1983 export of military equipment was considered as conflicting with her 'non-alignment' status.

But this policy gradually changed. "In August 1986, the Minister of State (Defence) Mr. Sukh Ram, affirmed India's interest to export weapon systems but not to the areas of conflicts."[35]

A beginning has been made with the export figures for 1988-89 standing at around Rs. 57 crores.[36] Our export programme is still in the exploratory stage and might be expanding in near future.

Changes in 1990s and its Effects

In the post-cold war period of 1990s India lost its helping hand i.e. Soviet Union in defence modernisation programme.

The end of the cold war has changed global and regional strategic environment and is slowly crystallising to a multipolar world order.

Regional trading blocks and economic relationship are playing dominating role in international politics (multipolar world order). With the rise of multipolarity in international system economic power has become the most potent determinant of military power. The Gulf war has demonstrated that non - nuclear technology will now play a decisive role in the security of a nation. Non-nuclear technologies such as information, communication, computer technology, targetting and propulsion techniques, war head efficiency, stealth technologies, space oriented technologies etc. are emerging as the technologies of the 1990s and have assumed a significant role in military preparedness, industrial progress and economic competitiveness.[37]

The technology dominated environment is going to govern economic, political, and military relations. The rising costs of developing emerging technologies and their sophistication has forced the bringing together of developed counties like Japan, USA, and other Western nations. These countries have created co-development programmes. They have developed Technology Control Regimes like NPT, MTCR by which third world countries are denied of these technologies. India is a victim of MTCR in Cryogenic engine issue in 1990. All this has called for restructuring of India's economic, military and foreign policy programmes in 1990.

In the beginning of 1990s India faced economic crisis caused due to the budgetary deficit, widening fiscal deficits, imbalance in BOP, debt trap, slow economic growth rate etc. The Indian Government was quick to realise the imminent disaster and adopted restructuring of its policies. The financial restructuring, liberalisation, privatisation, globalisation programmes were adopted to correct various Indian economic problems since July 1991. It was followed by the devaluation of rupee, delicensing of all industries except 18 special ones, allowing automatic clearance for foreign equity investment upto 51 per cent and other liberalistion measures. All this was done with a view to respond to the fast changing external and domestic environment.

India's defence production in 1990s is in the consolidation stage and therefore India needs a major boost to indigenisation in defence production and development of emerging technologies. It can save foreign exchange and reduce dependency. India is directing her efforts in this direction. India has also entered the defence related export since 1987. An ambitious target of reaching a level of rupees Five Thousand Crores in defence export by the end of 8th five year plan was being chalked out. At the same time India wants to achieve self-sufficiency, upgradation of technology, developing dual purpose technologies etc. within the restricted defence budget.

Modernisation of the defence forces has already slowed down due to inadequacy of resources since 1988. Defence budgets are declining since 1987-88 in real terms. Therefore it is necessary to find out the alternative funding methods for this. Efforts are being made by the Indian Government to improve cooperation in economic and defence areas. India and USA are trying to cooperate in defence sector.

In June 1989 Indian defence Minister K.C. Pant visited Washington to develop Indo-US collaboration in submarine development project. The joint collaboration in the development of Light Combat Aircraft has already started and a prototype is likely to be ready by 1997. In 1991 Lt. Gen. Kickighter (USA) proposed Indo-US defence cooperation, which is being considered by the Government. Indo-US joint military exercises were carried out in 1990s. All this marks a change in India's defence and economic policy to meet the emerging challenges.

It would be fruitful to look at some problems of defence production sector. The production delays, cost escalations and finally going back to foreign suppliers for the state-of-the-art are common drawbacks of India's defence production sector.

In various projects, India still uses large scale import component. e.g. Mig 21 project, MBT-Arjun project, etc.

Defence Industrial Base in India

There were sixteen ordnance factories in India in 1947; today there are thirty six ordnance factories. These are divided into different groups such as: weapons, explosives, clothing and vehicles. The range of productive activities is wide incorporating small arm ammunition, explosives, armoured vehicles, rocket propellants, parachutes and military apparel. Along with the ordnance factories there are Defence Public Sector Units. The ordance factories and Defence Public Sector Units are the main constituents of the defence industry in India. They are organised and controlled by the Department of defence production within the Ministry of Defence. With the increased focus on local production of armaments during 1960s and 1970s the number of Defence Public Sector Units (DPSUs) had grown to 9 by the 1980s. In 1986 it was reduced to eight by transferring Praga Machine Tools Ltd. to the Ministry of Industry.

Distinction between the Ordnance Factories and the DPSUs

The distinction between the ordnance factories and the DPSUs is two fold. Firstly, the traditional military needs for basic equipment and stores are satisfied by the ordance factories. They mostly supply basic equipment, small arms, ammunition and uniforms – the bread and butter of military affairs. The DPSUs on the other hand, involve themselves in the manufacture of modern, sophisticated weapon system, in advanced electronics; and in the production of exotic metal alloys for aerospace projects. They are organised, as far as possible, to gain the benefits of operating on a private enterprise basis. In supporting the DPSUs bigger and more complex manufacturing programmes, in house design and development capabilities have been established. By comparison, the lower order activities of the ordnance factories require only limited design and development facilities, with much greater reliance on the institutional research base, the Defence Research and Development Organisation (DRDO) which is external to the ordnance sector. The second difference between the ordnance factories and DPSUs has to do with the destination of output. The ordnance factories are primarily oriented to produce for the Army; supplies to the air force and navy are small, and only about three per cent of production is to meet the requirements of the policies and paramilitary forces, sports (rifles) and civil undertakings (explosives). The DPSUs also, obviously, cater for the defence sector, but not exclusively as they look after the needs of the civil market as well.

Ordnance Factories

Now India has got 36 factories with a range of production which includes sophisticated anti-tank guns and all types of guns and ammunition except some newly acquired weapons like the Bofors gun. The range of production covers all types of explosives, optical instruments, fire control instruments, armoured vehicles and accessories, varieties of general stores and software items.

The organisational side of ordnance factories is controlled by a Control Board, the Director General of Ordnance Factory is the Chairman of the Board, who operates from Calcutta among with seven full-time technical members.

The Defence Public Sector Unit's in India

There are 8 Public Sector Units in India. The principle features and their major activities can be summarised as shown in the chart on next page:

Hindustan Aeronautics Ltd. (HAL)

This is the biggest DPSU in India. This unit was established by a pioneer industrialist Seth Walchand Hirachand in December 1940 in co-operation with the then Government of Mysore. The HAL designs, manufactures,

Chart 7
Defence Public Sector Units

	Company	*Mjor activities*	*Employees (Approx.)*	*Main Locations*
1.	Hindustan Aeronautics and Ltd. (HAL)	Aircraft, aero-engines avionics, radar	41,800	Bangalore Nasik
2.	Bharat Electronics Ltd. (BEL)	Radar, electronics electo-optics	18,200	Bangalore and Pune
3.	Bharat Earth Moves Ltd. (BEML)	Heavy engineering plant	13,700	Bangalore and Kolar Gold fields
4.	Mazagon Dock Ltd. (MDL)	Naval vessels, repair and maintenance	14,250	Bombay
5.	Goa Shipyard Ltd. (GSL)	Naval vessels, repair and maintenance	1,800	Goa
6.	Garden Reach Ship Builders and Engineers Ltd. (GRSE)	Naval vessels, rapair and maintenance plus General Engineering	10,600	Calcutta
7.	Bharat Dynamics Ltd. (BDL)	Naval ASW and artillery rockets, NST 58 terpedo Milan license production	1,200	Hyderabad
8.	Mishra-Dhatu Nigam Ltd. (*Midhani*)	Gun barrel forgings Specialised metals and alloys for weapons systems and aerospce	1,500	Hyderabad

Note: ASW - anti-submarine warfare.
(Mathew Ron, *Defence Production in India*, ABC Publishing House, p. 71, New Delhi)
Source: *International Defence Review* (April 1986), p. 437.

repairs, overhaul of various types of air crafts, helicopters, and develop related aero engines instruments avionics and accessories. Thus HAL provides the necessary service to Indian Air Force. The most important steps were taken in the 1970s to upgrade the technology and to raise the production capacity of HAL. The first step was taken in 1963 when HAL decided to manufacture MIG21 interceptor air craft. The licensed production was successfully established with the aid of the USSR and since then India has continued the licensed production of an improved version of MIG Series.

Besides, the MIGs, HAL has been producing under licence Chetak and Cheetah helicopters. A pilotless aircraft designed and built by HAL was successfully test flown on July 28, 1983. A proposal for the manufacture of Light Combat Aircraft is under consideration of HAL and it is trying to acquire technological and other aid from the USA.[38]

Bharat Electronics Ltd. (BEL)

The Government set up Bharat Electronics Limited in 1954 for producing radio, radar and other electronic equipment for the forces. BEL is the second biggest DPSU company. It concentrates on the production of electronic warfare equipment. Out of its total output 40% of its production goes to the civil market. The civil output includes TV broadcasting equipment, Radio equipment, Satellite receiver terminals etc.

Bharat Earth Movers Ltd. (BEML)

This unit was formed in 1964 for building railway coaches, a task transferred from HAL. BEML has since set up a unit (at Kolar) for manufacturing earth moving equipment. It now manufactures besides passenger and other rail coaches, heavy duty transportation trailers and earth moving equipments.

Mazagon Docks Ltd. (MDL)

Mazagon Docks was acquired by the Defence Ministry in 1960. Since the take over, the unit which was manufacturing harbour launches and similar craft besides undertaking ship repairs has become a full-fledged shipyard capable of building modern warships. The unit has been able to export ships and earn useful foreign exchange. Presently, around 70% of its output is for the civilian market with specialisation in ship repair, floating docks and cranes etc. and off shore technology associated with oil exploration and excavation.

Goa Shipyard Ltd. (GSL)

GSL commenced in 1957, was originally a Portuguese concern. At that time it provided repair facilities. It was incorporated in 1967 as Goa Shipyard Ltd. a subsidiary of MDL. One third of the ship-construction, repair, and general engineering business is for civil purposes.

Garden Reach Shipbuilders and Engineers Ltd. (GRSEL)

GRSEL is the third of the DPSUs whose activities are related to sea trade. Located at Calcutta, it has been engaged in ship-building, repair and general engineering work since 1884. There are 7 plants at Calcutta and other 2 situated at Ranchi and Nagpur. It produces civil oriented items including cranes, steel plant materials.

Bharat Dynamics Ltd. (BDL)

This unit was established in 1970 for the purpose of manufacturing anti-tank missiles, first under licence and subsequently for creating a base for producing guided missiles needed by the military. Indigenous sources of material for manufacturing components are also being located and developed. It is currently engaged in production of MILAN.

Mishra Dhatu Nigam Ltd. (MIDHANI)

MIDHANI was established in 1973 in order to meet the needs of different defence production and other public sector units for the supply of special metals and super alloys for fabricating components of air craft, electronic weapon equipment, rockets, missiles and other instruments.

Defence Research and Development

Science and technology is an essential precursor to economic development and defence capability development. India was fortunate in having visionaries like Nehru, Dr. Homi J. Bhabha and Sir Shantiswaroop Bhatnagar who understood the necessity of developing strong R&D base in science and technology. Nehru had implicit faith in application of modern science for the alleviation of most of the ills in society and betterment of mankind and he fully comprehended the necessity of science and technology for the benefit of the Indian people and encouraged establishment and expansion of both civilian and defence research units in the country.[38]

In the initial years of post-Independence India had to resort to external technical assistance and tried to secure products and not processes from outside. As a consequence of this, R&D in all fields including defence related industry suffered and received less funding. At the time of independence no separate institution or establishment was in existence to conduct R&D and to meet the needs of armed forces except a few Technical Development establishments which were located in the ordnance factories. The main function of these Technical Development establishments was inspection, quality control of Ordnance factory's products and only most infrequently were involved in the modification of imported equipments. Therefore, to create an indigenous defence R&D base the first step was taken on 12th July 1948 by appointing Dr. D.S. Kothari, a physicist at the University of Delhi as the first Scientific Advisor to the Minister for Defence.[39]

DRDO

In 1949, TDES were amalgamated to create Defence Science Organisation and a few scientists from classical disciplines were recruited to form a base. All these organisations related to Defence Research and Development amalgamated in 1958 to form the Defence Research and Development Organisation (DRDO) and started working under the administrative and financial purview of Ministry of Defence.[40]

The main objective of DRDO is to improve the quality of defence products, to reduce the cost of defence items, improvement indigenisation and modification of machinery, invention of new designs, weapon development programmes etc. Over the years DRDO is serving the purpose of providing defence related R&D and making the nation self-reliant. An element of interaction already exists between DRDO and civil industrial R&D organisations. e.g. Food preservation technology developed by defence food research lab is used by the civilian sector, vehicle technology development contributed to the quality control in defence vehicle technology. But there is a need to stream line spin of effects and optimise benefits of this R&D base for mutual benefits. Today, DRDO has more than 50 laboratories and establishments. It employs manpower of more than 30,000 people which includes 4,000 highly qualified scientists and technologists.[41]

The DRDO covers practically every spectrum of service research.

In the 1950s DRDO had undertaken projects related to minor equipment and production of low technology items. The major military hardware and complex weapon system continue to be imported.

During the 1960s and 1970s it adopted three level strategy to achieve the quest for self-reliance.

Since, 1968 the DRDO has been building up considerable infrastructure over a wide range of well demarcated thrust areas capable of embarking, designing and developing major weapon systems. In 1970s the DRDO ushered into major systems and subsystems for the development of military equipment. All this is due to some factors such as user's demand, availability of science and technology infrastructure, availability of economic resources, proper defence and science policy leading towards self-reliance.[42]

Simultaneously the Indian Civil Sector also supported the development of dual purpose technologies like nuclear, space, electronics, communication which consolidated Indian defence potential and R&D base in the 1970s. India has succeeded in the development of low and medium grade technology in all spheres but it has largely been unable to break ground into 'state of the art technology' except in a few fields. In the 1980s and 1990s India concentrated its efforts towards development of sophisticated major and complex weapon systems and continued its stress on indigenisation and more self-reliance.

Since 1980 DRDO expanded its activity covering following 12 sectors

1. Aeronautics
2. Armaments
3. Combat vehicles
4. Computer systems and analysis
5. Electronics and instrumentation including communication radars and electronic warfare.
6. Engineering
7. Life sciences and food preservation, nuclear medicine
8. Material technology
9. Navel test facilities
10. Navel systems

11. Rockets and Missiles
12. Training and information including artificial intelligence robotics forecast and control.[43]

In July 1983 Indian government sanctioned one of the largest and the most important programmes of the DRDO. This programme is meant to design, develop and manufacture the Light Combat Aircraft for Indian airforce indigenously with HAL. The maiden type of the first prototype was expected to be ready by the end of 1996 with the deployment in the IAF by the year 2006.[44]

The Light Combat Aircraft (LCA) project is expected to integrate modern design concepts and the state of art technologies. For some complex technologies of LCA India is still dependent on some foreign sources and it has been decided that they are to be developed in collaboration with U.S.A. The other notable achievement of DRDO is in the field of Aeronautics. It has developed and designed the 'Lakshya'– Pilotless target aircraft and the 'Nishant' – Remotely piloted vehicle. They are expected to be included into the defence forces by 1997. In 1992-93 'Arjun' – main battle tank underwent field trials for the first time. India has successfully developed missiles like Akash, Trishul and Nag during 1990 to 1995. These are only some of the notable examples of DRDO successful programmes. There are many other programmes in which DRDO has succeeded in complete or partial self-reliance in terms of technology and material development. At the end of 1980 and 1990s DRDO has slowly changed its earlier strategy from import substitution to the design and development of high technology weapon systems and equipment indigenously. It is expected that Indian armed forces in the present era will place greater reliance on indigenous R&D for their weapon systems. In the view of the vast experience and growing self-confidence of DRDO along with appropriate science and technology policy India can really achieve almost total self-sufficiency but still we must remember that there is a long way to go to achieve complete self-reliance in different equipments. We are steadily but surely moving towards self-sufficiency and are on the right path.

In April 1994 the Indian Government approved a major 10 year self reliance plan in the critical sphere of defence to be completed by the year 2005. This ambitious plan aims to increase self reliance in Indian Armed forces from the present level of 30 per cent to 70 per cent by 2005 in terms of Defence equipment and acquisition. In this endeavour, a self reliance implementation council has been constituted under chairmanship of Dr. A.P.J. Abdulkalam (new Preseident of India) and other senior officers of the Ministry of Defence.[45]

In this attempt there is a strong need to integrate the defence R&D with civil R&D in the country. This step may introduce an element of competition and can lead to optimum utilisation of human and material resources. It also provides intellectual simulation and can curtail R&D effort cost. The resource constraints seems to be a major problem for such ambitious plan in India in 1990s.

It seems that in spite of various difficulties of resource constraints and Technology Control Regimes from developed countries India has decided to concentrate on achieving self-sufficiency.

The following table (on next page) gives the defence R&D position in India.

The table shows the level of funding given to defence R&D from Defence Budget is gradually increasing since 1980. Till 1970s defence R&D was given only 1 per cent of the defence budget of the country. In 1980-81 only 2 per cent of the defence budget was allocated to R&D: Defence R&D rose to about 3 per cent of defence budget only in 1984-85. Indigenous defence R&D accounted for over 4 per cent of defence budget for the first time in 1986-87. This increased to 4.6 per cent in 1987-88.

Table 11
Table of Expenditure on Defence R&D in India

Year	*Expenditure on defence R&D in crores of rupees*	*Percentage of total defence expenditure*	*Percentage of GDP*
1980-81	77.34	2.00	0.06
1981-82	96.00	2.06	0.06
1982-83	110.00	2.03	0.06
1983-84	164.00	2.59	0.08
1984-85	213.00	3.20	0.09
1985-86	315.00	3.94	0.12
1986-87	431.03	4.11	0.15
1987-88	549.39	4.59	0.16
1988-89	577.78	4.33	0.15
1989-90	607.67	4.19	0.13
1990-91	670.29	4.34	0.13
1991-92	682.86	4.17	0.11
1992-93	788.26	4.48	0.11
1993-94	1,046.00	4.86	0.12
1994-95 (RE)	1,175.00	5.10	0.13
1995-96 (BE)	1,348.48	5.28	0.13

Source: Defence Services Estimates and the Economic Surveys of the Government of India for various years

In view of the limited resources provided to defence sector after 1987-88 the budgetary share of R&D also started declining till 1993-94. In 94-95 R&D received 5 per cent of defence budget to move towards the objective of self-reliance. Nevertheless the expenditure of defence R&D has not reached even 0.2 per cent of Gross Domestic Product. In 1994-95 it was 0.10 per cent of GDP and in 95-96 it was only 0.13 per cent of GDP.[46]

This shows that funding for defence R&D still continues to be exceedingly poor in India. It seems that the present level of funding of R&D is inadequate to meet defence self reliance plan. It should at least rise to 0.5 per cent of GDP in near future. The acquisition of design skills and high technology from abroad has become high-cost-exercise in 1990s and therefore we need to develop self-reliance in the crucial areas.

There is need to streamline and integrate the defence and civil R&D efforts for mutual benefit. It will avoid duplication of efforts, rationalisation of expenditure, increase in private and defence R&D, reducing the costs and it can help in concentrating on the basic and critical technology areas by the defence sector.

NOTES AND REFERENCES

1. Singh, Jasjit, "Defending India in 21st century", *Strategic Analysis,* vol. XIX, No. 7, Oct. 1996, (New Delhi) p. 977.
2. Singh, Jasjit, *Ibid,* pp. 971-972.
3. Khanna D.D. and Mehrotra P.N., *Defence vs Development: A Case Study of India,* (New Delhi: Indus Publishing Co., 1993), p. 65.
4. Bhattacharya B.B., *Defence and Development Strategy in India,* IDRC Workshop, Allahabad, April 1992.
5. Deger Saadet and West Robert, *Defence Security and Development,* (London: Francis Printer Publishers, 1987), pp 6-8.
6. Deger Saadet and West Robert, *Ibid.,* p. 8.
7. Khanna D.D., and Mahrotra P.N., *Defence vs Development: A Case Study of India,* (New Delhi: Indus Publishing Company, 1993), p. 35.
8. Khanna D.D. and Mahrotra P.N., *Ibid,* pp. 35-36.
9. Benoit, Emile, *Defence and Economic Growth in Developing Countries,* (London: Lexington Books, 1973) p. XIX.
10. Subramanyam, K., *Defence and Development,* (Calcutta: The Minerva Associates, 1973), pp. 1-4.
11. Quoted in Schmidt, C and Blacking, Frank (eds.), *Peace, Defence and Economic Analysis,* (New York, st. Martin's Press, 1987), p. 45.

12. Deger Saadet, *Human Resources, Education and Military Expenditure in Developing Countries, 2nd World Congress Social Economics, Report,* August 1981, pp. 3-5.
13. Kukreja, Veena, *Civil Military Relations in South Asia Pak B.D. and India,* (New Delhi: Sage Publications, 1991), p. 185.
14. Mathews, Ron, *Defence Production in India,* (New Delhi: ABC Publishing House, 1989), pp. 6-7.
15. Kennedy, G. *The Military in Third World,* (London: Duck Worths, 1974), p. 301.
16. Subramanyam, K. *Defence and Development in India IDRC Workshop,* April 1992, Allahabad.
17. Malik, V.P., "Defence Planning System in India", *Strategic Analysis,* volume XIII, No. I (New Delhi), April 1990, p. 29.
18. Malik, V.P., *Ibid.,* p. 29, 30.
19. Singh, Jasjit, "Defending India in the 21st Century: issues of affordability and credibility", *Strategic Analysis,* vol. XIX No. 7, (New Delhi), Oct. 1996, p. 982.
20. Malik, V.P. *op. cit.,* p. 31.
21. India, Ministry of Defence, *Annual Report* 1963-64 and 1964-65 (New Delhi: Government of India) pp. 18, 19.
22. Malik, V.P., *op. cit.,* p. 33.
23. Singh, Jasjit, *op. cit.,* p. 981.
24. India, Ministry of Defence *Annual Report,* 1991-92, (New Delhi: Government of India) pp. 13-16.
25. Singh Jasjit, "Defence Doctrine and Policy Planning in India", *Strategic Analysis,* Vol. XVI, No. 6, (New Delhi) Sept. 1993, p. 643.
27. India, Ministry of Defence, *Estimates Committee 19th Report of Tenth Lok Sabha,* (New Delhi: L.S. Secretariat), 1992 p. 6.
28. *Military Year Book 1981-82* p. 134.
29. Mathews, Ron, *op.* cit., p. 12.
30. Mathews, Ron, *op. cit.,* p. 38.
31. Mathews, Ron, *op. cit.,* p. 53.
32. Roy, Choudhary Rahul Roy, "Defence Production in India", *Asian Strategic Review 94-95* (New Delhi: IDSA), p. 223.

33. Rao, B.N., "*Defence production in the Private Sector*", *USI Journal* April-June 1991, (New Delhi), p. 189.

34. India, Ministry of Defence *Annual Report 1987-88,* (New Delhi: Government of India), p. 25.

35. *Times of India,* (New Delhi), 10 August, 1986.

36. India, Ministry of Defence, *Annual Report 1988-89* (New Delhi: Government of India), p. 31.

37. As quoted in H.K. Shrivastava, Vital factors in India's strategic planning, *Indian Journal of Strategic Studies,* Vol. XVIII, (Allahabad: University of Allahabad), p. 103.

38. Rao, Rama, *Self-Reliance and Security: A Role of Defence Production,* (New Delhi: Radiant Publishers, 1984) p. 49.

39. A Nagratnam and N.S. Venktesan, Prof. Daulat Singh Kothari: A profile, *Defence Science Journal,* Vol. 44, No. 3 (New Delhi) July 1994, pp. 191-193.

40. India, Ministry of Defence, *Defence R&D,* (New Delhi: Government of India), 1986, p. 11.

41. India, Ministry of Defence *Annual Report 1986-87* (New Delhi: Government of India) p. 23

42. Sharma, G.S. (ed.), *R and D Special Digest,* (New Delhi) Jan. 1984, p. 12.

43. Indian' Ministry of Defence *R & D,* (New Delhi 1986) p. 23.

44. Aneja, Atul, LCA–A technological leap, '*The Hindu*' Jan. 28 1993 p, 6 and India, Ministry of Defence, *Defence R & D Organisation,* (New Delhi: Government of India) 1993, pp. 3 and 4.

45. India, Ministry of Defence, *Annual Report — 1994-95.* (New Delhi: Government of India), p. 38.

46. Roy, Chowdhary Rahul, *Defence Research and Development in India, Asian Strategic Review 94-95,* (New Delhi, IDSA), p. 225, 226.

CHAPTER 6

External Security Factors

In the preceding chapter, the rationale for defence expenditure was analysed in the context of economic capability, external and internal security threats with the help of an integrated model. The issue of economic capability is already discussed in Chapter 5. This chapter now focuses on external security environment which constitutes a major segment/area as a determinant for defence expenditure.

This chapter presents a broad survey of the important factors in India's external security environment at the global and regional level. It also presents a comparative study of defence expenditures of India, China and Pakistan; China and Pakistan do constitute one of the key external security threats to India. This chapter also provides the structure of defence budget in India and also provides a phasewise analysis of India's defence expenditure for the period 1970-71 to 1994-95.

EXTERNAL ISSUES

Changes in the International Security Environments

There are fundamental changes in the global security scenario due to the end of cold war between the two super powers. The cold war is over and now a new international world order is in and is yet to overvalue its manifestations. This has added new dimensions to India's security problems and has increased the sphere of potential conflict for the country. The disintegration of the erstwhile USSR has resulted in the loss of a friendly veto member of the United Nations Security Council for India. This has badly affected rupee-rouble trade and has also initiated spare part acquisition problems for high technical weapon systems.

The Gulf War (Iraq-Kuwait 1991) demonstrated the technological supremacy of the West. It also was the turning point for unipolar world order where USA is the only superpower and its stand is supported by all in the UNO including USSR. As a result of the Gulf war USA will have a permanent presence in the Gulf region and it certainly affects Indian security environment. The Islamic fundamental ideas of Iran and internal problems of Indonesia, Malaysia and other Indo-China states loom large on Indian security perimeter.

The process of economic globalisation is shrinking the world into one entity which has paradoxically broadened the parameters of security. Economic power and Technological power are becoming the most important indicators of security alongwith military power. There is a growing realisation about this in the world. India has taken bold steps in this direction. But it seems that it is difficult for India to catch up with the developed nations in the sophisticated military technology for quite some time. There are various reasons which compelled India to adopt economic restructuring programme in the 1990s. This is based on free-market ideology and it includes package of measures related to liberlisation, privatisation and globalisation of the Indian economy. In this way India adapted herself to changing international scenarios.

The post World War II international order has been called a bipolar system. This era was characterised by two relatively rigid blocs of states organised around competing ideologies of USA and USSR. The Western bloc, led by USA and its nuclear arsenal consisted of economically developed capitalist democracies and had security alliance called NATO (North Atlantic Treaty Organisation) The Eastern bloc led by USSR and its nuclear arsenal consisted of East European and other communist states and their security alliance was known as WPO (Warsaw Pact Organisation).

The rivalry between these two super powers continued as a cold war till 1990 and it affected international economic and political order. The origins of cold war can be found in power rivalry, conflict of interests and ideologies, economic and military superiority over each other. In this environment newly independent states of Asia, Africa and Latin America were forced to join either the Eastern or Western bloc. The ideology and military power became important features and this led developing nations to increase their defence expenditure and defence acquisitions of security alliance. At the same time only a handful of states from the Third World notably India, Yugoslavia, Egypt, Indonesia determined to avoid joining either the Eastern or Western bloc. They had chosen the path of Non-alignment i.e. NAM (Non-Aligned Movement).

During the fifties and sixties many third world countries became member of this movement and it had become a permanent organisation called Non-Aligned Movement group. Non-aligned countries have consistently and continuously made every effort to reduce the tension between two super powers and tried to build international understanding and peace. But this NAM group could not achieve much success in its objectives and it has become redundant in the present international environment.

In the initial years of independence, India was facing challenges to the security from cold war politics. The then Prime Minister and the architect of India's foreign policy Pt. Jawaharlal Nehru thought that non-alignment was the best guarantee for peace and national security of India. The choice before India was either to adopt a policy of alignment or to adopt an independent non-aligned foreign policy and stay away from the bloc politics. The two superpowers were busy in building the military blocs in the world but India kept herself away from them.

India's Regional Security Environment

At the contiguous level the external security threat came to India from her immediate neighbour Pakistan which resulted in Indo-Pak conflict over the Kashmir issue in 1947-48 in the initial period after independence. Pakistan joined the US sponsored alliances CENTO and SEATO in 1954 and brought cold war to the Indian subcontinent. In the initial years of independence India decided to concentrate more on the development than on defence and tried to assure its security through diplomacy and non-alignment.

India faced the challenge from China and adopted the strategy of Panchsheel (five principles) of peaceful coexistence. India signed Panchsheel Agreement with China in 1954 and accepted Chinese occupation of Tibet. This type of national security strategy proved a great failure in 1962 because it ignored geo-political compulsions and national interests of India. In 1962 China attacked India over the border dispute issue and the Indian defeat awakened the Indian leadership. This made India to realise that Non-Alignment and peaceful co-existence require adequate defence preparedness for the defence of the nation. The Chinese military operations humiliated India and damaged its position in the international sphere. Therefore in post–1962 period India tried to strengthen its defence capabilities with many restructured, reorganised and reequipped military programmes. Since 1947 there is a permanent hostility between two states stemming from territorial disputes, religious grounds, arms race, political and military aid, international alignments, regions roles etc. One finds increase in defence expenditure according to the then needs of security. India and Pakistan have gone to war in 1947-1965 and 1971.[1]

India tried to build up the structure of durable peace with Pakistan on the principle of non-use of force and bilateralism through Tashkent Treaty (1966) and Simla Agreement (1972) but this problem has remained unresolved.

The 1971 war created Bangladesh cutting Pakistan to size and introduced democracy in that country under the leadership of Shaikh Mujibur Rehman.

These achievements marked a change in the balance of power in South Asia and India acquired a preeminent position for herself in the region. In the post–1971 period Pakistan vigorously continued its rearmament programme from various sources like USA, China, France etc. showing that it was under threat due to the Afghan Crisis. USSR intervened militarily in Afghanistan in late 1970s.

There were certain other important developments in the global strategic horizons which affected Indian defence budget. Out of them one of prime importance was the security threat due to the improvement in the Sino-American relations which started after a secret visit of Dr. Henry Kissinger to Beijing in July 1971. It evolved a strategic triangle consisting of China, Pakistan and USA against India. In such circumstances India was forced to move closer to the Soviet Union and signed Indo-Soviet Friendship Cooperation and Peace Treaty in 1971 for 25 years. This brought in a new era of economic and military cooperation and weapon acquisition from Soviet Union to India.

In 1974 India carried out its first underground peaceful nuclear explosion. This possibly was designed as a counter against Chinese increasing nuclear capability and strengthening India's regional power status. This type of nuclear status attainment by India created concern in the neighbouring countries and Western bloc countries.[2]

The USA and countries of the Western Bloc wanted India to sign Nuclear Non-Proliferation Treaty (NPT) of 1948 but India refused to do so putting forth many valid reasons and continued its peaceful nuclear programme. India's adversary Pakistan reacted to it and speeded up its nuclear programme by giving an Islamic colour to it.

The nuclear collaboration between China and Pakistan was brought to light in 1982 for the first time by American press reports. In 1986, a formal agreement on nuclear cooperation between Pakistan and China was established which indicates the level of commitment to Pakistan's security by China. Reports of Chinese assistance in Pakistan's missile programme seems to be valid, for Pakistan is believed to have signed a Memorandum of Understanding with China in 1989 for a ten year cooperation in the field of military procurement, R & D, technology transfer and co-production. This contributes to missile proliferation in South Asia.[3]

China and India are both great Asian powers often regarded as threshold superpowers. China has global ambition. But it cannot suddenly leap to the status of a global power so it is trying to achieve its immediate goals in the Asian region. It has strategic interest in South Asia and it wants to contain India through establishing closer relations with India's neighbours and exploiting their bilateral problems with India to hilt. Both Pakistan and China are interested in South Asia and their nexus has posed a security threat to India for a very long period of time and it seems to continue for the future too.

India was one of the first countries to recognise Communist China in 1949 immediately after the Chinese revolution and extended goodwill. Nehru did not consider China to be either an immediate threat or a serious security problem in 1950.

In the 1950 Sino-Indian Treaty on Tibet, the Indian negotiations accepted the inclusion of reference to the 'Tibet region of China' and allowed annexation of Tibet by China.[*4] India tried to consolidate its special relationship with China by the Bandung conference of 1955 and *Hindi-Chini Bhai Bhai* became the slogan of those days but it hardly succeeded.

In March 1959 the Dalai Lama fled to India and set up a Tibetan Government in exile in Dharmsala (Himachal

Pradesh), which China took as an interference in its internal affairs. In 1960 the Chinese Government began to question blatantly the legitimacy of the MacMahon Line, (the border between Tibet and India which had been recognised by both parties in 1913-14) by sending patrols into the disputed areas.[5]

The Sino-Indian relations deteriorated rapidly but Nehru and his advisors continued to misread most of the warning signals and Chinese intentions. In July 1962 India faced the Sino-Indian war and her defeat in this war has had numerous ramifications.

In 1964 China demonstrated its nuclear capability which increased our security concerns. In July 1971 Dr. Henry Kissinger visited Beijing and started normalisation of Sino-American relations. Pakistan played an important role in it. This led to the formation of China-Pak-USA axis. Since 1980 China has tried to normalise its relations with Japan seeking technological aid from it for its modernisation.

In 1980 China adopted modernisation programme which has an important element of upgradation of military-power. China is a major arms supplier to the countries in the neighbourhood of India and this has been a source of great security concern to India. China has become the fourth largest arms exporter in the world. Chinese arms sold at "friendly" prices and on easy terms of payments, are capturing the markets in various countries in South-East Asia, Asia, Africa, South America and South Asia. So India has to be very vigilant while handling the Chinese threat.

China's nuclear capability grew steadily since 1964 and now it possesses sophisticated nuclear weapon inventory including IRBM (2500 km. range), SLBM (Sea launched Ballistic Missiles), and ICBM (Inter-Continental Ballistic Missiles).[6]

China has initiated a programme of reform and modernisation in the military that would reduce its size but eventually increase its combat capabilities and led to qualitative improvements. At the same time China is consolidating its economic capability by international trade, industrialisation, liberlisation and open door policies for foreign investors. It has attempted to normalise its relations with Japan, Soviet-Union (CIS) for economic advantages.

India also has kept aside her border dispute and is trying to normalise relations with China since Rajiv Gandhi's period (1984-88). China is very secretive about its defence matters and therefore it is very difficult to asses the magnitude of its technological and economic advances.

In spite of Tiannaman Square students riots of 4th July 1989 and disputes over Taiwan elections, USA also cautiously warning China, yet it has declared China Most Favoured Nation (MFN) status to China in international trade in 1965. This indicates Chinais significant military and economic capability.

Another major cause of concern for India from China and Pakistan is the Siachen glacier issue. This region has always been of strategic importance to the three countries i.e. India, China and Pakistan. The Chinese interest in the region is that it provides a cushion to the Chinese positions in the area and de facto occupation of Siachen by Pakistan would weaken any future Indian negotiations on border issues with China. "The Pakistani perception is that if Siachen comes under their control they would be in an advantageous position, for its possession would lead to their domination of Nubra valley sandwiched between Siachen Glacier and Northern Ladakh and the routes going down to Leh. Therefore to avert any threat, the Indian army occupies a commanding position in this region and it requires huge expenditure."[7]

External Arms Supply to Pakistan

Pakistan has been continuously receiving military aid from USA, China and West Asian countries during the 1970s.

Pakistan has exploited the 'Kashmir issue' to spurread hate India sentiment in the world and it is making every effort to destabilise and disintegrate India. Indo-Pakistan relations also has an added dimension of nuclear threat because of clandestine nuclear programme of Pakistan.

Pakistan plays a strategic role in the context of US's Asian interest. Despite earlier refusal of the US aid to Pakistan, yet we find that it is receiving the required military and economic aid from USA. The main reason behind equipping Pakistan's armed forces with all modern sophisticated weapons is to cultivate Pakistan as a military ally in the global US strategy in South Asia, South West and West Asia. In 1991, the USA continued large scale sale of military equipment to Pakistan despite the imposition of the Pressler Amendment in 1994. The U.S.A. claims that it is helping Pakistan just to avoid Pakistan from making its own nuclear weapons but India cannot get any assurance from such hollow statements and Pakistan continues to pose immediate threat to India's security.

India and The Indian Ocean

Indian Ocean occupies key position in India's security policy determination. India is one of geopolitically the most important littoral states in the region. It lies at the very centre of an immense 'bay' reaching from the Cape of Good Hope around to the Australian city of Perth. In 1967 the British Government decided to withdraw armed forces from all points east of Suez. The big powers and the super powers continued their search for bases and other facilities in the Indian Ocean region with the littoral states which are weak both in military strength economically and therefore extra regional powers are taking advantage. There have been persistent moves by India and other littoral states for declaring this Ocean as a Zone of Peace since 1971 but unfortunately it continues to remain a playground for power rivalry.

India's overseas trade is carried through the Indian Ocean. She has a coastline of 7000 km. which occupies a dominating position at the centre in this Ocean. "More than 65 per cent of the world's oil reserves and 31 per cent of natural gas reserves are in this region and it has mineral wealth therefore India has a strong interests in this region."[8]

Since 1980 India has developed its oil industry and new oil fields in the Indian Ocean region and India needs to protect them. In 1987 India sent Indian Peace Keeping Force (IPKF) to Sri Lanka at the request of Sri Lankan Government to resolve the LTTE problem at the regional level. In 1988 Indian task force successfully prevented a *coup-d'-etat* in the Maldives. These events indicate India's security concerns in this region.[9]

In 1980 the USA has developed permanent presence of Rapid Deployment Force under its central command head quarters at Diego Garcia. This base maintains sea based nuclear deterrents against the USSR and others. The other US bases are designed to have adequate controls on sea routes. The Soviet interests in the Indian Ocean emerge from commercial and security perspectives. Russia has one of the largest merchant fleets at sea since 1975. In order to spread its influence in the littoral states, the USSR provided or sold arms to these countries. This help enabled the USSR to gain access to military facilities of its client states.[10]

The Indian Ocean states including India are deeply apprehensive of the naval presence of big powers in this region. Therefore India has to take steps to enhance its naval capability to meet security challenges from the Indian Ocean region.

The Gulf war has given an opportunity to the USA and its allies to strengthen its presence in the Indian Ocean. Thus extra regional power presence will remain active and be a source of security threat to India even in the 1990s.

India and Sri Lanka

Indian security and India-Sri Lanka relations are intimately connected. Sri Lanka's geopolitical location is an important factor that compels India's anxiety over the destabilising developments in the Island. Sri Lanka is barely thirty km. from the Southern tip of India. Its ethnic Tamil population, its earlier cultural communality with India and the current political turmoil in that country all have a serious relevance to India's security environment. A stable Sri Lanka ensures Indian security and India would not like any other extra regional power or any other power hostile to India getting involved in Sri Lankan matters. The single issue that strained the relationship between India and Sri Lanka is the Sinhalese-Tamil ethnic conflict which has simmered since 1965 but became acute in the summer of 1983. Due to Sri Lanka's British and Israeli military forces the conflict could be internationalised. The Indian government therefore repeatedly offered assistants for a peaceful settlement of this separatist problem. "On July 29, 1987 India and Sri Lanka signed an accord (Rajiv Gandhi-Jaywardhane Accord) wherein India decided to help Sri Lanka in fighting the LTTE (Liberation Tiger of Tamile Ealam) led insurgency. For the implementation of the agreement the then President of Sri Lanka Jaywardhane invited the Indian Peace Keeping Force (IPKF)."[11]

The IPKF's task was perceived to be simple as India thought that the LTTE could be persuaded to surrender arms to IPKF. However, the IPKF operations turned out to be a very costly affair to India in terms of lives, material and money. The IPKF failed to counter insurgency operations and Sri Lanka wanted IPKF to withdraw.[12]

V.P. Singh's government decided to withdraw the IPKF in 1990. IPKF did not achieve much success with the LTTE. It is in the national interest of India to get this problem solved and to normalise Indo-Sri Lankan relations. India is making every effort to bring peace in Sri Lanka and supporting it economically to evict the outsiders. India has also tried to help Maldives in 1988 in the event of a *Coup-d' etat* by mercenseries. This was in the interest of India's security and to establish her influence in South Asia.

India and Bangladesh

India has always desired to have stable and friendly Bangladesh so that geostrategically it did not nurture a potential enemy in the eastern underbelly. India resolved the outstanding problems between two peacefully like the Farraka Barrage, demarcation of border, Chakama refugee problems etc. India has given massive economic support to Bangladesh because India wants a secular democracy in Bangladesh. It is also found that the belligerent attitudes are adopted by Bangladesh, China and Pakistan and they are adopting anti-Indian stand. Due to this India has to deploy adequate forces on the Bangaldesh border but India has never felt insecure from Bangladesh.

India and Myanmar

Mayanmar is geostrategically important to Indian security. The Chinese can pose a threat to the Brahmaputra valley through Burma. India's geopolitical and geo-economic interests lie in having an independent, democratic and friendly Myanmar. Myanmar is one of the heroin producing centres of the world and could call for Narco terrorism. The military leaders of Mayanmar are refusing to transfer the power to the elected people so restoration of democracy is an important issue in Myanmar. The military leaders have kept Myanmar isolated from the world and India would like to make it a full member of SAARC so that it could interact with South Asian nations on a different plane. This would add to the security of India.

India and Afghanistan

Afghanistan is located in a very strategic region and through this country one has full access to Central Asia and

Russia. Because of its very important strategic location it is imperative that the government in Afghanistan should be democratic and moderate and that this country should have very cordial relations with India.

The Bloodshed in Afghanistan continues in 1997 which endangers security environment. The Russians intervened here in 1979 and left Afghanistan in 1989 but the Afghan problem remains unresolved. After the end of the cold war USA does not want Pakistan to train these Mujahideen terrorists and therefore it has stopped its economic and military aid. Afghan extremist and came to power pose a grave security threat to India.

India and the Himalayan Kingdom

Nepal is a land locked country and is surrounded by India from three sides and Tibet from one side. India provides transit facilities for overseas trade to Nepal. It is economically dependent on India and it has to have political coordination with India. Nepal is a buffer state between India and China and China can cause security threat to India through Nepal. India has a peace treaty with Nepal according to which India has taken upon itself to safeguard the security of Nepal for its own security against China. The treaty revision and renewal went through an unpleasant phase in 1989-90 but now the problems have been solved. The USA, China, Israel and Britain are trying to woo Nepal with economic and military aid. However China is not able to create any serious rift between Nepal and India. It is imperative for India to ensure that Nepal is not used as tool for pursuing an anti-India policy by countries outside South Asia.

Sikkim, east of the Nepal until 1975 was a protectorate of India and is now state of the Indian Union. Between Sikkim and Tibet there are several passes which can be used throughout the year. The strategic 'chumbi valley' lies in this area. Bhutan has been loosely integrated into India's Defence system and India has tried to minimise security threats to the Himalayan kingdoms. India has strengthened its economic and political relations with other Himalayan kingdoms like Bhutan.

India and other Asian Neighbours

India also has to take into account West Asia and South East Asian countries for its security perspective. Indonesia, Thailand, Malaysia, Vietnam, Cambodia and other countries want South East Asia as a Zone of peace. India sought to meet the challenges from these countries through upgrading economic and political relations, "India has shown its desire to become a member of ASEAN and got the membership of ASEAN Regional Forum in 1996. Now India can try to curtail US and Chinese influence in this region by mutual cooperation."[13]

The Gulf war of 1991 has challenged India's principles. India had successfully evacuated its nationals from Kuwait but there was much more left to be done. India's national interest in this region was restoration of 'Kuwait' as a country and pulling out Iraq forces from Kuwait without a war. But this could not happen. The war in the Gulf has had a devastating effect on the Indian economy and security. India will be required to put in efforts to sustain its stable and friendly relations with the countries of West Asia even though they are war torn and divided after war. The USA and its Western allies are going to have permanent military presence in the Gulf and Indian Ocean due to this war. Pakistan is likely to get advantage by this presence and it might become a "frontline" state in West Asia for the USA. This might also lead to strengthening of the Gulf cooperation council, the Arab League Indian Ocean community and other regional forums.

India has to be more pragmatic and safeguard its national interest in such a situation. India needs to make efforts to become self-sufficient in oil products in near future and it will be long-term security perspective.

POST-COLD WAR SECURITY SCENARIO

The most significant factor changing the international security environment has been the end of the cold war between former Soviet Union USSR and the USA in 1989-90. A new international post-cold war order is in the making. It seems that in this new order there will be wide spread diffusion of political, economic, and military power. The post cold war world order has neither come as a result of any violent military confrontation nor has it been a follow up of any international conventions of summits. Instead, it has come about in the form of slow moving processes of certain related and unrelated events like collapse of communist regimes in Eastern Europe, disintegration of Soviet Union, Unification of East and West Germany, rise of Germany and Japan as economic super powers, integration process of Europe, USA as a sole military superpower.[14]

The post-cold war order or new world order will be multipolar and or complex interdependence of big or medium powers for economic, political, and physical existence. This is because in the new world order there will be no super power as such but there will be 20 odd big powers in the world. The USA will be only a military superpower. Japan, Germany and unified Europe will be economic superpowers. In Asia big powers will include China, Japan, India, Iran, Indonesia, Pakistan, Vietnam and these will create a regional system of survival.

Due to domestic compulsions the Soviet Union had chosen to shed its role as a superpower and has decided to reduce its military commitments in Europe in 1990. This policy certainly had an impact on its Third World friends who always looked upon it in times of crisis in the bipolar world. Slowly the USSR disintegrated. Russia and all other Eastern bloc countries wanted economic and technical aid from the West. Thus the special relationship which India had with erstwhile USSR is undergoing a radical change. The former USSR had all these years been India's time tested friend and ally providing moral and material support whenever required. "The Soviet equipment accounts for over 70 per cent of India's defence procurement. But in the changing situation there are disruptions in this support. Russia today is ready to sell its military equipment to India but it is no longer as powerful as the former Soviet Union was. India is aware of this development."[15]

The changing equations at the global levels have a direct bearing on India-USA relations. It seems that both countries have decided to keep aside confronting issues like nuclear non-proliferation and recognised the areas of cooperation. The Economic issues have superiority over the military issues in the present world order and accordingly Defence, Industry, Energy and Commerce secretaries of USA have visited India in 1994-95. "On 13 January 1995, William Perry, Defence Secretary of USA signed the Indo-US Memorandum of Understanding (MOU) for defence cooperation. This shows that security component is the most crucial aspect of Indo-US ties in the present situation."[16]

This is likely to begin an era of cooperation in two countries in terms of joint armed forces exercises and training, joint research and development projects, active participation of US companies in Light Combat Aircraft and other projects. Despite differences regarding issue of military aid and economic aid to Pakistan, India is expanding its trade relations with USA and realising the present world situation. It is mainly because of economic compulsions faced by both the countries that they are coming closer to each other. By June 1995 the USA has emerged as the largest trading partner and largest foreign investor in India. The US also desires to liberalise countries like India for her own economic recovery. However, it will be long time before India and USA develop trust and cooperation in vital security areas, as the USA has had long standing security alliance with Pakistan and the US is extremely reluctant to give up that alliance in favour of new military cooperation with India.

Role of SAARC in the 1990s

In the changing security equations the role of South Asian Association for Regional Cooperation (SAARC) becomes very important to Indian security. SAARC created in 1985 suffers from a symmetry of power between giants like India and other smaller nations like Nepal, Sri Lanka, Bhutan, Bangladesh, Maldives and hostile Pakistan. India has to develop a feeling of 'Trust' among these nations and has to work hard to include Afghanistan and Burma into the orbit of SAARC. The economic aspect must be a unifying factor in SAARC which will safeguard the security interests of this region. Therefore at the Dhaka Summit in April 1993 SAARC nations adopted South Asian Preferential Trade Agreement (SAPTA). Pakistan was not keen to implement it but was persuaded by other members to sign it. "The eighth summit of SAARC was held in Delhi in May 1995 and India expressed the desire to run SAPTA into South Asian Free Trade Agreement (SAFTA) very soon. This type of regional cooperation is the need of the hour."[17]

This will help India in developing friendly, cooperative and economically fruitful policies towards its smaller and other regional neighbours and that can save India's military expenditure and safeguard security interests for the long run.

Chart 8
Important Events in the External Security Environment

Year	*Developed World (USA, USSR, Europe and other countries)*	*Developing & Underdeveloped World Countries (Asia, Africa, South America)*
1945	End of the Second World War, Establishment of UNO, emergence of two super powers the USA and the USSR, beginning of cold war.	De-colonisation and process of independence to these countries.
1947	Truman Doctrine and Marshal Plan for gaining	Independence to India, Asian countries conference at

	and economic military influence over the developing world.	New Delhi.
1949	Establishment of NATO by the USA Establishment of Comecon (Warsaw pact countries) by the USSR, nuclear capability demonstration by the USSR.	Communist revolution's success in China, recognition given to China by India.
1950	Korean War	China-USSR friendship treaty.
1951	USA-Japan defence pact, steel and Iron industries common development in Europe.	
1952	Anzus Treaty between Australia, New Zealand and USA.	
1953	Death of Stalin in USSR, End of Koreant war, Hydrogen Bomb capability demonstration by both USSR and USA.	
1954	SEATO Treaty between South-East Asian countries and USA.	peaceful co-existence principles in Indo-China relations, accession of Tibet by China and acceptance by India.
1955	Baghadad Treaty by USA Warsaw Pact Treaty by USSR.	Pakistan jointed SEATO and CENTO and became ally of the USA, Bandung conference for co-operation of Asian and developing countries, Birth of non-aligned policy.
1957	Beginning of space weapon era by the USSR in the form of Sputnik, Emergence of European Common Market.	

(contd...)

Year	*Developed World (USA, USSR, Europe and other countries)*	*Developing & Underdeveloped World Countries (Asia, Africa, South America)*
1958	Flight of USA's satellite and enhancement of space capability Gaulle came to power in France.	
1959	Camp David Treaty in USSR and USA Antarctic Treaty.	
1960	First disarmament conference at Geneva and U2 Aircraft incident in super powers.	
1961	Problem of Berlin Wall in West & East Germany.	First Non-aligned Summit at Belgrade.
1962	Cuban crisis	China-India war
1963	Partial nuclear test ban treaty between USSR and USA.	Humiliating defeat of India in the war and rethinking of security strategy.
1964	Cold war clashes in USSR and USA.	China demonstrated its nuclear capability. Non-aligned confe ence at Cairo, Setting up of UNCTAD for economic cooperation. Death of Nehru, L.B. Shastri became Prime Minister.
1965	—	India-Pakistan war.
1966	—	End of the war by Taskhand Treaty, death of Shastri, Indira Gandhi became Prime Minister of India.
1967	Outer space ban treaty in super powers.	Arab-Israel war, formation of ASEAN group in Asia.

1968	Nuclear Non-proliferation Treaty (NPT), revolution in Czekoslovakia.	India criticized the NPT India continued rearmament & licensed defence production withdrawal of British Naval Forces from Indian Ocean area.
1969	Brezeneve's policy for common Asian security, conflicts in USSR and China.	
1970	Strategic arms limitations talks (SALT) between two super powers.	Influx of Bangladesh refugee to India
1971	Visit of Dr. Kissinger (USA) to China, normalisation of Sino-USA relations through Pakistan, USS Enterprise seen in the Bay of Bengal, spare part diplomacy in the Bangladesh war by the USA and Western countries.	India Pakistan war and birth of Bangladesh, India getting a status of regional power in South Asia, proposal of India Ocean as a zone of peace by littoral countries including India.
1972	US President Nixon's visit to China, SALT-I agreement in USSR and USA.	Shimla Treaty, Treaty of co-operation and friendship between USSR and India for 20 years.
1973	Oil price hike shock	Arab Israel war, price hike in oil, OPEC group becoming powerful.
1974	Acceptance of New International Economic Order (NIEO) in UNO.	Non-aligned conference at Algierae, peaceful nuclear explosion (PNE) by India at Pokharn.
1975	Heleski Treaty	
1976	End of SEATO Treaty	Death of Mao in China, End of Vietnam war, non-aligned summit at Colombo.
1977	—	Lifting of emergency in India and Janata Party came

(contd...)

Year	*Developed World (USA, USSR, Europe and other countries)*	*Developing & Underdeveloped World Countries (Asia, Africa, South America)*
		to power, some shifts in economic, defence and nuclear policies.
1978	—-	Conference on West Asian countries security at Camp David.
1979	Salt-II Treaty, Soviet Intervention in Afghanistan, elections for European Parliament.	Islamic fundamentalism in Iran Khomeni came to power, Iran-Iraq war started, Pakistan started getting more military aid under name of Afghan crisis Development of Rapid Development Force by USA in Indian Ocean Region.
1980	US bycott on Olympic Games held at Moscow.	Arms supply by superpowers to both Iran and Iraq in the war, Modernisation programme in China started.
1981	Ronald Regan became President of the USA.	South–South Nations Conference at New Delhi. Israel and Lebanon conflict.
1982	Death of Brezhnev	India's Space programme got success in SLV-3 programme development of indigenous. nuclear rector started in India.
1983	—	Integrated Guided Missile Development Programme started in India, Sri Lankan Ethnic crisis took dangerous turn.
1984	Britain and China agreed to the transfer of Hongkong to China after 1997.	Assassination of P.M. Indira Gandhi in India, Rajiv Gandhi comes to power.

1985	Gorbachev came to power in the USSR.	Asia-pacific Region declared as nuclear free zone, establishment of SAARC for regional cooperation in South Asia.
1986	Reforms started in USSR under Gorbachev Regime.	Non-aligned conference at Harrare.
1987	INF Treaty between USA and USSR Integration of Europe Act.	India-Sri Lanka Accord-Indian Peace Keeping Force sent to Sri Lanka. Nepal-India trade issue resolved, normalisation of Sino-Indian relation started.
1988	The process of reforms in USSR speeded up.	Palestinian Liberation Organization succeeded in getting independence, Rajiv Gandhi visited China.
1989	Soviet Army withdrawn from Afghanistan, revolution in East European countries and they left communism, disintegration of USSR started.	
1990	Economic integration of Europe started, end of the cold war, integration of West and East Germany.	Political and economic crisis in India, death of Rajiv Gandhi.
1991	Revolt against Gorbachev Regime, Yeltsin becomes President of Russia, Gulf-War on Iraq-Kuwait issue, emergence of USA as only superpower in military terms.	Narasimha Rao came to power and process of economic reforms started in India.
1992	Complete disintegration of USSR Gorbachev thrown out of power, formation of CIS.	Non-Aligned conference at Jakarta.

(contd...)

Year	*Developed World (USA, USSR, Europe and other countries)*	*Developing & Underdeveloped World Countries (Asia, Africa, South America)*
1993	START-II Treaty.	Yeltsin visited India, John Major visited India, PVN Rao visited China, Indian Economy opened up for foreign capital.
1994	World becoming multipolar in economic aspect and so various regional economic organisations formed. Dunkel proposal, GATT, received more importance than other issues.	India established multilateral economic relations.

Source: Kissings contemporary archives, Encyclopedia Britannica, India–Year book, Data India, Asian Recorder (of various years).

The above chart gives a list of important events in India's global and regional security environment but for the analysis one has to take into account the only major external security threats.

Comparative Analysis of Defence Expenditure—India, Pakistan and China

The major external security threats to India arises from Pakistan and China and therefore, comparative analysis of defence expenditure of these countries is attempted here.

Defence Expenditure/GDP ratio and Defence Expenditure/Central Government Expenditure ratio of India, Pakistan and China are given in the Table No.12 on next page.

The glance at the table shows that India is spending the lowest amount on defence as its defence expenditure/GDP ratio inspite of hostile security environment around it. Pakistan spends almost double the percentage of GDP on defence.

Table 12
Comparison of Defence Expenditure—India, Pakistan & China

Year	TDE Share in CGE in India (%)	TDE as (%) of GDP in India	TDE Share in FGE in Pak. (%)	TDE AS (%) of GDP in Pak.	TDE Share in CGE in China (%)	TDE AS (%) of GNP in China
1	2	3	4	5	5	7
1978-79	17.27	3.52	34.50	5.79	33.53	10.70
1979-80	19.18	3.78	33.35	6.02	32.81	10.78
1980-81	18.19	3.34	33.01	6.19	32.41	9.06
1981-82	18.31	3.25	36.45	6.43	35.18	8.47
1982-83	17.74	3.40	39.31	7.08	34.30	7.85
1983-84	17.53	3.39	35.31	7.13	30.40	6.97
1984-85	15.18	3.19	35.30	7.31	26.10	5.96
1985-86	15.04	3.42	34.75	7.10	23.81	5.27
1986-87	16.37	4.04	36.94	7.57	19.30	4.76
1987-88	17.02	3.59	34.53	7.61	19.50	4.20
1988-89	16.39	3.37	32.64	8.56	20.00	3.80
1989-90	15.26	3.19	33.43	7.62	19.10	3.60
1990-91	14.69	2.97	34.63	7.16	18.80	3.70

(contd...)

1	*2*	*3*	*4*	*5*	*5*	*7*
1991-92	14.50	2.68	38.67	7.51	17.30	3.30
1992-93	13.76	2.50	37.91	7.58	16.90	3.20
1993-94	15.58	2.44	34.31	6.81	16 50	3.00
1994-95	15.15	2.53	34.52	6.78	16.40	2.90

TDE = Total Defence Expenditure
PAK = Pakistan
FGE = Federal Government Expendniture of Pakistan
CGE = Central Government Expenditure

Source: Based on US Arms Control and Dis-armament Agency, World Military Expenditure, Washington DC for various years. Jasjit Singh, "Trends in Defence Expenditure," *Asian Strategic Review 94-95*, New Delhi, IDSA, p. 52.

India's Actual Defence Expenditure—Analysis Defence Budgets and it's Structure in India

Defence expenditure does not serve any economic purpose directly but one must accept that it is essential and an utmost important expenditure for the survival of a nation because no country is completely safe and secure from threats to its integrity and sovereignty. India is no exception to it and it could not turn a blind eye to its security concerns. The responsibility for conventional defence in India, as established by the Constitution is vested in the Union Government which is responsible for all aspects of defence and national security. This includes not only the prosecution of war but also defence preparedness and defence production. To carry out these functions effectively India has a separate Ministry i.e. the Ministry of Defence. It is responsible for the Defence of India and every part thereof including preparation for Defence and all such acts as may be conducive in times of war for its prosecution and after its termination, to effective demobilisation. The administration of the Armed Forces, namely, the Army, the Navy and the Air Force and the reserves of these forces is therefore, the main function of the Ministry of Defence. The matters related to other organisations, like Territorial Army, Coast Guard, the Auxiliary Air Force etc. are also looked after by the Ministry of Defence.[18]

Although the three Branches of Defence services are under the general control of the Ministry of Defence, they normally function directly under their respective Chiefs of Staff who are assisted by their Principal Staff Offices.

The Ministry of Defence is responsible for obtaining policy decisions of Government and for transmitting them to the three service headquarters, ensuring their implementation and watching their progress. The Ministry of Defence is also responsible for obtaining the necessary finance for Defence Expenditure and for its allocation among the three Branches of Defence services.

The details of India's Defence Expenditure and posture are published every year for legislative scrutiny and approval of the Parliament in the form of Defence Service Estimates. The Defence Service Estimates give estimated budgetary allocation towards defence for the current year, revised estimates for the previous year and actual net expenditure incurred on defence for the year before last.

Due to the constitutional and legislative limitations the three Services Army, Navy and Air Force operate independently and the Ministry of Defence is only a coordinating control over these services. Therefore Defence Service Estimates (DSEST) are presented to the Parliament as separate from that of Ministry of Defence.

The Defence Service Budget Estimates represented in five demands for grants; four on Revenue account (one each for Army, Navy, Air Force and Ordnance Factories, and one for capital account). The expenditure for which provision has been made in Defence Service Budget Estimates falls broadly into following categories-

(a) Pay and allowances of personnel of armed forces.
(b) Payments to Industrial Establishment employed in stores, Depots, Factories etc.
(c) Transportation and Miscellaneous expenditure.
(d) Store purchases.
(e) Work Expenditure.
(f) Capital outlay such as capital works, purchase of vessels, plant and machinery.

The expenditure under categories (a) to (e) represents part of revenue account of defence budget. The expenditure under (f) category represents capital account of defence budget. It mainly consists of outlay of expenditure on (1) Land, (2) Construction works (3) Military farm (4) NCC (5) Air craft and Aero Engine (6) Heavy and medium vehicle development (6) other equipment (7) Naval fleet (8) Naval dockyards (9) Rashtriya Rifles and (10) Procurement of rolling stock.

There are some changes in the concepts and demand for grants in the 1980s. The component Rewards and Pensions was removed from Defence Service Estimates since 1985-86 and is shown under a separate head of accounting. Since 1987-88 a separate demand for ordnance Factories has been opened for better budgetary control.

There is a separate Finance Division of the Ministry of Defence for dealing with all defence matters having a financial bearing since 1975. The head of this Division is the Financial Advisor. The Financial Advisor or his representative is a member of various Committees of the Ministry of Defence and the service Head Quarters and normally attends all high level meetings of various Committees dealing with defence matters whenever the proposals having financial bearing are discussed. The Financial Adviser (Defence Services) and his officers function as Associate Finance and are responsible to and have the right of access to the Ministry of Finance and to the Finance Minister through Secretary (expenditure). The financial control exercised by the Financial Adviser and his officers is really a careful and intelligent scrutiny of all proposals involving expenditure from the public funds, the objective being the safeguarding of economy, efficiency, and propriety in public finance. The Financial Adviser prepares the Budget and other estimates for the Defence Services. He is also fully associated with formation and implementation of Defence plans. The Financial Adviser is also the Chief Accounting officer for Defence services and in this capacity he prepare the Appropriation Accounts for Defence Services.

Each year the budgets for Ministry of Defence and the Armed Forces are scrutinised by the legislature in the Parliament as per India's democratic commitment. In principle the legislature can demand increase or decrease in defence allocations. The Defence Service Estimates and the Annual Report are placed before the Parliament and it gives an exhaustive over view of India's defence expenditure and defence policy. Almost two days in April are given to the discussion for annual defence budget. In addition to this, the Ministry of Defence frequently produces press releases about defence matters, defence purchases, defence decisions or military exercises. In this way substantial information is made available on defence matters in India.

In addition to this the Public Accounts Committee (PAC) examines autonomous public sector defence enterprises and Estimates Committee scrutinizes organisational efficiency. The reports of the Public Accounts Committees and the Estimates Committee are published and they are presented to the Parliament. It must be noted that the international publications like those of SIPRI Year Book, IISS (Military balance), IMF (Government Finance Statistics), US Arms Control and Disarmament Agency (ACDA Report), World Development Report by World Bank have published data about military expenditures of various countries of the world including India. It is pointed out by the experts like G. Balachandran (Dec. 1991), Jasjit Singh (1991) etc. that these publications have cited high figures about India's military expenditure. The discrepancies in these figures can be detected by careful study of India's budget documents, Defence Service Estimates and other reports. Therefore we have used the primary sources in the study as far as possible.

Phases in Defence Expenditure

A linear trend was assumed for defence expenditure (1970-71 to 1994-95). It shows that defence expenditure has 13.31% of exponential growth rate per annum at current prices at 4.56 per cent of exponential growth rate per annum at (1980-81) prices.

On the basis of graph and expenditure table one finds that Defence Expenditure has four phases in this period. (1) 73-74 to 79-80 (2) 79-80 to 84-85 (3) 84-85 to 87-88 (4) 87-88 to 94-95.

The years 1971-72 and 1972-73 were the war year and immediate year following it and therefore the increase in defence expenditure was expected for war efforts. Therefore the phasing of defence expenditure in the further period is taken into account for analysis.

I-Phase

In first phase defence expenditure is continuously showing an increasing trend till 87-88. After 87-88 in the fourth phase defence expenditure is showing a declining trend.

In the period 73-74 to 79-80 defence expenditure had exponential growth rate of 10.30 per cent per annum at current prices and 4.95 per cent per annum at (1980-81) prices. In 1973-74 the actual total defence expenditure was Rs. 1681.00 crores and in 1979-80 it rose to Rs. 3356.00 crores at current prices. In this period Indian economy was recovering from 1971 Bangladesh war effects. The declaration of Emergency in 1975, the defeat of Congress party and Indira Gandhi in 1977. General elections also contributed to the moderate defence expenditure. "Some changes were expected in defence policy, planning, international relations with other countries, economic policies, nuclear policy etc. during this period."[19]

But the Janata Government could not survive for five years so before bringing about any major change on the defence scene, it collapsed.

In 1973-74 Indian economy suffered from international oil price hike and stagflation.[20]

In addition to this Indian economy suffered from the economic burden of refugees from the erstwhile East Pakistan and the increase in current prices could not be sustained in real terms. In 1973-74 actual defence expenditure was Rs. 1681.00 crores in 1979-80 it rose to 3356.0 Rs. crores in current prices. In (1980-81) prices defence expenditure was Rs. 3083.27 crores and in 1979-80 it rose to Rs. 3951.49 crores.

Table 13
India's Defence Expenditure

(*In Rupees Crores*)

Year	*At Current Prices*	*At 1980-81 constant prices*
1970-71	1199.00	3072.78
1971-72	1525.00	3699.66
1972-73	1652.00	3643.58
1973-74	1681.00	3083.27
1974-75	2112.00	3094.05
1975-76	2472.00	3660.59
1976-77	2563.00	3718.26
1977-78	2634.00	3632.10
1978-79	2868.00	3954.77
1979-80	3356.00	3951.49
1980-81	3867.00	3867.00
1981-82	4652.00	4236.79
1982-83	5408.00	4694.85
1983-84	6309.00	5093.65
1984-85	6661.00	5051.19
1985-86	7988.00	5820.03
1986-87	10477.00	7190.30
1987-88	11968.00	7590.05
1988-89	11341.00	6693.62
1989-90	14416.00	7923.49
1990-91	15427.00	7690.04
1991-92	16347.00	7164.39
1992-93	17582.00	7001.43
1993-94	21844.00	8028.22
1994-95	23245.00	7811.60

Source: Defence service estimates for various years.

Graph 1

Defence Expenditure at Current Price and (1980-81) Constant Prices

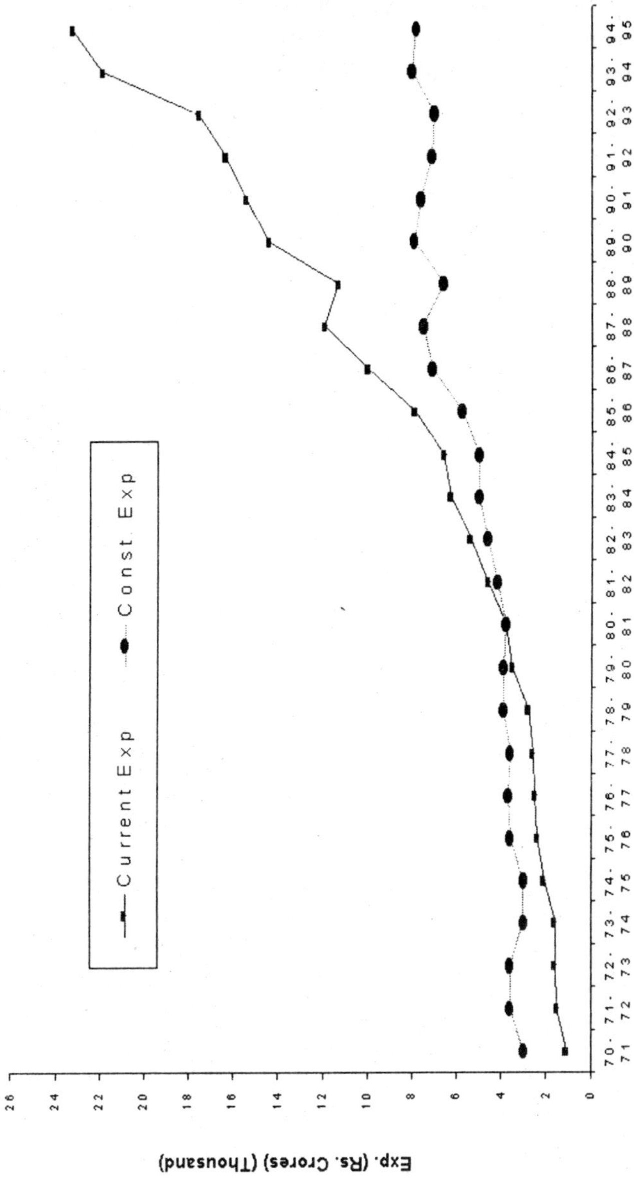

II Phase

In the second phase (1979-80 to 1984-85) Defence Expenditure has an exponential growth rate of 15-48 per cent per annum at current prices and 6.35 per cent per annum at (1980-81) prices. Defence Expenditure in 1979-80 was Rs. 3356.0 crores and it rose to Rs. 6661.0 crores in 1984-85 in current prices. At (1980-81) prices defence expenditure in 1979-80 was Rs. 3951.49 crores and it rose to Rs. 5051.19 crores in 1984-85.

In 1980 Indira Gandhi returned to power. India was stabilised as regional power in South Asia since the 1971 war and has created adequate defence and dual purpose infrastructure in the decade after the war. Indian economy also recovered. But the security environment at international and domestic levels started deteriorating. Pakistan's quest for nuclear status, Chinese modernisation programme, superpower rivalry in Indian Ocean region, Russian intervention in Afghanistan, normalisation of Sino-USA relations of Sino-USA relations through Pakistan continued to be India's main security concerns. Pakistan became a frontline state in Afghanistan crisis and USA continued to supply military aid on this ground and the cold war came to the door step of India.[21]

Domestically the disturbances in Assam, Punjab, Gorakhaland, continue to pose threats to security. The separatist movements in North-Eastern-Region continued to revive and got fuelled by external support.[22]

All this called for increase in defence expenditure since 1980. Internal security problems became more serious than ever. The Indian defence equipment also required replacement and so reequipping in the defence sector was necessary. At this time India wanted to modernise its defence sector. This also required huge expenditure on defence.

III Phase

In the third phase (1984-85 to 1987-88) defence expenditure has exponential growth rate of 22.49 per cent per annum at current prices and 15.40 per cent per annum at (1980-81) prices. This period has the highest growth rate of defence expenditure in the period under consideration. In 1984-85 Defence Expenditure was Rs. 6661.00 crores and it rose to Rs. 11968.00 crores in 1987-88 in current prices and at (1980-81) prices in 1984-85 it was Rs. 5051.19 crores and it rose to Rs. 7590.05 crores.

This increase was due to various reasons. A few of them can be summarised as – "In 1984 the operation 'Blue Star' was conducted with the help of military to control the terrorist activities from the Golden Temple in Amritsara. The internal security problems in this period took serious turns all over the country."[23]

This was followed by the assassination of Prime Minister Indira Gandhi on October 31, 1984. Internal disturbances grew and threatened to tear apart the fabric of Indian society. The political instability was revived by giving Prime Ministership to Rajiv Gandhi. He vigorously continued modernisation programme of defence sector and started adding sophisticated weaponry to Indian arsenal. More expenditure was diverted to technology upgradation, Research and Technology and other areas. Domestically Rajiv Gandhi continued to face internal security threats supported by external forces from all the directions. He tried to resolve them but could not succeed fully.

At the international level external threats from Pakistan, China, Indian Ocean region continued. India sent Indian Peace Keeping Force (IPKF) in July 1987 to Sri Lanka to resolve ethnic problem based on separatist movement but could not do much. "India also helped other neighbours like Maldives, in 1988 in warding off the security threat demonstrated and its regional security interests in South Asia"[24]

This period witnessed four major war-like situations or localised wars. They include the localised war in Siachen,

Jammu and Kashmir with Pakistan, the border skirmishes in Arunachal Pradesh and Pakistani belligerence at the time of Exercise Brass tracks (1986-87). Alongwith this External Support from Pakistan, China, Bangladesh, Nepal continued for internal separatist movement which caused increase in internal security expenditure.[25]

"The defence expenditure on revenue account increased during this period due to the implementation of the fourth Pay Commission's recommendations and subsequent revision in pay and allowances of the armed forces."[26]

IV Phase

The Fourth phase (1987-88 to 1994-95) witnessed a sharp decline in the exponential growth rate of defence expenditure. In this period defence expenditure had exponential growth rate of only 11.76 (which is almost half of the third phase growth rate) per cent per annum at current prices. In (1980-81) prices also defence expenditure had growth rate of 4.19 per cent per annum only. These defence expenditure growth rates are more or less equivalent to the (1973-74 to 1979-80 First Phase) period.

This decline has various reasons. The important one being that Indian economy started facing grave problems. The resource crunch led to these defence expenditure cuts.

The inflation level in the country continuously remained double digit in this period and it affected real term expenditure. The devaluation of rupee was done in July 1991 which added to the inflation.[27]

India faced critical situation on the economic front. Liberalisation, Privatisation, Globalistion measures were taken for restructuring the Indian economy. The foreign exchange reserves condition was the worst in the Indian history since independence during 1990.

In the political area instability continued after the assassination of Rajiv Gandhi in 1990. The internal security threat continue to be dominant. Jammu and Kashmir experienced love intensity warfare supported by Pakistani aid. Terrorism in Punjab was controlled to some extent and positive responses were received from various anti-terrorist moves. But other internal security problems continued with a few more additions.[28]

At the international level sea changes occurred which have long-term effects on Indian security. The process of Soviet disintegration lost an important friendly ally to India. India lost its easy access to military technology/weapon systems. Rouble-Rupee trade was also affected badly. The Indian armed forces started facing the problem of spares. The USA, the only superpower left tried to dominate International world order. India tried to develop Indo-US collaboration areas in defence and other fields. "The Missile Technology Control Regimes (1983) came to use and India suffered in the Cryogenic Engine Technology case. The Gulf war (1991) demonstrated supremacy of technology in the electronic warfare. The Gulf war has large ramification on the security system in Asia."[29]

The end of the cold war brought the issue of ideology to the end and the economic issue has acquired primacy over all other issues. The international economic conditions led to the shrinking of the world resources and debt trap continued to pose great threat to international security.

Pakistan tried to build its relations on the basis of religion with the Central Asian Republics of the former Soviet Union. Pakistan gave them immediate recognition. It might help in getting ex-Soviet military equipment, nuclear material, technology and equipment to Pakistan. Pakistan is also strengthening its influence in Afghanistan via military aid and support to Taliban.[30]

International world order is yet in the making and India still has to readjust itself within it. In the possible multipolar economic world order economic capability will have far greater role than before. In this period India is going through economic crisis and so it could not allocate adequate resources for defence.

Indian defence expenditure responses to Pakistan's defence expenditure and one finds that there is two/three years lag and is guided by short-term perceptions rather than long-term one. We generally "managed" our defence effort in relation to that of Pakistan rather than planned it independently in the long run.

As we have already analysed various external security threats to India's National Security. One must remember that external security can not be discussed in isolation without any considerations to the problems of internal security. These two need to be taken together. In the next chapter discussion on internal security is now being done.

NOTE AND REFERENCES

1. Sreedhar, "*Defence and Development Dilemma in India in 1990s,*" *Strategic Analysis,* vol. 14, No. 11, Feb. 1991. (New Delhi) pp. 1238-40.
2. Nanda, Ravi, *National Security: Perspective Policy and Planning,* (New Delhi: Lancer books, 1992) p. 18.
3. Beri, Ruchita, "*Ballistic Missile Proliferation,*" in *Asian Strategic Review 1991-92* (New Delhi: IDSA Publication, 1992) p. 177.
4. Khera, S.S., *India's Defence Problems* (New Delhi: Orient Longman, 1968) pp. 165-171.
5. Smith, Chrish, *India's Ad hoc Arsenal,* SIPRI Study, (New York: Oxford University Press, 1994) pp. 74-75.
6. Pradhan, Pradyot, "*People's Republic of China; A security threat to India*", *Strategic Analysis,* Vol. No. (New Delhi), January 1988, pp. 1996-97.
7. Subramanyam, K., *India's Security Perspective, Policy and Planning,* (New Delhi: Lancer Books, 1991) pp. 37-59.
8. Singh, Bhupinder, *Indian Ocean and Regional Security* (Patiala; BC Publishers, 1983) p. 3.

9. Athawale, Sanhita, *India's Indian Ocean Islands* (New Delhi: ABC Publishing House, 1991) p. 1.

10. Braun, D, *The Indian Ocean: Region of Conflict or Zone of Peace?* (New Delhi: Oxford University Press, 1983) p. 97.

11. India, Ministry of External Affairs, *Annual Report 1987-88* (New Delhi: Development of India) p.12.

12. Smith, C, *op. cit,* p. 29.

13. Mohan, Dr. Kashikar, in Daily *Tarun Bharat,* (Pune), 29th May 1996, p.4.

14. Singh, Swaran, "*Post Cold war world order and India's National Security,*" *Strategic Analysis,* (New Delhi), Vol, XVIII No. 4, July 1995, pp. 522-23.

15. Singh, Swaran, *Ibid.,* p. 529.

16. Singh, Swaran, *Ibid,* p. 529.

17. Mathur K. D. and Kamath, P. M. *Conduct of India's Foreign Policy* (New Delhi: South Asian Publishers Pvt. Ltd., 1996) p. 166.

18. Based on information given in Government of India, *Defence Service Estimate 1996-97,* Ministry of Defence, p. 93.

19. India, Ministry of External Affairs, *Annual Report 1977-78,* (New Delhi: Development of India), p. 9-11.

20. India, Ministry of Finance *Economic Survey 1974-75,* (New Delhi) p. 7-9.

21. On the basis of information given in, India, Ministry of Defence, *Annual Report 1980-81,* (New Delhi: Government of India), p. 7-9.

22. *Data India – Weekly event Diary,* various weeks, 1979-80 to 1983-84, (New Delhi: P.T.I.)

23. Justified on the basis of information given in India, Ministry of Defence, *Annual Report 1983-84,* (New Delhi: Government of India) pp. 11-13.

24. India, Ministry of Defence, *Annual Report 1987-88,* (New Delhi: Government of India), p. 10-13.

25. India, Ministry of Defence, *Annual Report 1987-88* and *Ministry of Home Affairs, Annual Report 1987-88,* (New Delhi: Government of India), pp. 7-9.

26. Singh, Jasjit, "Trends in India's Defence Expenditure," *Asian Strategic Review 1992-93* (New Delhi: IDSA Publication) p. 35.

27. India, Ministry of Finance, *Economic Survey 1991-92,* (New Delhi: Government of India), p. 5.

28. India, Ministry of defence and Home Affairs, *Annual Report 1991-92,* (New Delhi: Government of India) pp. 7-8.

29. Based on the information given in, India, Ministry of Defence, *Annual Report 992-93,* (New Delhi; Government of India) p. 7-8.

30. India, Ministry of External Affairs, *Annual Report 1992-93,* (New Delhi: Development of India), p. 9-11.

CHAPTER 7
Internal Security Factors

Introduction

Internal security is an area which has recently been accepted as an important dimension of the problem of security or security perception of a nation and consequently moves to be one of the crucial aspects in the analysis of defence expenditure in the Indian case, as in the most of Third World Countries. There has been a shift from the problem of border wars/conflicts as the key to the problem of security. Internal security may at one level be considered as the problems of militancy, insurgency, low intensity conflict etc. At another level it needs to be considered from systemic prospective. This chapter looks into the problems of internal security in the Indian context and analyses the problem of internal security from the perspective of socio-economic, political and other factors. It also goes into the ways in which internal security problem escalates over a period of time.

This chapter presents details about internal security management both in terms of crisis management and crisis resolution in India. More important is that this chapter focuses on the expenditure of various agencies which look after the problem of internal security when it becomes the crisis. It is at that point the issue of defence expenditure gets related to the management of internal security. In that context, the expenditure on paramilitary forces, police, intelligence etc. need to be taken into account. This expenditure would not fall under the proper defence budget in India. It falls under the Ministry of Home Affairs. This chapter includes these diverse expenditure to have more holistic understanding of the defence expenditure.

The domestic environment of a nation has an important place in the security system of nation. The economic, political, military capability is built from domestic environment and domestic resources. No developing nation can fulfil all sided aspirations of its people fully. There exists gap between the expectations and the satisfaction level and this increasing gap turns out to be a source of threat to the security of nation.

The sources of threats are from political, economic, social, psychological, ideological, technological and religious dissatisfaction. The external support received from the adversary country adds to the problems of internal security. They are called external factors of influences.

Chart – 9

Sources of Threat to Internal Security in India

External sources	*Internal sources*
a. Various types of Interventionist policies of super powers and their linkages in neighbourhood.	a. Religious dissimilarities.
b. Extra territorial loyalties of political and religious parties.	b. Ethnic dissimilarities
c. Economic and technological dependence indebtedness of the developing world.	c. Cultural dissimilarities
d. Aid to insurgencies by arms, money, organisation and instigation from others.	d. Linguistic dissimilarities
e. Inflow of subversive literature.	e. Ideological dissimilarities
f. Regional disputes, culture of terrorism at international level.	f. Political instability
	g. Economic dissimilarities and problems regional economic imbalances, high incidence of poverty and unemployment etc.
	h. labour/student/farmer unrest
	i. Political, industrial and criminal collusion.

Manifestations of these threats into

↓

a. Communalism/fundamentalism
b. Regionalism/Separatism

c. Parochialism
d. Violence
e. Insurgency
f. Sabotage/subversion
g. Espionage
h. Secessionism
i. Terrorism

Therefore it seems that every nation needs to develop greater homogeneity in its economic, political and social structures to safeguard and survive in the modern world and India is no exception to it.

We know that Indian democracy has survived for nearly 50 years and 10 general elections. This is the positive side of political effort to bind India as a nation. India has all the 12 great religions of the world 15 languages with more than 250 dialects, 26 states, 6 union territories all operating within the constitutional norms.

"All the efforts are directed in building a strong democratic socialistic society. India also has achieved considerable economic, social and technological progress. In spite of this progress it is difficult to fulfil fully all sided aspirations of a diversified society like India and this has led to various internal security problems in India."[1] India's internal security perspective revolves around its core values such as democracy, secularism, political stability, economic stability, removal of poverty and unemployment, equal rights and justice, social cohesiveness, social justice, self-sufficiency in science and technology, religious, economic and ideological freedom, balanced development, protection of environment and security. As we probe into the internal situation we find that India is being divided from within on various grounds. These are not only problems of internal stability but they are of internal security the major internal security threats to India arise from the terrorism, subversion, insurgency, secessionist movement in the different parts of the country.

Near insurgency situation prevails in Jammu and Kashmir, West Bengal, Punjab and Assam. Earlier insurgency in Nagaland, Mizoram, Tripura, the Gorkhaland movement in West Bengal. Bodoland in Assam all show the fissiparous tendencies in the social structure. In the initial phases these movements started only with small fraction of dissatisfaction but slowly grew into a big challenge to internal security in the form of terrorism. The Jharkhand Movement and the Utrakhand movements continues to cause great internal security concerns.

North Eastern Insurgency Movements

Insurgency movements in North Eastern part i.e. Manipur, Tripura, Nagaland, Assam were initially treated as an extension of Chinese subversion and the Indian Government was able to successfully control them. But since 1970s the fight against insurgency is becoming more difficult in a democratic society and is creating perpetual unrest.

Nagaland

The Naga insurgency movement is based in the hill areas of Myanmar adjoining Nagaland, and is functioning since 1956 under the legendary A.Z. Phizo. The objective of this is the achievement of an independent Nagaland through violent struggle. There are two groups – National Socialist Council of Nagaland and Naga Federal Government (NFG). The situation at present is well under control but the politicians use the bogey to get more funds from Central Government. NSCN guerrillas have taken on the security forces time and again and killed many of them. The army says that the NSCN has the patronage of the Pakistani International Service Intelligence. It also operates in the hill districts of Manipur.

Manipur

There are half a dozen diverse insurgents groups operating in Manipur. The political instability and social underdevelopment is the main cause. From 1971-1981 the state has witnessed 13 Chief Ministers. Mr. Rishaing Keishing came to power in 1981 and has brought stability and economic development to the state to some extent which helped to control insurgency and it was limited to only Ukhral (North Eastern Bordering Nagaland and Burma). The Peoples' Revolutionary party of Kangleipak (PREPAK) and Peoples Liberation Army (PLA) are some of insurgent groups and they had attacked the security forces and police many times. The combined operations between Indian and Burmese forces could once and for all heal the running sore of insurgency in Manipur. The insurgent groups get aid from across the border from China and Myanmar. This is the worst example of insurgency caused by Internal problem. Bloody clashes of Kukis and Nagas add to it. (The insurgency situation is under control despite sporadic acts of violence). On 29th November 1987 the ambush on CRPF near almost revived the insurgency in Manipur again. The supporters of Greater Mizoram and Greater Nagaland are believed to propel this insurgency attacks. The problems of unemployment and poverty have helped the insurgents to strengthen their movement.

Mizoram

In Mizoram the insurgents are based in the Chittagon Hill and have so far been aided and abetted country by the Bangladesh Government. Indira Gandhi tried to find out a political solution during the talks with Lal Denga, leader of Mizo National Front, the main leader of the insurgent group. Rajiv Gandhi had peace talks with the insurgent group which has resulted in a final settlement on paper in 1988. This has helped to creates peace and some control on the insurgency in Mizoram. India has taken nearly three decades to control the Nagas and two decades to control the Mizos. A long International border with Myanmar makes it vulnerable for drug trafficking from the Golden Triangle located to the east of Myanmar.

Tripura

Two main groups today are the All Tripura Tiger Force and National Liberation Front of Tripura (NLFT). Self-loading rifles, and automatic weapons are used. Kidnapping for ransom is also resorted to. The Tribal National Volunteers have stepped up the extremist activities and have intensified violence in Tripura. Since the late 1970s 14 insurgent groups operating in the state. TNV actions were supported by Bangladesh and the Mizo National Front. The Tripura Government has used paramilitary forces and local police to control insurgency. They could achieve only limited success. So in 1988 the Central Government stressed the need of central-state cooperation in dealing with insurgency. Mr. Buta Singh (Union Home Minister in Rajiv Gandhi Ministry) signed an agreement with the state chief Minister Mr. Nripen Chakravarty on 4th January 1988 to give full support to deal firmly to finish insurgency and the anti-National elements.[2]

The new strategy to curb insurgency includes induction of more soldiers in the Assam Rifles, CRPT units and redeployment of Army in trouble areas and to make efforts to find out a political solution. The TNV is threatening to relaunch the Tripura movement. Tripura Gramin Bank was closed down due to the unreasonable demand for money from these groups.

The Chakama Problem

The Chakama question in the North Eastern states remains hopelessly tangled. The Chakama refugees are spread in Tripura, Mizoram and Arunanchal Pradesh.

Since 1950 they have been staying in Camps in Tripura. In Mizoram and Arunanchal Pradesh they have stayed for decades but face the prospect of eviction as foreigners. They have refused to go back to Bangladesh saying that the conditions in Chittagong hill tracts which had been their home were not yet congenial. The Chakamas are Buddhists and the Hajogars are Hindus. In Arunachal Pradesh (A.P.)

the government wanted to deport the Chakamas from the state before 31st December 1995. Employment opportunities in the state government of Arunanchal Pradesh were denied to them since 1980. Trade licences were also cancelled. Ration cards were taken back in 1991 to stop them from voting. However in 1996 the Supreme Court Judgement directed the Arunanchal Pradesh Government to maintain the right of Chakamas to apply for Indian citizenship.

The Young Chakama association presented a memorandum to the Prime Minister in October 1995 which demands the formation of a separate union territory for Chakama. The Chakama who came to India after 26th January 1950 should be considered as foreigners is the demand of Mizo National Defenders. A Chakama Autonomous District Council has been provided under the 6th schedule of constitution.

The Jharkhand Movement—21 Tribal districts in South Bihar, West Bengal, Orissa and M.P. have been demanding a separate state for them under Jharkhand Movement since 1937.[3]

The main reason for a separate state is that the natives are being oppressed by the other people. The oppression is compounded by the exploitation of mineral, forest and human resources of the region. It is argued that coal, iron, manganese, mica, uranium and a variety of other minerals and metals vital for India's economy have been extracted from Jharkhand without proportionate benefits of development not having reached the natives. The main allegation is that the local people have been subjected to oppression and have been converted into bonded or semi slave labourers. The Jharkhand party was founded in 1937 by Jaipal Singh and has gone through many twists and turns and has had many factions till today. But the demand for a separate 'Jharkhand' state continues even today and Jharkhand Mukti Morcha. No government, has paid adequate attention for the economic development of the tribal people in this area. Things continuing as they are, will increase the growing tribal anger leading to an explosive situation which will make the creation of a Jharkhand state unavoidable.

The Jharkhand Coordination Committee has given a signal to the Union Government in 1988 that if this demand of a separate state is not conceded than a parallel provisional government will be established. The Union Government has tried to resolve this issue through various peaceful talks. As a result of prolonged movement *Jharkhand state is created.*

The Uttarakhand Movement

In November 1987 the demand for separate hill state covering eight hill districts in U.P. was voiced at the rally in New Delhi by the Uttarakhand Kranti Dal (UKD).[4]

The Tribal Movement is not a new development but only the format of the movement is changing since 1915. The hill area people are demanding separate hill state and seeking an identity of their own since 1957. In 1979 the UKD was formed which emerged as a regional party and is sustaining itself on separate hill state's demand. In 1982 the UKD leaders met the late PM Indira Gandhi and discussed the issue with her. On 22nd August 1987 a delegation of UKD met Rajiv Gandhi and pressed for their demand and conveyed that the agitation would take a serious turn if the Government ignored their demand. The eight hill districts are: (1) Naini Tal, (2) Almora, (3) Pithoragarh, (4) Chamoli, (5) Puri, (6) Tehri Garhwal, (7) Uttarkashi, (9) Dehra Dun. The hill districts have a population which is more than that of the neighbouring Himachal Pradesh. Now as a result of great strife a new State with the name Uttaranchal has came into existence.

Secessionist Movement

The Gorkha National Liberation Front (GNLF) demanded the creation of a separate Gorkhaland state in the Darjeeling hills and the adjoining areas in 1980. The GNLF leader, Mr. Subhash Gheising wanted to create an ethnic identity of Nepali speaking minority in the hill districts of Darjeeling, Kurseong, Kalimpong and part of Jalpaiguri to be formed into a separate state. This is a strategic area from the point of security on the Sino-Indian border and between Bhutan and Sikkim. In December 1983 GNLF leader Cheising wrote a letter taking Birendra to support the Gorkhaland Movement on Nepali grounds. In 1985 the letters were sent to all heads of state of the UNO. In December 1985 Rajiv Gandhi started discussion with GNLF leader about their demand. In Septemper. 1987 Mr. Rajiv Gandhi, the West Bengal Chief Minister Jyoti Basu discussed a package with the GNLF leader and established the Hill Development Council. This Council, would give sense of participation to Nepali speaking people in ensuring economic and social development of this region. The neglect of economic development was the main issue raised by GNLF. The Council exercises control over municipalities and Panchayat in the subjects related to transport, education, health and tourism. But the militant sections are opposing this arrangement. The infighting among the factions of GNLF is creating difficulty and Gheishing is losing control of this movement. The militants among the GNLF under the leadership of Mr. R.P. Waiba have set up arms training camp inside Nepal near Darjeeling-Nepal border. Open help from Nepal is a major problem concerning this issue. Mr. Gheising is also in favour of fresh agitation which would be undemocratic and has called his followers to take to the field and be ready to die for Gorkhaland. It seems militancy has increased to a far greater degree than before.

Bodoland and Assam Problem

In 1985 Assam experienced a prolonged state of civil disturbances and violence based on ethnic, linguistic religious and economic factors by AAGSP. In 1985 the Assam Accord was signed with Assam Gan Sangram Parishad and the Assamese problem of Indian citizenship to foreign nationals in state was resolved.

Assam Problem

This problem started in August 1979 with the ostensible purpose of deleting names of "Foreigners" from electoral rolls since then the agitation has been continued till 1988 with varying degrees of intensity by all Assam Gansangram Parishad (AA GSP) and All Assam Students Union. (AASU). There has been influx of foreign nationals in Assam across Indo-Bangladesh border continuously since independence. These foreign nationals who came over from Pakistan or Bangladesh many years ago have since been living in Assam. The issue started with the citizenship of these foreign nationals and their electoral rights. The root cause of this agitation can be found in economic, social, cultural and ethnic identity of the Assamese people. There was considerable escalation in violence and extremist activity that jeopardised the development and economic well being of the people of Assam in the early 1980s. The Central and the State Government tried to resolve the problem peacefully within the constitutional framework and Late Smt. Indira Gandhi held various rounds of talks with the leaders of AASU and AAGSP who were spear heading the agitation. Ultimately on 15 August 1985 the Assam Accord was signed between AASU, AAGSP and the Government under leadership of Late Mr. Rajiv Gandhi and the issue of citizenship was resolved. But then the internal problem of the state arose.[5A]

The entire Bodo dominated areas of lower (six districts on Brahmputras South bank) Assam are demanding a separate Bodoland for Bodos. The 'Bodoland Accord' was signed on 20th February 1993 but it failed to bring peace in Assam and created further violence to causing turmoil and turbulence.[5B]

This accord was signed between the Bodos, the Assam Government and the Centre. The Bodo Autonomous Council (BAC) had been formed immediately after the accord but the area of BAC has not been demarcated. The Bodo people are demanding that 550 villages near Indo-Bhutan border also should be handed to BAC along with other 2500 villages.

The state has denied it on security grounds. All non-Bodos have been ordered to quit Bodoland by March 15, 1996 and the militants are implementing accord. The Bodo Security Force has been formed. The United Liberation Front of Assam (ULFA) movement in Assam is demanding independent Assam as a nation. They are warning the non-Assamese to leave Assam within one month and this has spread panic among the non-Assamese in the state. The ULFA has militant leaders like Shashidhar Chowdhary and lawlessness is rampant in the state.

Separate Jammu Movement

The Jammu & Kashmir state had been facing Terrorist problem for a long time. The people of Jammu are fed up with militancy had been driven away from their homes in the valley. They are now demanding 'secession' from the valley. People of Jammu have formed an organisation, Jammu Mukti Morcha (JMM) in 1990 under the leadership of Dr. Gupta (JMM) argue that Jammu, Kashmir and Ladakh have different political, linguistic social and cultural characters. Politically the Jammu and Ladakh regions would like to remain with India whereas Kashmir valley wants a separate identity.

Therefore there is no point in keeping these three regions together. Three independent units should be created, within the Indian Union to resolve the Kashmir problem. This is the demand of the JMM. But all do not endorse the JMM's point of view. The Buddhist Ladakhs are agitating too for more autonomy and for the creation of a separate state.

Terrorism in India

India's internal security problems are aggravated by terrorism in Punjab, Jammu & Kashmir. Although these problems have domestic roots the external forces and factors aggravate the situation. Pakistan has been supporting and spreading armed violence, militancy in these two states since 1980.

Punjab Problem [Khalistan]

Punjab presents a different sort of internal security problem in India. In the last few years terrorism has reared its ugly head and has continued to be a major problem to the government and the people. Terrorism in Punjab can be attributed to bitter factional state politics; religious fundamentalism; politicising of religion; corruption in the state agencies; smuggling across the Indo-Pak border; unemployment; weak, and ineffective law enforcing machinery. The Punjab problem basically started with the concept of a separate ethnic identity of the Sikhs. Out of the total population of Punjab 52% are Sikhs. As early as 1971 the demand for an independent Sikh state was put forward by Dr. Jagjit Singh Chauhan, a former Finance Minister of Punjab and General Secretary of 'Akali Dal' who then migrated to England.

In 1972 his follower Mr. Balbir Singh Sidhu formed a provisional National Council for a separate Sikh State i.e. Khalistan and Started issuing currency passport from the head quarters i.e. Golden Temple at Amirtsar. In 1973 to resolve the economic disparity issue and other ethnic and religious problems a resolution was passed called as 'Anandpur Sahib resolution. But it was found that both Center and State government neglected its implementation and unrest to some extent continued. In 1979 it erupted in the formation of 'Dal Khalsa' [a militant Sikh youth orgnanisation] under the leadership of Gajendra Singh with the objective of establishing a separate 'Khalistan'. During this period various political parties including the Congress supported verifications of the Sikhs who dominated political parties and the Akali Dal groups for the electoral gain and political power. Till 1980 Sant Bhindranwale — a militant supporter of Khalistan created a strong base of civilian support for the separatist movement. Pakistan and other anti-Indian nations fuelled the Khalistan movement by providing training to militants, weapons, money and other help. They were successful in creating Hindu-Sikh divide.

Since 1980 the Khalistan movement posed a great security threat to India and terrorist activities became a day to day affair in the state. In 1981 a well known journalist Lala Jagat Narayan was shot dead because he criticised the Khalistan movement. Saint Bhindranwale allegedly murdered the Nirankari Sect Saint Guru Bachan Singh and took a refuge in the Golden Temple of Amritsar which became a centre for conducting terrorist activities. On September 29, 1982 an Indian plane flying from Delhi to Srinagar was hijacked by the Khalistanis. The counter strategy against terrorism could not succeed. In an attempt to curb this terrorism 'Operation Blue Star' was conducted by the military forces on 6 June 1984. The Indian soldiers fought a day long battle fiercely on in their way to the Golden Temple. This extreme measure was necessary to end prolonged and mounting violence in the state. Jarnail Singh Bhindranwale, the leader of Sikh militants died in this operation. Unrest continued in the country. On 31 October 1984 Prime Minister Mrs Indira Gandhi was assassinated in New Delhi by two Sikh members Satwant Singh and Beant Singh of her bodyguard. In 1985 Rajiv Gandhi tried to solve the Punjab problem by signing an accord on July 24 with Sant Longowal [Akali Dal] which aimed at ending the period of confrontation. Various demands of Sikh including transfer of Chandigarh, economic measures, rehabilitation and employment program for youth were accepted, but the militant sections of Akali Dal denounced it and August 20 1985 Sant Longowal was shot dead by the terrorists. On 10 August 1986, Khalistani supporters assassinated General Arun Vaidya the then Chief of the Army Staff when troops entered in the Golden Temple in 1984. Various measures have been adopted on political, economic and social grounds to counter terrorism. J.F. Ribeiro the then chief of police tried to control the situation. The common people are tired of terrorism and are now responding positively to the government measures. But it will take a long time to achieve normalcy.

Kashmir Problem

Jammu & Kashmir is geostrategically important from the point of view of security of India. For the last 9 years India is facing low intensity conflict in this region which has deep roots. In October 1947 Kashmir faced the invasion of the state by armed raiders from Pakistan to liberate the Muslims of Kashmir. The ruler Maharaja Hari Singh and the leader of political party in 1947 requested India to accept the accession of Kashmir and to intervene with her armed forces. India accepted the accession of Kashmir which became a part of Indian territory.

The matter was taken to UNO by India and a cease fire was brought about in December 1948. But since then Kashmir has continued to be an issue of dispute between India and Pakistan. In 1972 India and Pakistan arrived at the Shimla Agreement on the principles of durable peace and bilateralism as the basis of resolving the Kashmir issue. This agreement had frozen the borders of Kashmir to the line of actual control resulting from the cease fire of December 17, 1971 and shall be respected by both sides.[6] But Shimla Agreement could not resolve the problem fully and it has been further aggravated by the militancy supported by Pakistan in this region.

Jammu & Kashmir has three regions Kashmir, Ladakh and Jammu having different religious and regional aspirations. A recent study by P. Stoban states that, "Out of total area of J&K 54.4% area is under control of China and Pak occupied Kashmir and 45.6% area is only under Indian control.

J&K Inside India	*Outside India*
Jammu-11.8% of total area	16.9 of total area occupied by China
Ladakh-26.6% of total area	20.3% of total area ceded to China by Pak for Karakoram Highway.
Kashmir-7.2% of total area	35.1% of total area in Pak occupied Kashmir.

Source: P. Stoban, Kashmir Key Issues, *Strategic Analyses,* Vol. XVVI, No. 1, April 1996, p. 117.

As a result of such distribution various centrifugal pulls and pressures operated in the state J&K causing internal instability. The state Government till today has appointed three commissions to fulfil the demands and grievances of these three regions."[7]

In 1975 Mrs. Indira Gandhi and Sheikh Abdullah had offered six point package with the regional Kashmiri party, The National Conference and Sheikh Abdullah as its leader who formed the Government, in the state. The National Conference confirmed its stand that Kashmir is an integral part of India. Pakistan continued to question the Indian claim of voluntary acceptance by Kashmir of the accession to (Kashmir: An on the spot study Indian Defence Review summer 1994). Pakistan has always tried to destabilised the state by waging a 'Proxy War' in some form or the other. For a long time Pakistan has waited for Kashmir to ripen for an Islamic Revolution but it failed. Therefore since 1977, Pakistan has started sending tribesmen, Pakistani nationals and foreign mercenaries in the valley for spreading militancy and terrorism. The Inter Service Intelligence (ISI) motivated these mercenaries with the euphoria of 'Jihad' to liberate the land of Allah from the infidels. They forced Kashmiri locals to help them by promising Azadi to them. As per one estimate, "In 1993 there were approximately 600-1000 foreign mercenaries or guest militants in J&K and 10,000 militants were trained militants."[8]

According to one study there are 100 odd militant groups in J&K. The few important groups were formed after 1975 are:-

(1) *Jammu Kashmir Liberation Front* (JKLF) founded in 1977 with an aim to re-establish Kashmir to the pre-1947 borders. This group became active in 1988 when its leader Aminullah Khan joined with Islamic Student League Hamid Sheik Yasin Malik. These leaders wanted to review Islamic ideology and gets help from ISI.

(2) Hizb-ul Mujahdeen (HM) — A major insurgent group formed in 1990. An Islamic force and it is pro Pakistani group aided by ISI.

(3) Haarkat Al-Ansar (HAA) - Radical group based in Islamabad which believes in the global supremacy of Islam. It has members from Afghanistan, Arab countries, Pakistan and Kashmir. The other groups are Karkat ul Jihad, Al Faran, Janbaz-Mujahadeen, Jammat, Pakistan spread force, Al Jihad, Al Barg, Jihad Force, Allah Tiger, Khalifas etc.

The major terrorist training camps are conducted in Pakistan occupied Kashmir at Kahata, Rawalkot, in Pakistan occupied Kashmir Mirpur, Muzzafarbad and Peshawar. In this way Pakistan is spreading low intensity warfare in J&K since 1988. The Indian Army has been conducting counter insurgency operations and is getting success since 1993. Pakistan also raised a hue and cry over alleged human right violations by Indian security forces in Kashmir in all international forums but failed in March 1994 in moving a resolution on Human Rights Violation at UNO. In 1993 Indian Security forces resolved the problem of Hazarat Bal crisis and in 1991 resolved the issue of Kidnapping of daughter of Mufti Mohammad Sayeed the Home Minister at that time.[9]

In this way since 1987 the Kashmir problem has become a major internal security concern for India. Like any other internal insurgency problem this problem also has its roots in economic issues like unemployment and lack of industrial development, misguided religious perceptions, identity crisis as Kashmiris etc. But other than these external factors and active role of Pakistan in supporting terrorism deteriorates the internal security scenario.

Internal Security Management in India

Role of Union and State Governments in Internal Security

In India the primary responsibility of the three Defence Services is to safeguard the sovereignty, territorial integrity

Analysis of Internal Security Threats in India

Chart 10
Issue and Ladder of Internal Security

Escalation ladder (Issue Areas)	*Level One (Basic demnds/issues)*	*Level Two (Rising demand)*	*Level Three (Crisis/Major threat to security)*
1	2	3	4
1. Political	Political identity/ sub-nationalism.	Separatist movement and self-determination demands (Political level).	Militant Insurgency/Sabotage terrorism.
	e.g.- Punjab problem-1972 - Kashmir problem till 1975.	'Khalistant' demand in 1980 Jammu Kashmir Libertation front other groups and their demands since 1977 to 1987	Continued terrorism in Punjab since 1982 with external support Continued Violence and terrorism with external support 1987 to date.
	- Bodoland - Bodo people demands in 1985.	Separte Bodoland and Bodo Autonomous council demand 1990 to 1993.	Continued activities of Bodo Security force since 1993 to date.
	- Separate Jammu movement - since 1990. Demand of Buddhist Ladakhi for Ladakh Autonomous Council.		-

(contd...)

1	2	3	4
	- Gorkhaland movement in 1983.	Gorkhaland movement since 1985 till development council and Accord.	Low level violence and dissatisfaction sicne 1990. Aid from China and Nepal.
2. Social/Cultural	Religion/Caste/language /culture and other social problems.	Religious identity formation. Integration on social and religious basis, pressure group formation.	Caste and religious riots. Rise of fundamentalism/ communalism.
	e.g.- All North-Eastern Region insurgencies in 1970-75. Bodoland, Punjab, Gorkhaland Assam and other problem at the inception stages.	North Eatern Region insurgencies in 1975-1985 and their talks and solutions during Rajiv Gandhi and Indira Gandhi peiod, Assam accord in 1985.	Rising demand and continued activities of insergent groups with external support since 1987.
3. Economic	Disparity in development other economic problems	Call for development Boards participation in economic decision process.	Militancy in economic demands strastegies and external help.
	e.g.- Jharkhand Movement in 1965 to 1975. Uttarakhand Movement in 1979.	Demands of Jharkhand co-ordination committee in 1988. Demands of Uttarakhand Kranti-dal in 1987.	Continued demands of Jharkhand Mukti Movement, Uttarakhand Movement.

Assam problem in 1979.	Demands of AASU and AAGSP in 1980-85 on economic issues and disparities.	
'Gorkhaland' movement's demand in 1980-85.	'Hill council development' in 1988.	Miliancy in economic demand since1988.
Demands of Punjab and Kashmir insurgents for economic progress since 1980.	Measures to improve economic conditions and to restore peace for it and people's positive support in Punjab since 1990.	More concentration on economic demands since 1989.
Demands of all North Eastern insurgencies since 1985 are focusing on economic disparities and economic backwardness.	Accepting economic bargains with goverment.	Militancy in economic demands since 1988.

and to tackle external securtiy threats to the country. This responsibility of the internal security is shouldered by the police, the para-military forces and intelligence agencies of both the Union and State Governments.

The founding fathers of the Constitution have delineated the responsibilities of external and internal security in explicit terms. On the basis of the Government of India Act of 1935 the Constitution of India has listed centre-state and concurrent subjects which demarcated the activities of the Union, State and Union Territory governments. As per this demarcation the external security is the responsibility of the Union Government while the internal security considered akin to the maintenance of law and order is the preserve of the provincial (State and U.Ts) Government.[10]

Agencies involved in Internal Security

Since the attainments of independence a large variety of paramilitary forces have been raised in India on an ad hoc basis to meet or overcome the immediate Internal Security challenges consequently the budget for paramilitary forces of the Union Government increased from Rs. 3.2 crore in 1950-51 to 1500 crores in 1985-86. A comprehensive internal security policy has never been evolved which could take care of India's long-term and medium-term needs. It is seen that whenever a contingency arose a force was raised to meet it.[11]

The internal security in India is managed by the police, paramilitary and intelligence agencies of both union and state governments. These agencies are charged with the responsibility of identifying, preventing, containing and eliminating threats to internal security. As mentioned earlier the structure and organisation of Internal Security forces is not cohesive and some of these forces continue to exist even when the task for which they were originally raised remains ceased to exist.

The normal police force in the country is primarily under the control of state/union territory government while the centre only maintains a number of paramilitary forces to guard the borders during peace and to augment and assist the State Government in maintaining law and order. National Intelligence is developed by all the Government departments and at the highest level and it is co-ordinated by the Joint Intelligence Committee (JIC).[12]

These agencies are governed by the Ministry of Home Affairs (Union Government) and Home affairs Ministries of State/UT. Government. In India each state has its own peculiar law and order and internal security problems. Each state is authorised to have its own armed police forces. At the centre there are nearly fifteen to seventeen types of paramilitary forces which can be reinforced in any situation to help and support the State Government in tackling the law and order and Internal Security problems. At present there-exist a diversity in organisation in the agencies that are used to combat the threats to Internal Security of India and they also lack an overall controlling and coordinating authority. The Ministry of Home Affairs or Cabinet Secretariat is not equipped to fulfil this rule to the desired extent.[13]

The other countries like the USSR, China and Pakistan which have long sensitive land borders also maintain para-military forces but they are well integrated with their defence system. In all these countries paramilitary forces are officered by the army or defence department. This helps in developing a common culture and values so that integration of military and para-military forces becomes almost automatic and helps in building a cohesive team. India lacks this type of integration.

We have seen that threats to Internal Security do not originate only from within the frontiers of the country but also from outside, therefore it is urgent need to create a separate professional body/department to tackle these issues in integrated manner. We also need to restructure para-

Chart 11

Classification and Summary of Internal Police and Para Military Agencies

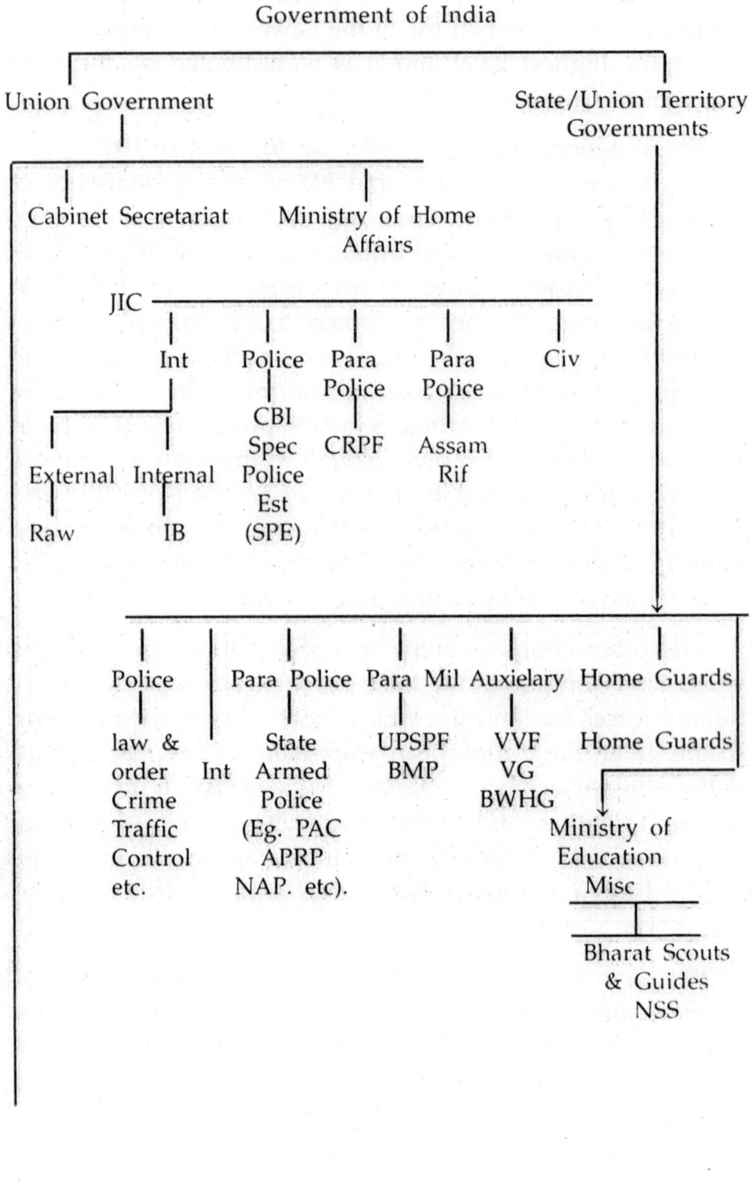

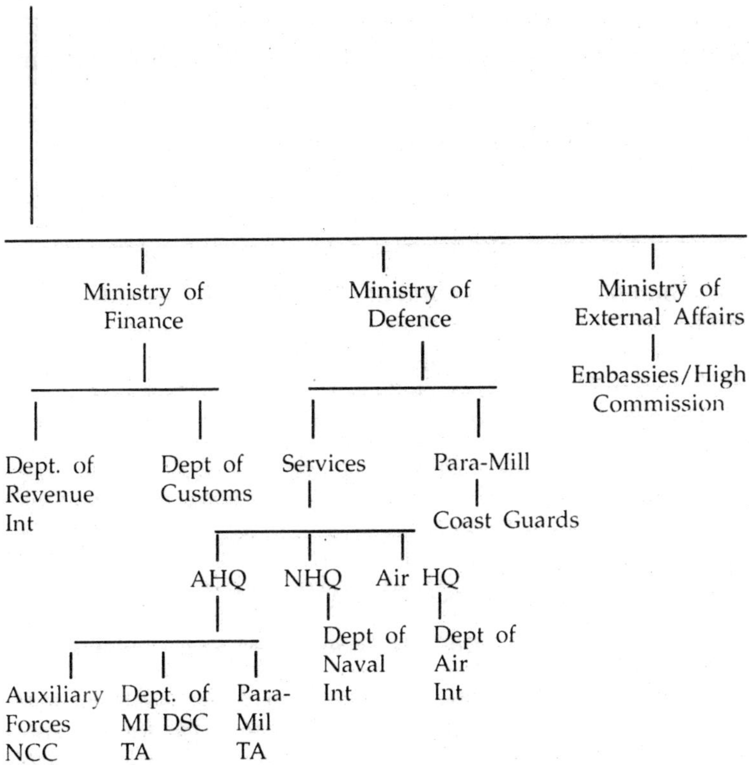

(*Source*: Prasad B.A., Re-structuring Forces to Combat Threats to Internal Security, *Strategic Analysis* Vol. XIV - No. 9 December 1991, IDSA Journal, IDSA New Delhi, p. 1110)

military forces and integrate them with the Army/defence forces in such a way that it would create a "Well integrated cohesive team".

At present we have ad hocism, lack of coordination of various agencies, lack of well defined rules and consequent anomalies in organisation, force structuring, training and equipping of internal security forces. Therefore there is an urgent need for reorganisation, restructuring and rationalising of the Internal Security forces to obtain optimum efficiency of the various constituents of these forces individually/or collectively.

The Important Constituents of Internal Security Forces

- It includes the police, paramilitary, auxiliary and intelligence forces.

These forces can be grouped into three categories on the basis of their broad functions as follows:-

(A) Forces Guarding Borders

The primary duty of the internal security forces is on the borders and they are expected to fight to a limited extent with enemy. This groups includes the B.S.F., Indo-Tibetan Border Police [ITBP], Special Frontier Force, Special Security Bureau, N.C.C., Assam Rifles, Territorial Army, Rashtriya Rifles, Coast Guard for sea frontiers and Intelligence forces.

(B) Forces Meant for the Maintenance of Law and Order

These forces function in the interior of the country and can be more appropriately called as para-police forces. This group includes Police, CRPF, the state armed police, the village guards in Nagaland, Village Volunteer force in Manipur, CISF, different Section Corps., National Security Guard Railway Protection Force, and the Bihar Military Police.

(c) Forces Meant for Country's Discipline

They are developed at auxiliary forces to create a national awareness among the Civil population and the students. It includes the Border Roads Organisation, Civil Defence, National Service Scheme, Scouts and Guide, etc.

All these agencies are not under a central control and coordinating agency and therefore could not function as a united cohesive body to the maximum efficiency.

History of Para-Military Forces

The Para-Military forces were raised in India in the 18th and 19th century essentially to extend the control of the British rule to the north eastern and north western parts of the country at the minimum cost. These forces were assigned the duty to garrison the newly conqured territory of British Empire in the north-east. The Assam Rifles initially named the Kacher Levies came into being and in the north-west a number of levies from the Pathan Tribes were raised.

These forces were locally recruited but commanded by Army officers. After independence Assam Rifles stayed in India and others were transferred to Pakistan[*14]

Assam Rifles

This is the oldest para-military force in the country. Bulk of this force operates in the north-eastern region under operational control of the Army. As a result of this their fighting potential is the highest among all para-military forces.

Border Security Force (BSF)

BSF was created in December 1965 consistuing of men and patrol the land borders of India in order to relieve the Army from this responsibility in peace time so that they can carry out formation training. Military organisation manning the borders is not indicative of any aggressive design of India as perceived by our neighbours but it provides effective assistance to local administration in maintaining law and order. The BSF works under the Home Ministry and it was commanded by the police in the initial period but now its own cadres are created. The BSF comes under the command of the Army during war operations and it comes under the Home Ministry force in peacetime.

Central Reserve Police Force (CRPF)

It was created to provide the central government with a police force. It has enabled the Union Government to intervene and police the trouble spots inside the country. It assists the State Government, in the maintenance of law and order. It also assists the Army authority where they are operationally in charge for maintaining internal security. This force is used in relief operations in natural calamities. It was used in Sri Lanka and Maldives and other operations. Lt. Gen. M.L. Chibber opines that, "This force is found to be inadequately trained in riot control, of to contain terrorism. It lacks arms, equipment, training and leadership. Hence there is a need to split this force into specialist training units for the different roles it has to perform."[15]

Indo-Tibetan Border Police (Patrol)

It was created for policing the Indo-Tibetan Borders in U.P., H.P., J. & K. sectors. This force is specifically trained and equipped to patrol high altitude areas knowing the local language, and acquainted with the hill people, duly trained to carry out this task. This force is also deployed in bank security and VVIP establishments.

National Security Guards

This is a specialised force to combat terrorism in all forms. It was raised in 1984 after the assassination of Mrs. Indira Gandhi as a Federal Force to tackle any specific situation requiring special skills to counter increasing terrorism in all forms.

The best volunteer officers from the Army were picked to man the NSG which has been interested with the task of providing security to high risk VVIPs.

Rashtriya Rifles

Since 1970 the army has been increasingly employed in anti-militant operations and for the maintenance of law and order for a long period of time. Keeping this in view a new para-military force under the ministry of defence has been created. The Government of India has decided to use R.R. as an anti-terrorist force since 1991. The R.R. force has been trained by the experts and deployed in Punjab and Kashmir. The sanctioned strength is 36 Battalions, two Sector headquarters and a counter insurgency headquarters etc.

Coast Guard Services (C.G.)

An interim Coast Guard was formed within the Indian Navy on 1 February 1977. The (C.G.) was established for taking over peace time duties in the country's maritime zone from the Navy. It was formally constituted as an armed force of the Union under Coast Guard Act 1978. The C.G. is to the Navy what the BSF is to the Army.

The Coast Guard checks smuggling and poaching by foreign vessels, it protects offshore rigs, Indian fishing, marine pollution and conducts general surveillance of nearly 7000 K.Ms of the Indian Coast line. The force is geared to switch over from a peace time role to war time responsibilities in support of the Navy. While the CG is under the administrative control of the Defence Ministry its budget comes from the Department of Revenue, Ministry of Finance. It has three regional headquarters at Mumbai, Chennai and Port Blair.

Police Forces

Presently the rate of crime and other law and order problems have increased multifold due to the population growth, problems of urbanisation, illiteracy, poverty, unemployment etc. The rule of police forces have become more complex and have undergone a substantial change. To quote the renowned police chief, K.F. Rustamji the policy is called upon to "Keep the terrorist at bay, to fight against corruption, provide protection to minorities and unlike any other forces it does more than just policing".[16]

The main function of preservation of order and enforcement of law by the police forces has increased substantially therefore State/Union territory Government and Union Government had to increase parapolice forces.

The present organisation of police forces is shown in the chart on the next page.

Chart 12
Organisaton of Police Forces

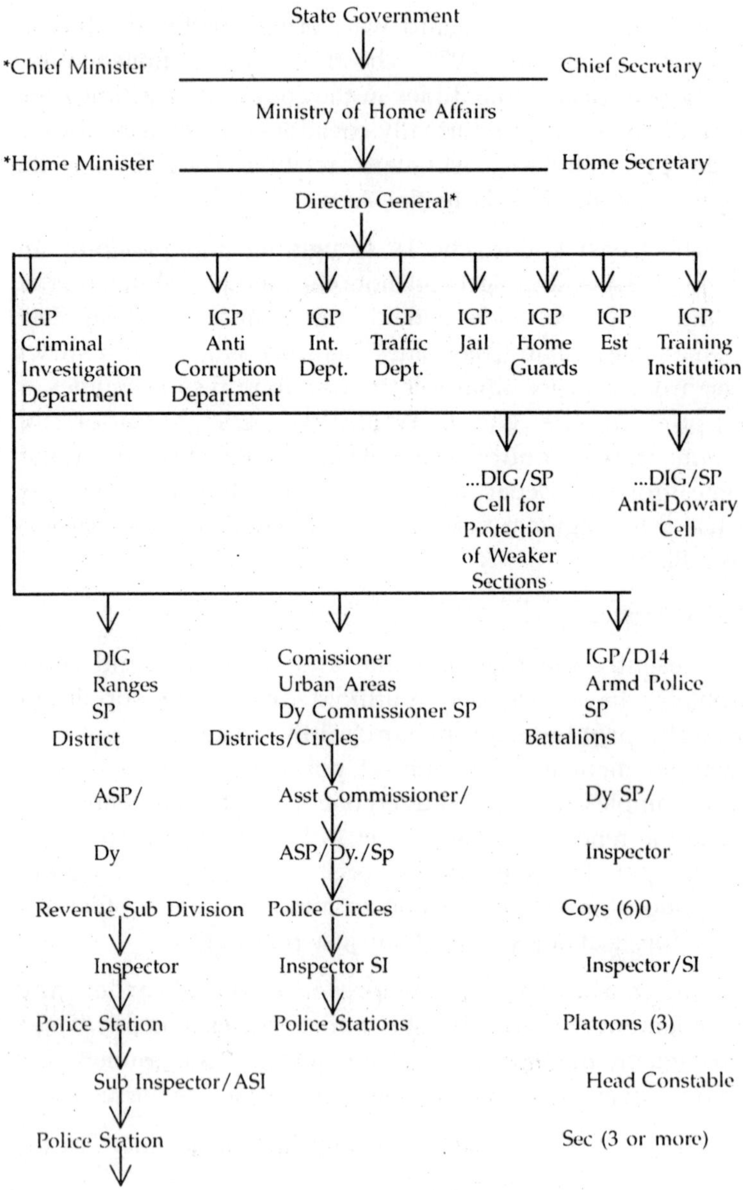

ASI/Head Constable

↓

Police Out Post

↓

Haad Constable

↓

Sections

Legend

* Elected Representative

= IAS

= IPS

Provincial Police Service

(Source: Prasad B.A., "Re-Structuring Forces to Combat Threats to Internal Security, *Strstegic Analysis* (New Delhi IDSA Pub) Vol. No. 9 December 1991, p-1111)

In spite of broadening of various tasks assigned to police forces there is very little attempt to evolve specialised training, restructuring and modernisation tasks requires superior mental ability, training and specialisation but in India the same less educated police officer is required to perform any or all the tasks assigned to the officer during his duty hour. This causes deterioration in efficiency. Along with this it is often found that intelligence branches of policy establishments are completely neglected and they have inadequate staff and equipment. This is coupled with long hours of duty, poor public image, political pressures, outdated equipment, and a low morale has made the police force a mere spectator to the growing crime and disturbances. Therefore there is an urgent need to modernize police force effective for their functioning. The Government of India has undertaken a programme of modernisation. The technological developments have increased the power of the criminals and anti-social elements tremendously through latest weapons and means of communication etc. Hence police forces are now equipped with sophisticated weapons to combat threats from them. There is also a need for coordination from the national level to the district level for the effective working of police force. Police intelligence needs to be strengthened. In the game of power and politics criminal collusion, the honest police officers have became common victim. All this needs to be corrected for the effective use of police force as an Internal Security force.

Apart from this there is the Railway Protection Force, used to maintain law and order rule in JandK, Punjab, Assam, and West Bengal. This force is also used for handling communal riots all over the country. Further Defence Security Cores, Village Guards, Bihar miliary police and Village Volunteer Force are also raised for the maintenance of law and order.

Auxiliary Forces

Home Guards (H.G.)

It is a statutory voluntary organization raised all over the country at the time of the Indo-China War of 1962. The H.G. serves as an auxiliary police in maintaining law and order, Internal Security, guarding lines of communications, vital plants and installations etc. They help the community in any kind of disaster such as floods, cyclones, earthquakes etc. They promote communal harmony and give assistants to the administration in protecting the weaker sections of the society and provide essential service in times of disaster. The H.G. also assist the BSF and are known as the Border wing of H.G. in 1983-84 the strength of H.G. was over Five and half lakhs. The Government of India and the State Government share H.G. expenditure on a 50 : 50 basis. For the Border wing H.G. the entire expenditure is met by the Government of India and in some Western States of Punjab, Rajasthan and Gujarat. H. G. expenditure is shared on 75 : 25 basis.

The role of the Territorial Army, V.V.F. and V. Guards, and the NCC is well defined but their potential is not fully utilized. Therefore, they are not very successful in controlling disturbances or preventing crime, sabotage or subversion.

Territorial Army

The Territorial Army is a voluntary part time force working under the Ministry of Defence. It offers excellent opportunity to civilians from all walks of life to serve the nation while carrying out their civil vacations. It provides the country a reserve force that can assist the Regular Army during operations and emergent situations as and when required.

The Territorial Army consists of Departmental and Non-Departmental Territorial Army units. The total authorised strength is approximately 40,000 all ranks. Departmental units are raised from amongst the employees of Government Departments and Public Sector Undertakings. Ecological task force and wasteland development force comprises of only External Servicemen. There are 28 departmental units of Territorial Army.

Non-Departmental Territorial Army units are the Infantry Battalions which are financed entirely by the Ministry of Defence. There are 25 such units. The Territorial Army is developed in J & K for Internal Security under operations Rakshak for road opening, convoy protection, search operations, guarding vulnerable areas/points etc. series of measures taken to improve the service conditions of Territorial Army.

National Cadet Core (NCC)

A premier youth movement which has emerged as an extremely dependable and disciplined youth orgnanisation which aims at all round growth and development of the youth. It motivates cadets to strive for national unity, discipline and excellence in all walks of life and was formed in 1948. Girls units were introduced in 1949. The strength of NCC was 11.5 lakhs in 1994 and is expected to reach 11.7

lakhs by the end of 1997. It covers 6684 schools and 4665 colleges.

Civil Defence Scheme

It aims at maintaining the continuity of production and minimising damages to property in the event of hostile attacks. It also aims at maintaining the morale of the people in difficult situations. The Government of India has laid down the policy that Civil Defence measures should be confined to certain selected places. Early warning system both by Radio and TV and speedy Blackout measures are being implemented gradually in a phased manner. C.D. measures are being planned under Nuclear Environment. The C.D. measures cover 27 states/UT in this country. Under this scheme 251 selected towns recovered which are vulnerable to hostile attacks as per government sources the strength of the C.D. Volunteers is more than 5 lakhs and Ministry of Home Affairs shares the expenditure with the State Government on 50:50 basis except in the North Eastern States. Mobile civil emergency Force in Delhi and Calcutta have engaged themselves in multiple activities such as rescue and Fire calls etc.[17]

Intelligence Agencies

National intelligence is developed by all Government deptartments and it covers the broad aspects of National Security. The coordination of all Intelligence agencies of the armed forces and other ministries at the highest levels is done by the Joint Intelligence Committee (JIC) which forms an integral part of the Cabinet Secretariat. However this oganisational set up is quite inadequate and suffers from many lacunae. The acquisition of external intelligence is handled by (RAW) of the Cabinet Secretariat i.e. Research and Analysis Wing while the internal intelligence is assigned to the Intelligence Bureau (IB). Besides this, various other departments have their own Intelligence branches catering for their own peculiar intelligence requirements. This has created a plethora of intelligence agencies each of which works in watertight compartments and generally at varying purposes. Thus many times there is a duplication or triplication of efforts which causes of wastage of resources and lack of coordination.

Research and Analysis Wing (RAW)

RAW was created in 1963. Before this IB used to undertake the external intelligence through the Director General of Security. Head of the RAW is the ex-officio Director General of Security as well Raw is not involved in Internal Security matters except in so far as they are related to external security matters. In such cases RAW works in cooperation which and the approval of internal intelligence agencies.

Chart 13

Structure of Structure of Intelligence Services in India

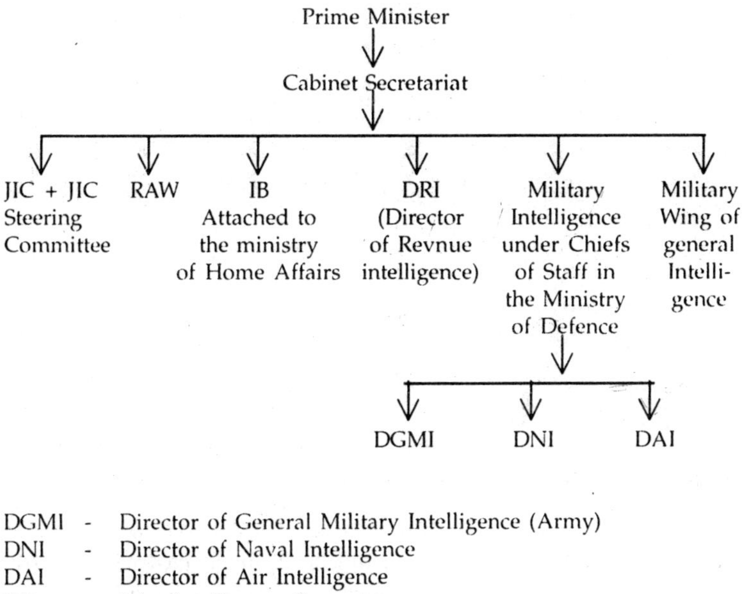

DGMI - Director of General Military Intelligence (Army)
DNI - Director of Naval Intelligence
DAI - Director of Air Intelligence
JIC - Joint Intelligence Committee

Source: Bhashyam Kasturi, *Intelligence Serices: Analysis Organisation and Functons,* (New Delhi, Lancer Publishers and distributors, 1995) p.57.

India has political, economic and other interests abroad and its the external security has to be safeguarded, it also needs to know the strategic environment outside its borders therefore RAW is entrusted with the responsibility of collecting external Intelligence for these objectives. RAW has an officer posted in each of the embassies abroad. These officers appoint agents, get information and transmit the same to their superior headquarters and then it is analysed for specific objectives.

Intelligence Bureau (IB)

It is the oldest intelligence agency of India. The main function of this agency is to gather intelligence related to the security and stability of the country. IB is also assigned the role of assessment of the public mood and temper.

IB has a representative in each district of the country who reports to the IB head in the state. It has a number of senior officers of the rank of a DIG or higher level in each state. Most of the middle and higher levels officers of IB and RAW are drawn from the officers of the IPS on a tenure basis from the state cadres. This type of migration from one service to another affects the permanent cadre of intelligence. We also need to understand that the gathering of intelligence is not a purely police function but it requires wider understanding of the issues.

The IB Director reports to the PM and CM on a regular basis. The reports collected by IB staff reach the PM the very next day. Great importance has been given to the IB. IB watches all those whom the party in power or the bureaucracy of the sate wants to be observed. IBs' activities have always been justified on the grounds that they are obliged to report back to the Government.

In India the coordination of the work of various intelligence agencies is neglected to a large extent. The JIC fulfills two task only in a peripheral manner and it is often influenced by the Director of IB, RAW and Security Adviser to the Prime Minister Prasad B.A. is of the view that, "India has many times suffered greatly due to intelligence failures which consequently turned to internal or external security threat. The staff of these agencies need to be like a healthy combination of men from the police, foreign service, military, scientific, trade and revenue establishments."[18]

This is necessary because good intelligence is a basic prerequisite for the security of a nation in modern world.

Central Bureau of Investigation (CBI)

The CBI is the investigation agency of the Government. Every Government has an investigative agency to keep the people under watch and carry out detailed investigations in doubtful cases. The main function of the CBI is to protect the people and public resources. In addition to this, there is the Director of Enforcement and Revenue Intelligence which to has been given more powers by the Government to conduct raids and adopt other such measures. The Intelligence set up also exists with BSF, CRPF, NSG special protection group and military. They function on parallel lines of other intelligence agencies. Now-a-days counter intelligence has become important counter intelligence means safeguarding and protecting our own information from falling into the hand of the enemy.

In India we need to avoid duplication and contradiction. At the same time we need to improve coordination of various intelligence agencies and military intelligence agencies. India's expenditure on IB, RAW, CBI and military intelligence is increasing day by day. These agencies are only accountable to their political bosses who are from the party in power. We require to re-oganise the structure and means in which NSC shall define the objectives of intelligence and these agencies shall provide detailed assessment before the formulation of policy. This will avoid duplication of efforts and will provide comprehensive and timely intelligence.

Table 14

Internal Security Expenditure Police/Internal Security Expenditure

Year	*At Current prices in Rs. Crores*	*At 1980-81 prices in Rs. Crores*
1970-71	345.00	884.16
1971-72	389.00	943.72
1972-73	424.00	935.16
1973-74	470.00	862.06
1974-75	557.00	816.00
1975-76	654.00	968.46
1976-77	696.00	1009.72
1977-78	764.00	1053.15
1978-79	834.00	1150.02
1979-80	955.00	1124.46
1980-81	1163.00	1163.00
1981-82	1376.00	1253.19
1982-83	1634.00	1418.53
1983-84	1894.00	1529.14
1984-85	2165.00	1641.77
1985-86	2544.00	1853.55
1986-87	2955.00	2028.00
1987-88	3535.00	2241.88
1988-89	4086.00	2411.62
1989-90	4833.00	2656.37
1990-91	5657.00	2819.90
1991-92	6563.00	2876.36
1992-93	7815.00	3112.05
1993-94	8789.00	3230.18
1994-95	9848.00	3309.47

Source: India Budget for various years and CAG report: Appropriation account for various years.

Graph 2

Police Exp Current Prices & Constant Prices

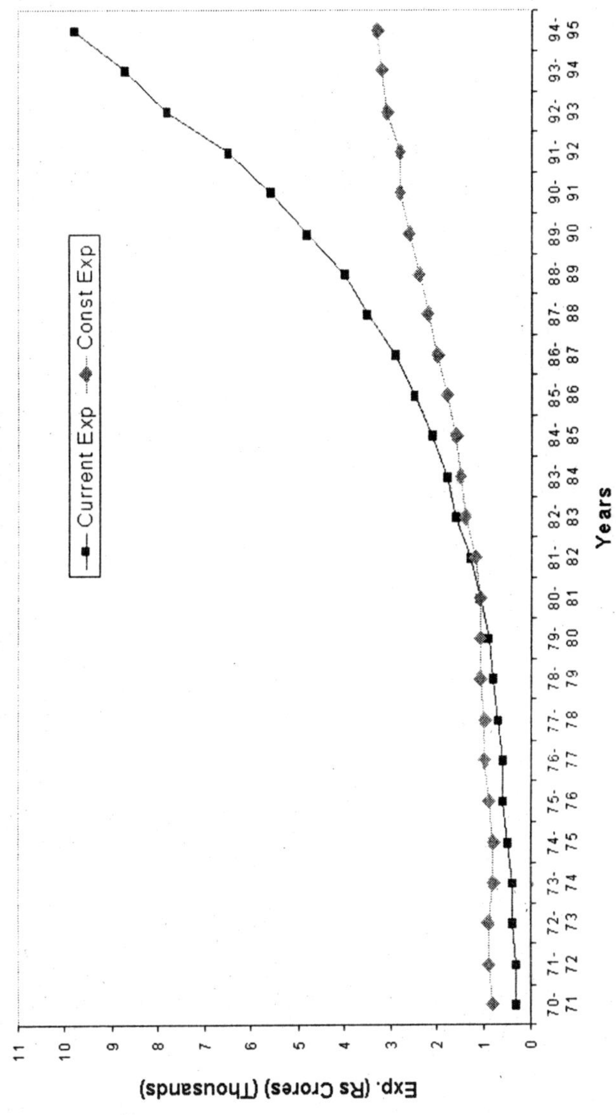

Internal Security Expenditure Break-up

Table 15
Internal Security Expenditure Breakup

(Rupees in crores)

Year	*C.R.P.*	*B.S.F.*	*I.T.B.P.*	*C.I.S.F.*	*Assam R.*	*I.-B..D. Border Works*	*Punjab*	*Mod. of Police*	*I.B*	*Civil Defence*	*Home Guard*
1	2	3	4	5	6	7	8	9	10	11	12
63-64											
64-65											
65-66											
66-67											
67-68											
68-69											
69-70											
70-71	26.62	34.86		0.92	15.16				6.50	0.35	3.00
71-72	32.32	51.60	5.06	1.44	14.63				7.81	0.36	2.50
72-73	37.14	52.07	8.36	4.30	14.25				8.32	0.36	2.70
73-74	38.78	54.11	8.42	5.14	14.91				8.77	0.48	2.50

74-75	45.59	70.67	9.24	7.04	18.59				10.42	0.96	3.10
75-76	56.53	80.74	11.50	10.98	30.20			5.02	13.56	0.95	3.25
76-77	53.45	84.17	13.09	13.43	31.29			6.00	12.06	0.80	4.00
77-78	55.81	87.87	12.02	14.77	32.32			3.50	12.90	0.65	6.11
78-79	57.37	94.00	13.00	14.82	34.38			7.09	13.34	0.73	4.50
79-80	63.49	104.33	14.21	18.60	34.34			2.25	15.02	0.82	4.90
80-81	73.97	116.06	16.94	22.50	38.67			3.75	16.14	0.83	5.50
81-82	94.87	135.93	20.42	26.06	42.37			4.00	18.44	0.77	6.50
82-83	112.34	153.17	22.78	32.90	50.99			3.75	23.09	1.09	6.70
83-84	124.54	180.10	24.34	42.50	60.13			3.90	25.00	1.26	7.10
84-85	161.92	215.50	29.55	53.67	68.14			4.06	33.86	1.34	10.00
85-86	170.97	221.16	30.27	62.66	82.72			5.00	45.89	2.05	15.80
86-87	250.83	328.33	41.02	90.13	108.77	5.00		9.41	60.09	4.01	120.50
87-88	272.58	370.24	63.24	100.00	130.00	9.43		15.00	69.89	5.75	20.70
88-89	328.99	422.01	73.50	110.00	141.00	18.64	71.19	16.00	85.40	4.77	19.50
89-90	362.62	489.88	86.90	119.00	150.75	20.22	19.00	10.00	99.34	5.96	23.13
90-91	437.27	615.00	104.70	162.00	180.00	28.00	79.00	10.00	101.65	7.36	22.50
91-92	579.15	709.00	113.25	186.97	195.00	48.29	74.00	20.00	129.82	7.47	23.75

(contd...)

1	2	3	4	5	6	7	8	9	10	11	12
92-93	644.00	763.35	136.47	232.37	229.82	91.27	78.00	15.00	130.70	8.04	24.60
93-94	759.70	905.24	152.71	291.51	266.61	136.42	53.00	15.00	144.07	8.34	25.50
94-95	813.00	925.00	164.00	323.45	296.00	150.18	80.00	24.00	149.19	2.10	26.00
95-96	848.00	994.00	177.00	344.45	303.20		80.00	24.00	150.50	2.28	28.00

Source: India Budget for various years & CAG report:
Appropriation account for various years. These are only revised estimates.

I.-B.D. = Indo-Bangladesh, Mod. = modernisation, Ib = Interlligence Bureau,

Note.: The figures show the starting of separate account.

Police Expenditure/Internal Security Expenditure

On the basis of graph and expenditure table one finds that there are four distinct phases which have more or less similar time period like defence expenditure (external security expenditure).

(1) 1973-74 to 1979-80
(2) 1979-80 to 1984-85
(3) 1984-85 to 1988-89
(4) 1988-89 to 1994-95

(1) 1973-74 to 1979-80

In the first phase police/internal security expenditure grew at the exponential annual rate of 11.66 per cent in current prices and 5.74 per cent (1980-81) prices. The North-Eastern Region's insurgency movement was at a lower of pace. The Assam problem was in the first level the insurgency movement. The Punjab issue was posing internal security threat, the evidence of Pakistan's support were coming to the forefront. The political, economic and social anti-insurgency measures were used to resolve the issues by Indira Gandhi. These gave positive results in some areas during the emergency.[19]

(2) 1979-80 to 1984-85

In this second phase the police expenditure had an exponential growth rate of 17.77 per cent per annum at current prices and 8.43 per cent per annum at (1980-81) prices. In this period domestic security situation worsened and so expenditure on internal security was increased. The Punjab problem turned into a terrorist movement. The wide-spread violence and terrorism prevailed in Punjab, Assam state. In June 1984 the military was sent in the Golden Temple in Amritsar from where the Khalistani terrorists conducted their activities under the leadership of Sant Bhindranwale. In the history of India this was the first time that armed operation was used as an anti-terrorist measure. This spread violence in some parts of India between the Hindus and the Sikhs, but it was controlled immediately.

(3) 1984-85 to 1988-89

In this third phase police expenditure had exponential growth rate of 17.58 per cent per annum at current prices and 10.78 per cent per annum at (1980-81) price which is the highest in the whole period. The police expenditure continues to remain more or less the same as in the last phase which shows that domestic security threats remain dominant throughout the 1980s. On October 31, 1984 the then Prime Minister Indira Gandhi was assassinated and Rajiv Gandhi came to power. He resorted to various accords, peace treaties with the insurgent groups and separatist movement leaders to arrive at political solutions to these internal problems e.g., the Assam Accord, Development of Autonomous Hill Development Council for Gorkhaland, Rajiv Gandhi Sant-Longowal accord etc.[20]

But he could not achieve much success. The internal security situation continued to put pressure and called for more expenditure on internal security during Rajiv Gandhi's regime. In this period India was involved directly in external problems like sending IPKF to Sri Lanka and that also cost India considerably.

The modernisation of police forces, purchase of sophisticated equipment and creation of additional Para-military Forces such as Rashtriya Rifles, National Security Guard etc. was done during this period which led to increase in expenditure on police.[21]

(4) 1988-89 to 1994-95

In this fourth phase expenditure on police had exponential growth rate of 16.00 per cent per annum current price and 5.27 per cent per annum at (1980-81) prices. In 1980-81 the total expenditure on the police was Rs. 4086.00 crores which rose to Rs. 9848.00 crores incurrent prince. This shows cent per cent increase in police expenditure at current prices during this period.

Before completion of the General Elections of 1990, Rajiv Gandhi was assassinated in a Bomb blast in Tamil Nadu with the support of Liberation Tiger of Tamile-Elam (LTTE) by a human bomb. This caused instability in the political scene of India and the world witnessed international terrorism during National Front Regime (1989-90 of V. P. Singh and Chandrashekhar Government (1990-91) in India. India lacked major policy decisions. The Narasimha Rao Government came to power in 1991 and country went through the worst economic crisis ever.[22]

The resource crunch was the basic reason for decreasing expenditure on internal and external security. At the same time the supply of military equipment at concessional rate from the USSR was stopped. India had to really come to terms with the changing environment so the internal security preparedness also got affected.

During this period, Pakistan opened up large sçale weapon aid to the terrorists in Jammu & Kashmir. The separatist movement or Jihad for Azad Kashmir continued vigorously. Indian Government openly critcised Pakistani support on this issue and reported that "The ISI (Pakistani Intelligence Agency) sent foreign and Pakistani Terrorists in the valley of Kashmir and unrest in the Kashmir was spread. It affected the normal life of the people of Jammu & Kashmir and badly affected the economy and tourism in that area, therefore the Army was called for help."[23]

The Hindus from this valley started migrating to other parts of India and a separate Jammu Movement came to the forefront. The disputes in the Home Ministry between the Cabinet Home Minister Shankar Rao Cahvan and State Home Minister Rajesh Pilot on Kashmir issue were highlighted during this period.[24]

The Hazarat Bal Crisis, Kidnapping of Mufti Mohammed Sayeed's daughter, and foreign tourists etc. were notable problems in this period posed by the terrorists in Jammu & Kashmir.

The Punjab terrorist Movement was controlled but in Assam demand for a separate Bodoland was put fourth and it took a violent turn. The Gorakhaland supporters also denounced and criticised the working of Hill Development Council and threatened to revive separate Gorakhaland movement. The North Eastern Region troubles continued from insurgency to militancy movement. "On 6th December 1992 demolition issue of Babari Masjid and after that Bombay Bomb Blast brought a divide in Hindu and Muslim and religions fundamental groups came to the forefront."[25]

The increasing incidence of corruption, drug trafficking, unemployment remained as main problems in the development process. The foreign exchange crisis continued but situation improvised under guidance of Dr. Manmohan Singh's reforms programmes. The process of economic reforms slowed down after 1993. The inflation and slow rate of economic growth continued inspite of various efforts. So in real terms India started facing the problems of resource crunch and it has to slow down or overlook at certain internal threats.

NOTES AND REFERENCES

1. Nanda Ravi, *National Security Policy and Planning*, (New Delhi: Lancer Books, 1991) p. 103.
2. *Indian Defence Review Comment* Vol-1 Alpha Jan 1988, (New Delhi: Lancer Publications) p. 8.
3. *Indian Defence Review*, Vol. I, (New Delhi: Lancer Publications, January 1987) p. 12.
4. *Indian Defence Review, Ibid.*, p. 14.

5A. India, Ministry of Information and Broadcasting *Assam Events in Perspective*, Pub by DAVP, (New Delhi: Government of India, April 1986) p. 25.

5B. *Data India*–Weekly event Diary, (New Delhi: Press Trust of India (P.T.I.), 13-20 February 1993, p. 758.

6. *Data India.*–Weekly event Diary, (New Delhi: P.T.I.), 17 to 24 December 1971, p. 589.

7. Stoban, P., Kashmir Key issues, *Strategic Analysis,* Vol. xvii, No. 1, April 1996 (New Delhi), p. 126.
8. *Times of India,* (Bombay) 1 January 1996.
9. This information is based on, M.L. Kotru, *The Kashmir Story,* Government of India, Ministry of External Affairs, New Delhi, pp 49-51.
10. (Constitution of India, as cited in Prasad, B.A. "Restructuring Forces to Combat Threats to Internal Security", *Strategic Analysis,* Vol. xiv, No. 9, December 1991, (New Delhi), p. 1087.
11. Chibber M. L., "The rationalisation of Para-Military Forces", *Indian Defence Review, Digest* vol. II, March 1992, New Delhi p. 36.
12. Prasad, B.A., *op cit.,* p. 1088.
13. Prasad, B.A., *op cit.,* p.1090.
14. Chibber, M.L., *op cit.,* p. 36.
15. Chibber, M.L., *op cit.,* pp. 37 to 39.
16. Rustamji, K.F., "What is wrong with Delhi Police", *Hindustan Times"* (New Delhi) October 15 1978.
17. This is based on the information given in, India, Ministry of Finance, *India Budget 1983-84, Demand for grants of Home Affairs,* Home Guard and Civil Defence, New Delhi, p. 3 & 5.
18. Prasad, B.A., *op cit.,* p. 1093.
19. India, Ministry of Home Affairs, *Annual Report 1977-78* (New Delhi: Government of India), pp. 7-15.
20. Based on the information given in these reports and other government documents.

    India, Ministry of Home Affairs, *Annual Reports 1985 to 1987* (New Delhi: Government of India).
21. India, Ministry of Finance *India Budget 1987-88, Demand for Grants Ministry of Home Affairs-* Demand No.: police, (New Delhi: Government of India), pp. 6-9
22. Based on information in, India, Ministry of Defence *Annual Report 1990-91,* (New Delhi: Government of India) p. 9 and on the survey of economic condition of India at the at time.
23. India, Ministry of Defence, *Annual Report 1993-94,* (New Delhi:Government of India) p. 11-13.
24. *Times of India,* (Bombay 15 December 1994.
25. This is based on information given in, *Data India*—Weekly event diary, various issues of December January 1992, (New Delhi: P.T.I).

CHAPTER 8

Dual Purpose Technology Programmes and Expenditure (Nuclear, Space, Tele-Communications, Electronics Programmes etc. As modern factors contributing to Defence Capability)

Introduction

Over the last several years dual use technology has started to achieve a peculiar status in the discussions on National Security. Areas like nuclear science, space research, telecommunication, electronics, biotechnology etc. have been areas which have traditionally been in the civil sector in terms of private enterprise or in the civil sector controlled by the government. A very little have been written and analysed about the interactions of these areas with the military establishments. Traditional approaches to defence expenditure have not included nuclear, space, telecommunication, electronics etc. expenditures in their calculation of defence expenditure. However, over the past several years the modernisation that has taken place in the defence sector, the technological changes which have taken place in the defence sector have brought to the attention the role of this dual sector and the interaction of this sector with the military. The concept of dual use basically means that this may be the technology for civilian purposes but this has uses in defence sector also. Given the increasing importance of the dual purpose sector it was thought necessary to include expenditure on this dual area in the calculation of defence expenditure. It is true that the entire expenditure on nuclear, space, telecommunication, electronics, science and technology, ocean development etc. is not for defence sector. It is also not possible to separate defence use and non-defence use programmes and their expenditures. But it is equally true that there is a growth in the interaction between dual purpose technology sector and defence sector. This dual purpose technology capability is considered as one of the most important potential defence capabilities. Therefore, one must take into account the growth in the expenditure in the area of dual purpose technology. This chapter goes into the study of expenditur on nuclear, space, electronics, science and technology, ocean development etc.

Concept of Dual Technology and its importance for National Security

Development in science and technology are extended to every human aspect including security. In fact technology has become the key to the progress and power. The military and economic power of a state rests on the level and development of technology. Technology is often defined as an applied science and it involves the discovery and development of new technical tools, developing better ways to use existing tools and dissemination of knowledge. Any type of technology has offensive and defensive uses and these inherent dualities often create difficulties in technological spread and technological cooperation among various states in the world. We see historically that developments in science and technology gave superiority in terms of economic and military power to European countries through the Industrial Revolution in the 18th and 19th centuries. The two World Wars demonstrated the supremacy of technology over all the other aspects of war. In the post-second world war era the international relations and systems are revolving around technological capabilities and economic capabilities. The developed countries tried to devise strategies to prevent Third World countries from sharing advantages of technology. The developed countries developed technology control regimes by treaties like Nuclear Non-proliferation Treaty (NPT), Comprehensive Test Ban Treaty (CTBT), Missile Technology Control Regimes (MTCR) etc. But the objectives of such technology control regimes failed. The third world countries or developing nations developed their indigenous technologies of similar nature or found out some ways of access to such technologies. Zubhari H. and Kalyan Raman opined in their writing that, "advanced technologies were used as power tools by both USA and the Soviet Union during the cold war period. In this period science and technology had become a major driving force behind the arms race. Both super powers tried to attract underdeveloped countries in their bloc through the technology transfer deals. One can say that during this period the focus was on military uses of science and technology."[1]

At the end of 1980s US started losing its technological dominance and this was followed by the collapse of the Soviet Union and the end of the cold war. This is slowly leading to the decline in the monopoly control power of erstwhile super powers on advanced technologies and has started the process of diffusion of technology throughout the world. Yasushi Akashi in UN Disarmament Paper has taken a view that "In the present times, it is increasingly realised that equitable distribution of existing technologies can build durable global peace."[2]

Developments in technology, the pace of technological changes Research and Development, Technology transfers, modernisation and sophistication of hi-tech strategies have become important facets of national security. In the 1980s nuclear, space, electronics telecommunications, Bio-technology, materials technology etc. have been identified as non-conventional technologies which are crucial for power building base. These technologies are often termed as advanced technologies.

All advanced technologies have dual use i.e. they can be used in civilian and military spheres. Both civilian and military applications cannot be clearly separated from each other.[3]

Military applications of such technologies are often stressed and their civilian applications are often ignored. Therefore the expenditure on dual purpose technologies such as nuclear, space, electronics, biotechnology, material development, telecommunication etc. are considered as a hidden defence expenditure has become important part of defence expenditure and is sometimes called as non-conventional military build-up.

N. Vitthal has rightly pointed out that, "We all know that the resources are limited and therefore resources constraint forces the development of dual use technologies. They are economically reasonable and they have both military and civilian uses."[4]

In an underdeveloped country like India these dual–use technologies can be utilised for socio-economic development of the country and therefore India has systematically developed these advanced dual-use technologies for civilian application too.

It is often found that military spin offs from such dual purpose technology programmes are mainly used as a deterrent against the potential threats to the security. Most of the states including India, have been using nuclear, space and other advanced technological capabilities as a deterrent to tackle their security threats. They are considered as non-conventional strategies and a part of military build up.

It is often found that once civilian technology is available, it may be possible to either use it directly or by upgrading the same for military purposes. Therefore this becomes supportive or hidden defence expenditure. In the present atmosphere of economic liberalisation in India, we should try to attract direct foreign investments in such dual use areas which will ensure and enable us to upgrade our non-conventional military capability indirectly.

Therefore, in defence expenditure analysis this area deserves special consideration.

Nuclear Technology Programme

Nuclear science and technology is of recent origin but it is a fast developing area of research. India was therefore not much behind the other nations in developing the know how in the area. Homi. J. Bhabha was one of the few Indian scientists who became internationally renowned as a nuclear scientist as early as 1940. He was instrumental in establishing the Tata Institute of Fundamental Research (TIFR) in 1945 which started the study of nuclear science and technology in India. Jawaharlal Nehru with great foresight realised the significance of development of nuclear science and technology and he rightly entrusted Dr. Bhabha with the responsibility of giving concrete shape to India's nuclear programme.

Nuclear Technology is most important in the dual Technology area. India's nuclear science and technology programme falls in the civil sector and the main objective of this programme is peaceful use of the same. Therefore, the Indian government has always displayed an ambivalence on the issue of including India's nuclear capability in the country's national force structure. The extent of Nehru's ambivalence about nuclear weapon option was reflected in a statement he made to the Lok Sabha on 10th August 1960: 'So far as we are concerned we are determined not to go in for making atomic bombs and the like. But we are equally determined not to be left behind in this advance in the use of this new power."[5]

This type of ambivalence and contradictory interests were continued by the nuclear policy makers in India. The prime objective of India's nuclear programme as defined in the Atomic Energy Act of 1948, is the development, control and use of Atomic (nuclear) energy solely for peaceful purposes. Namely the generation of electricity and development of nuclear application in research, Agriculture, industry, medicines and other areas. A. Kapur points out that, "India's nuclear programme intentions are peaceful and entirely directed to beneficial uses but there is always a built in advantage for defence use if the need arises."[6]

From 1948 to January 1966 Dr. Bhabha was the Director of Department of Atomic Energy of which Nehru was Minister. He (Dr. Bhabha) very wisely used both his political power base, pre-eminent position within the scientific community and his personal relationship with Nehru to advance nuclear power programmes and kept open the option to produce nuclear weapons. The 1962 war with China resulted in a humiliating defeat for India and forced the country to serious thinking about nuclear weapon option with the conventional defence build up after 1962.

Stages in India's Nuclear Power Programme

The Department of Atomic Energy has fostered the nuclear technology in the country to quite a matured state of self-reliance fulfilling most of the aims of the planners. India has adopted a three stage nuclear power programme to use country's Uranium and vast Thorium resources.

This programme is as given below:

(a) The first stage started with natural Uranium fuelled in pressurised heavy water reactors (PHWRS) producing power and plutonium as a by product. India has developed PHWR technology to a developed state to design, construct, operate and maintain such type of reactors.

(b) In the second stage plutonium will be fuelled in fast breeder reactors (FBR) producing power, additional plutonium and/or additional uranium 233. For the development of FBR Indira Gandhi Centre for Atomic Research (IG-CAR) was set up in 1971 at Kalpakkam (Tamilnadu). Indigeneously developed FBTR (Fast Breeder Fort Reactor) of 40 mwt capacity has been operational here since 1985 and the centre is drawing up a plan to design and build a 500 Mw prototype FBR in 1990s.

(c) The Third stage of Indian Nuclear power programme will include development of an advanced power reactor system based on thorium cycle and development of reactor system capable of utilising U233. This is at the under development stage. The DAE aims at installing 10,000 MW of nuclear power generating capacity by 2000 A.D. which would then represent about 10% of the total electrical generating capacity in the country.[7]

Changes in Nuclear Environment

China's entry into nuclear club countries in 1964 changes Indis's strategic environment and enhanced threats to Indian security. Jain rightly points out this and states that, "The death of Nehru in 1964 and the liberal views of new Prime Minister Lal Bahadur Shastri has permitted a new and open political debate on nuclear option in changes strategic environment. Dr. Bhabha was quick to a changed environment and attempted to convince both the government and the public that "the explosion of a nuclear device by China is a signal that there is no time to be lost."[8]

This pushed India towards the nuclear threshold. In late 1965, Lal Bahadur Shastri approved in principle Bhabha's plan for an underground explosion which was not realised at that time. The death of Shastri and Dr. Bhabha in 1966 weakened the momentum of nuclear power programme. Dr. Bhabha's successor Dr. Vikram Sarabhai and Prime Minister Indira Gandhi did not show any inclination for nuclear device explosion at that time.

In 1968 India refused to sign the Non Proliferation Treaty (NPT) by arguing that the crux of the proliferation problem lay with the nuclear weapon states rather than with others who might display a future interest in nuclear weapon acquisition on the grounds of nuclear black mailing of non-nuclear states by nuclear powers and its inherent discriminatory nature.[9]

Simultaneously India showed keen interest in self-reliance and its lead in nuclear research and allocated adequate financial resources for the same.

Peaceful Nuclear Explosion and its Impact on Security

On 18th May 1974 India exploded a plutonium device at Pokharan (Rajasthan) which was its first and so far the only Peaceful Nuclear Explosion (PNE). This nuclear explosion had a yield of 12-15 Kilotons of TNT equivalent approximately to the same as dropped on Hiroshima.[10]

From 1962 to 1974 Indian public opinion appeared to favour the pursuit of nuclear weapons. None outside India seemed to have seen the event as a peaceful experiment and were critical about it. A few nations were even critical of the expression PNE and criticised the code name of PNE which was the 'smiling Buddha'.

There were many factors responsible for the decision to carry out a PNE. The national, regional and international events which took place in the early 1970s also contributed to in this decision-making. President Nixon's visit to China started the process of normalisation of relations between two nuclear power states i.e. China and USA in early 1970s. China is the only Asian country which has placed greater emphasis on the development of nuclear weapons than conventional weapons since its first nuclear test in 1964. In 1967 China also conducted the first explosion of China's H-bomb. China's nuclear missile and space programmes moved ahead with great speed although it had to go through various stages of failures and successes. For China nuclear weapons were the symbol of power, self-reliance and security because China wanted to neutralize the nuclear weapon threat both from USA and USSR.

The increasing nuclear capability of China certainly caused great security threat concerns to India. India tried to acquire an external nuclear guarantee from the declared nuclear powers against the possible Chinese nuclear threat. President Nixon's visit to China in the early 1970s represented the American interests in China. India was a less than a marginal factor in the US calculations of costs and benefits of establishing closer relations with China. This Sino-American defence brought the possibility of emergence of a US-China-Pak axis which could add to Indian security concerns and two geo-political change pushed India closer towards the former Soviet Union. At the regional level, Pakistan decided to pursue a rapid nuclear weapon programme, seeing the decisive victory of India in the 1971 Bangladesh war.

In 1971 India won the Bangladesh war and established itself as a regional power in Asia. Pakistan wanted to modernise defence forces to gain technological superiority and numerical parity with India and to avenge the defeat in Bangladesh War.

Pakistan's Nuclear Programme

Pakistan tried to give religious colour to it and called its nuclear bomb programme as 'Islamic bomb' and tried to acquire support of Islamic counties. This was coupled with the US tilt towards Pakistan to facilitate the normalisation of relations with China. Pakistan and China contributed to support each other's designs which were based on anti-Indian moves. India could not ignore this US-China-Pak axis.

It is the Chinese who have provided major nuclear technology to Pakistan in a clandestine way and therefore India needs to take into account Pak-China relations while analysing nuclear threat from Pakistan.[11]

There were some domestic considerations which led to PNE. During the early 1970s there was split in the Congress party and the former Prime Minister Smt. Indira Gandhi wanted to demostrate her political power to her political opponents.

The significance of the test was political rather than military to her. All such factors led to PNE in 1974. As a result, India lost most of the foreign assistance for its Nuclear energy programme but India continued her nuclear programme and nuclear research, in spite of sanctions and lack of supply of imported strategic materials from USA and Canada and also lack of foreign technical assistance. India's capability in nuclear science and technology has been viewed with apprehension by the West especially after 1974 PNE. Therefore India clarified its peaceful intentions of nuclear programme and rejected nuclear weapon option whenever possible in the international forums. Indian armed forces have been less enthusiastic about nuclear India and nuclear arsenal than their civilian counterparts.[12] In spite of many difficulties India continued to go ahead in her nuclear programme.

India's Nuclear Programme in the Post–1974 Period

The present nuclear capability shows that India enjoys a unique distinction of being the only developing country that has gained self-reliance in the entire range of nuclear fuel cycle activities in the midst of various difficulties and technology control regimes. India has effectively by-passed many of the international controls because they have not been rigid. India has built its own heavy water plants which are essential for nuclear programmes. This has helped India to create inherent nuclear deterrent capability in the 1980s. During 1970s and 1980s Pakistan continued enhancing its nuclear capability through clandestine means. It also continued to receive large amount of military and economic aid since 1979 from USA on the grounds of USSR's intervention in Afghanistan. During this period Pakistan has adopted the policy of nuclear ambiguity and USA had chosen to overlook the nuclear proliferation by its ally, Pakistan. Pakistan also had always denied its nuclear capability officially as it stands to lose much by declaring itself as an overt nuclear power. The US government did not take any desired steps to halt Pak's nuclear weapon programme. As a consequence India persuaded a policy of nuclear ambiguity. Throughout the 1980s Indian national leaders protested against the probable nuclear arms race in the Indian subcontinent.

India's regional compulsions forced it to maintain nuclear ambiguity and the right to continue with nuclear testing or nuclear weapon option open. This was repeatedly reiterated by India. India advanced tacitly its nuclear postures and in 1985 India commissioned DHRUVA, the largest research reactors of BARC. Most of the major components of the reactor were developed indigenously. This reactor serves as a tool for research in advanced areas of nuclear science and technology. The DAE has also set up a centre for Advanced Technology at Indore in 1984 for major research facility in nuclear science.

In 1987 the nuclear scenario in South Asia changed. In 1987 Dr. A.Q. Khan and Gen. Zia declared the possession of nuclear weapon (bomb) capability by Pakistan. India has never admitted of possessing a stockpile of nuclear weapons. However, as a result of Khan/Zia statements, Defence Minister K.C. Pant stated in April 1988 that, "India had not allowed a window of vulnerability to develop and the Indian armed forces would not be at disadvantage in the face of nuclear attack by Pak."[13]

Pakistan having nuclear weapons and India not possessing will create an adverse situation in South Asia and therefore India has to view Pakistan's nuclear capability and its China USA linkages in its own national security interests.

Changes in 1990s and it Impacts

In 1990s momentous changes occurred in the International and national systems. The USSR gradually abandoned its role of a major superpower and this had considerable implications for India because it lost its very close allies. In 1970s and 1980s the Soviets had been the major source of advanced conventional military technology and hardware to India at affordable costs and convenient terms. India also received a nuclear power sub marine from the USSR. In this changed situation India without the USSR assistance had to consider itself exposed and vulnerable and had to modify its security and nuclear policy.

The USA used the Gulf war (1991) as a means to prove its superiority and dominance in terms of military and political power over the world, and to show that it is a great super power of the world.

At the same time USA has been showing its favourable attitude towards China. It had stopped all aid and transfer of technologies to China after the Tiananmen square incident because of human right violations but now the USA has agreed to restore aid and technology transfer to China. It seems in the new world order the Chinese nuclear, military and economic capability will assume considerable importance. Two objectives of Chinese nuclear policy have been defined, by Savita Datta as, "firstly the preservation of its capability for nuclear retaliation and, secondly, to break up the super power nuclear monopoly. China is maintaining an impressive nuclear arsenal and pursuing its independent policies to fulfil its obejctives."[14]

Thus China would continue to place greater emphasis on the development of nuclear weapons in the near future and it would cause great security concern to India. The USA tried to slow down Indian missile programme through Missile Tech. Control Regimes in 1992. India needs to respond to these international needs and domestic developments where it has very few policy options. India has chosen to continue to remain outside the NPT.

In the 1990s internally India is unstable and there are no signs of insurgency, subversion, terrorism, communal riots and other disturbances going off the scene in near future. The Indian economy faces crisis situation.

In 1991 China agreed to accede to the NPT but it is not likely to cease its nuclear testing for research. If India accedes to the NPT, it would cause a great public outcry and it would require an acceptance of nuclear safeguards against which India has always argued. It seems that India cannot overtly pursue nuclear weapon programme because it would affect essential economic aid and it would be destabilising vis-a-vis both China and Pakistan. India has kept the option open for the employment of Nuclear Technology for military purposes. India continues to upgrade its nuclear science and technology, capability for civil purposes. But if circumstances force India to choose this nuclear option, it could assemble a bomb in a few weeks. "A report published in early 1988 and sponsored by the Washington based Carnegie Endowment for International Peace agreed with this assessment and added that India could if it so wished have more than 100 Hiroshima size bombs by late 1990."[15]

India has the Jaguar and Mirage 2000 aircrafts which are nuclear capable aircrafts. This provides India the ability to deliver nuclear weapons. In addition to this India's missile programme and space programme also support nuclear delivery system.

Nuclear Expenditure Phases and Explanation

On the basis of graph and expenditure Table 16 and 17 one finds that there are three distinct phases

(1) 1972-73 to 1979-80 (2) 1980-81 to 1986-87
(3) 1986-87 to 1994-95.

I Phase

In the first phase 1972-73 to 1979-80 the nuclear expenditure had exponential growth rate of 13.75 per cent per annum at current prices and 5.88 per cent per annum at (1980-81) prices.

Table 16
Nuclear Expenditure

(In Rs. Crores)

Year	*At Current Prices*	*At 1980-81 Prices*
1970-71	70.02	179.45
1971-72	103.11	250.15
1972-73	118.08	260.43
1973-74	116.25	213.23
1974-75	154.06	225.70
1975-76	193.50	286.54
1976-77	215.51	312.65
1977-78	241.44	332.93
1978-79	250.82	345.86
1979-80	260.23	306.41
1980-81	291.80	291.80
1981-82	358.00	326.04
1982-83	447.63	388.60
1983-84	759.56	613.00
1984-85	849.35	644.08
1985-86	963.00	701.68
1986-87	1102.70	756.78
1987-88	1110.09	704.00
1988-89	1347.63	795.39
1989-90	1178.13	647.53
1990-91	1095.20	545.94
1991-92	1209.12	529.92
1992-93	1399.10	557.14
1993-94	1505.33	553.24
1994-95	1223.50	411.17

Source:

(1) Government of India, *India Budget* (Expenditure Budget and demand for grants for various years (1970-95)) for Department of Atomic Energy, Ministry of Finance, New Delhi.

(2) Government of India, Comptroller & Auditor General of India Report: India Appropriation Account, for various years (1971-95) Ministry of Finance, New Delhi.

Note: All break-up tables after this table in this chapter are based on only revised estimates.

Graph 3

Nuclear Exp. Current Prices & Constant Prices

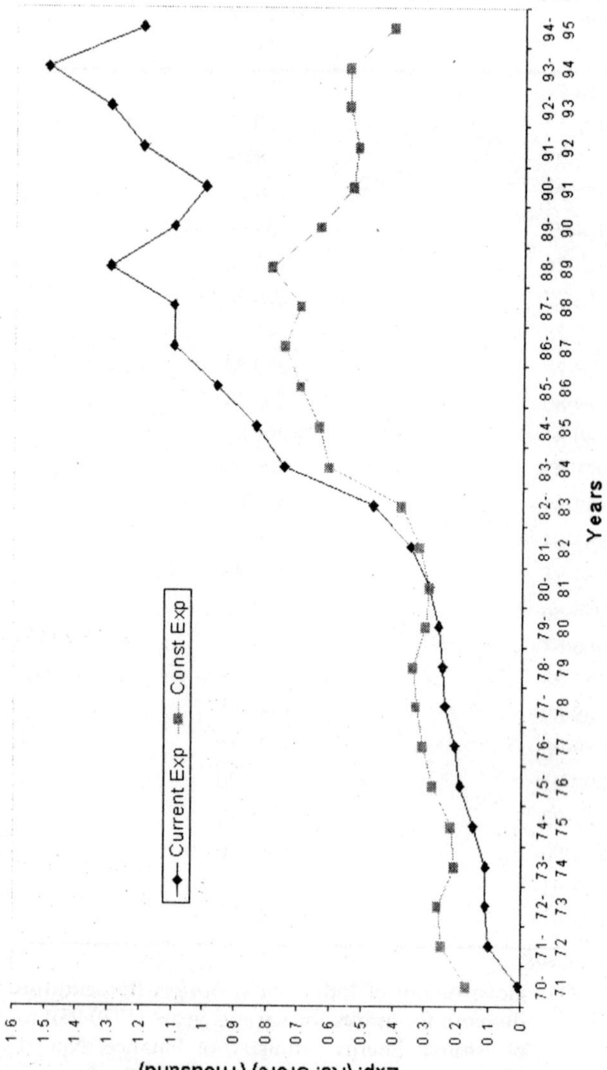

Table 17
Nuclear Expenditure Break-Up

(In Rs. Crores)

Year	*Total Exp.*	*Dept of A.E.*	*Atomic E. R & D*	*Nuclear Power*
1970-71	73.02	0.34	37.31	35.37
1971-72	99.59	0.35	53.26	42.76
1972-73	108.14	0.31	63.25	44.57
1973-74	117.14	0.32	69.74	47.08
1974-75	153.39	0.34	88.79	64.25
1975-76	193.49	0.39	113.12	77.97
1976-77	241.15	0.45	143.83	86.89
1977-78	241.54	0.47	155.36	85.70
1978-79	250.82	0.51	163.20	87.10
1979-80	268.23	0.54	154.60	113.22
1980-81	305.73	0.62	179.09	126.00
1981-82	357.80	0.69	207.01	150.28
1982-83	463.35	0.81	174.49	188.86
1983-84	587.55	0.92	350.45	236.18
1984-85	855.14	1.11	568.21	285.81
1985-86	1075.42	1.34	644.78	429.30
1986-87	1102.00	1.40	659.00	435.00
1987-88	947.10	—	696.02	251.08
1988-89	963.40	—	705.59	253.81
1989-90	1057.26	—	779.19	286.07
1990-91	1024.78	—	750.48	274.60
1991-92	960.15	—	717.88	242.67
1992-93	1095.20	—	844.59	250.61
1993-94	1505.33	—	931.88	573.45
1994.95	1223.53	—	928.35	295.18
1995-96	1402.15	—	1001.83	400.32

Source:

(1) Government of India, *India Budget* (Expenditure Budget and demand for grants for various years (1970-95)) for Department of Atomic Energy, Ministry of Finance, New Delhi.

(2) Government of India, Comptroller & Auditor General of India Report: India Appropriation Account, for various years (1971-95) Ministry of Finance, New Delhi.

Note: Only important items are taken in the break-up table so it will not tally with total nuclear expenditure. Due to changes in Budgeting method department of Atomic Energy is not shown separately since 1987-88.

Many experts feel that, "India had established its regional hegemony in the South Asia in 1971 war and in support to its regional power status it demonstrated its nuclear capability in 1974 by the peaceful nuclear explosion."[16]

This had some domestic reasons also. As a reaction to the peaceful nuclear explosion Indian Nuclear programme got a slight setback because the Western Countries stopped aid to our nuclear programme in terms of technology and strategic raw materials, heavy water etc. This was also seen in the issue of signing on Nuclear Proliferation Treaty (NPT) by India which came to the forefront.[17]

But despite these pressures India did not sign the Nuclear Proliferation Treaty and continued its nuclear programme. In this period economy was also recovering from the post war effects and therefore, India did not plan any major endeavour in this period.

II Phase (1980-81 to 1986-87)

In the second phase India's nuclear expenditure had exponential growth rate of 26.49 per cent per annum at current prices and 19.10 per cent per annum at (1980-81) prices. This period marks the highest increase in nuclear expenditure during this (1970-71 to 1994-95) period. During this period India expanded its nuclear programme by establishing new nuclear power plants. The indigeneously developed research reactor 'Dhruva' was set up, which proved self-sufficiency in designing Fast Breeder Technology Plants and heavy water projects was achieved during this period.[18]

'After regaining power in 1980 Indira Gandhi politically and financially gave support through her aggressive nuclear policy towards nuclear programme expansion. Rajiv Gandhi's quest for modern technology was depicted in his nuclear policy but he concerntrated more in space, Telecommunication and Electronics etc. Rajiv Gandhi provided necessary resources for nuclear technology and research programmes. It is found that "The indigenisation and self-sufficiency in nuclear technology were the main objectives of nuclear policy during this period. Pakistan's clandestine nuclear programme and China's increasing nuclear capability have forced India to upgrade and modernise its nuclear capability throughout 1980s.[19]

In 1987 Pakistan declared its nuclear weapon capability. The question of nuclear arms-race in the Indian sub-continent and its effect on security remained the main points of protest by India. On this issue Chris Smith feels that, "Both India and Pakistan used a policy of nuclear ambiguity to further their nuclear programmes. India reiterated that if required, still India has nuclear weapon option open but leadership of both countries restrained in real move towards nuclearization.[20]

As a sequel to Pakistan's declaration of nuclear capability India did not immediately react by increasing its expenditure on nuclear field. This was probably due to the fact that after 1974 and particularly since 1980 when Indira Gandhi regained power, it can be vividly seen that India continued her expansion of nuclear capability and adopted aggressive nuclear policy posture which must have created adequate nuclear capability to counter threats at regional level from Pakistan and others.[21]

During the period 1984-87 Rajiv Gandhi continued the stress on modernisation of nuclear technology, supported it and followed a policy of ambiguity rather than declaring any aggressive policy which could result in a chain reaction of India-Pakistan nuclear arms race etc.

III Phase (1986-87 to 1994-95)

During this phase nuclear expenditure had exponential growth rate of 2.40 per cent per annum at current prices and (-99.06) per cent per annum at (1980-81) prices. In 1986-87 total nuclear expenditure was Rs. 1102.7 crores and it rose to Rs. 9848.0 crores. This shows a high percentage of increase only at current prices.

The nuclear expenditure has the lowest growth rate in this period. It declined from 26.49 per cent per annum to 2.40 per cent per annum in current prices and from 19.10 per cent per annum to (-99.06) per cent per annum of (1980-81) prices.

There are several reasons for such a fall in nuclear expenditure. In 1987 Pakistan declared its nuclear weapon capability and as a reaction to it the Defence Minister K.C. Pant and Director of Department of Atomic Energy Raja Ramanna stated that, "India has kept nuclear weapon options open and could retaliate in a similar manner if faced with a nuclear attack."[22]

But inspite of such a loud declaration Indian nuclear expenditure started declining since 1986–87 because of initial stages of economic crisis in India and it seems that by that time India was assured of a minimum required nuclear capability which could be quickly converted to military use.[23]

Therefore, Rajiv Gandhi supported the consolidation of nuclear capability in the early phases and nuclear expenditure growth came to be as a plateau in this phase. At the same time one can point out that Rajiv Gandhi during his regime tried to modernise conventional defence capability, and other areas like Space Telecommunications, Electronics Ocean Development etc. which were comparatively lagging behind than laying stress on nuclear programme of Indira Gandhi's period. During 1989-90 there was political unstability and uncertainty about the direction of nuclear policy. So there were no diversions in the nuclear policy. In 1991 Narsimha Rao came to power but by that time economic crisis become the most important area and so nuclear issue was side tracked.

The nuclear issue brought some disturbances in US-Pak relations after 1987 and created confusion in the US Congress on giving military and economic aid to Pakistan but Pakistan succeeded in getting it. Later both India and Pakistan continued their nuclear programme but started facing resources crunch due to economic crisis. The collapse of USSR in 1989 and the victory of USA and other Allied powers in the Gulf War showed that the USA was a great military super power in the new world that emerged after the breaking up of the USSR. This led to increase in the pressure on India to sign the Nuclear Proliferation Treaty which it of course did not sign.

The Technology Control Regimes are becoming powerful and these controls are used against the less developed countries like India e.g. the Cryogenic Engine issue of 1992. Although India has resisted and not joined the Nuclear Proliferation Treaty, this has affected the progress of India's nuclear programme. The Operation Desert Storm (Gulf War) revealed that Iraq, a signatory of the Nuclear Proliferation Treaty had progressed covertly in nuclear weapon capability with the help of purchase of sensitive equipments from France, Germany and others. India took position that, "If a signatory to the Nuclear Proliferation Treaty could progress thus far, there is a need to change the attitudes and policy towards nuclear non-proliferation."[24]

The Indian government attempted to open a bilateral dialogue with the USA over the nuclear question in March 1992 but the outcome of this talk seems to be of little real use to either side.[25]

Indo-American difference over nuclear issue and the question of missile proliferation continued and are unlikely to be resolved soon.

Space Programme

The Govtrnment of India under the leadership of Nehru attached considerable importance to the development of science and technology in the country and to the achievement of technological self-reliance at the earliest. This thinking led to the decision of establishing a chain of various laboratories throughout the country to carry out scientific research in various disciplines and to the development of scientific manpower.

This scientific policy has helped India to make remarkable progress advanced frontier technologies such as nuclear, space, telecommunication, Biotechnology, electronic etc. The System Programme was conceived as an important component of this scientific endeavour. The space science and technology has dual uses i.e. Civilian and military uses, therefore, it is essential not only for socio-economic development but also for national integration and national security of the country. The military spin-offs from this programme cannot be ignored.

The year 1957 marked the beginning of the Space Age and four years after that in August 1961 the Government of India allocated the space research subject to the Department of Atomic Energy. In 1962 the Indian National Committee for Space Research (INCOSPAR) under the Chairmanship of Dr. Vikram Sarabhai was established. In 1963, India launched a 10 kg. rocket within the atmosphere from Thumba near Thiruanathapuram.[26]

This marked the formal beginning of the Indian space Programme after which the progress has been significant. The increasing scope for space research led to the establishment of the Indian Space Research Organisation (ISRO) at Bangalore in 1969. The ISRO and the Physical Research Laboratory (PRL) functioned as autonomous agencies supported mainly by DAE. Later these organisation were brought within the ambit of the Space Commission and a separate Department of Space (DOS) created in 1972 ISRO constituted as a Research and Development Organisation under DOS which has always been looked after by the Prime Minister.[27]

The National Remote Sensing Agency (NRSA) an autonomous registered society was transferred under the aegis of Department of Space (DOS) in 1980.

The role of Space Commission includes framing of policy approval of Space Programme budget and implementation of national policy in all matters related to outer space. The ISRO is responsible for planning, programming and management of R & D activities in space science and technology and Space applications. The PRL conducts research programmes in space related sciences and NRSA develops and uses modern remote sensing techniques for resources management. ISRO has various units and centres and ISRO headquarters provide overall direction to them.

The primary objective of the programme is to provide space based services in the areas of communication, meteorology, resource survey as integral to it develop satellites, launch vehicles, and associate ground systems. Indian space programme has made remarkable progress through a well integrated and self-reliant programmes.

Three distinct phases can be identified in the development of the Indian space programme. Phase one involved the setting up of Infrastructural facilities to provide necessary base and training to scientific personnel. This phase was an attempt to build scientific and technical manpower for space programme and establishment of number of units for space programme as per needs. This phase ended around 1975.

Phase II was marked by a series of experimental missions including satellite technology related projects, the Airlines Passenger Payload Experiment (APPLE), the Aryabhata and Bhaskara projects, satellite launch vehicle projects (SLVS) and other space application projects. In July 1975 a Soviet rocket launched the Aryabhata, India's first research satellite. It was followed by the Bhaskara project under which two satellite for earth observation were indigeneously developed and launched with Soviet rockets in June 1979 and November 1981. The utilisation of these satellite provided experience in obtaining, processing and disseminating remotely sensed data. Rajgopal has stated the utilities of these projects as, "The APPLE project helped in gaining experience in the design, development and operation of a geo-stationary satellite to provide telecommunication services. The SLV–3 project was designed to achieve competence in the sphere of satellite launchers and was to serve as a model for larger rockets which could launch geo-stationary satellites."[28]

This project was completed in April 1983 in spite of some failures in 1979 and 1981. From the military point of view SLV-3 programme was more significant. The achievement in this programme was considerable because India became the first developing country to launch a satellite into an orbit on its own launch vehicles. This was depicted in a few studies and writings e.g. Chris Smith has stressed the view that, "This had inherent military implication that India would be able to have an intermediate range ballistic missile (IRBM) capability which is of great importance."[29]

In addition to this India initiated its Integrated Guided Missile Development Programme (IGMDP) in 1983. The genuine regional compulsions forced India to develop IGMDP. India is confronted by nuclear China which had forced a war upon it in 1962. The Sino-Indian border problem is still unresolved and China has reportedly deployed IRBMS in Tibet and Sikiang.

China has also been providing assistance to Pakistan in developing nuclear weapons and missiles. Pakistan has reportedly acquired IRBM capability in 1989.[30] This caused great concerns to Indian security.

ASLV programme is India's endeavour at self-reliance in R & D in Space Science and Technology under aegis of DRDO. In the initial stages there were some failures in this ASLV programme but it continued getting financial support and other political policy support. Indian ASLV can put a 150 kg. Pay load into low earth orbit. The work is going on polar SLV (PSLV) stretched polar SLV (SPISLV) and Geosynchronous SLV (GSLV) which will enhance India's missile capability. A. Bhatia in his article opined that, "If the PSLV and SPSLV is converted for a launch on a ballistic trajectory, it could transform India in 1990s into a country with power potential of intercontinental ballistic missile (ICBM) capability."[31]

The developmental launch of PSLV–D2 took place on 15 October 1994 and it successfully placed IRS–P2 satellite into the intended polar orbit. Another four flights of PSLV-D3, PSLV-C1, PSLV-C2 and PSLV-C3 planned up to 1998.[32]

IGMDP

The fruits of Integrated Guided Missile Development Programme (IGMDP) under the leadership of Dr. APJ Abdul Kalam became known in late 1980s. IGMDP developed TRISHUL–surface-to–air missile (SAM) with a range of 9 kilometres for use by the army, Air Force and a naval version missile:

AKASH–The medium range surface to air missile (SAM) with a range of 25 kilometres to provide defence to vital areas, points and installations.

NAG–A third generation anti-tank missile with terminal guidance system with 4 to 6 km. range.

PRITHVI–A tactical surface to surface missile with a range of 250 km. and a pay load capacity of 500 to 1000 kg; tested in 1988.

AGNI–The IRBM (Inter range ballistic missile) was tested surface to surface mode, having range of 2500 to 5000 km. and a pay load capacity of one tonne.

Out of these, Prithvi is more relevant to Pakistan and Agni is more relevant to China. Agni has strategic importance as it can be mated with nuclear weapon. A second missile test of Agni took place in May 1992 and was by and large a failure but there is a strong political support for this programme. The response to this test in India was euphoric and India has become the sixth country to produce successfully an IRBM from indigeneous technology. However, the deployment of Agni in the military forces is not contemplated for the present.

The other missiles are under various stages of field and user trials. India is experimenting with a sixty km. range Air to Air missile [AAM] for the use with the Light Combat Aircraft and it should be able to make ICBM within couple of years. The Western countries feel that this missile development implies future nuclear ballistic weapon capability. The Indian government has consistently stated that, "these missile tests are nothing more than 'Technology Demonstrators' so far, India has not taken any decision to weaponise this technological capability."[33]

India's civilian space based capabilities could be used for military purposes and there perceived military applications should not be taken for granted because India has never shown explicit intentions of use of space programme for military purposes.

INSAT and other Programmes

Third phase of space programme saw the operationalisation of space services i.e. utilisation of satellites for telecommunications, weather forecasting, remote sensing, education etc. This phase stated in 1980s. Two separate satellites were used for this purpose. The Indian National Satellite (INSAT) series and Indian Remote Sensing Satellite (IRS) series.

INSAT: The first generation of INSAT–I represents India's first step towards implementing operational space system. The INSAT–I is multipurpose operational satellite system designed and developed by the Ford Aerospace and Communications Corporation of the United States and first launched in April 1982.[34]

INSAT is a joint venture of DOS, Department of Telecommunications, Indian Meteorological Department. All

India Radio and Doordarshan. The Marker control facility for INSAT satellites is located in Hassan district of Karnataka.

INSAT–I–B satellite successfully launched in August 1983 has completed its life of sever years in 1990.

INSAT–I–C put to orbit in 1988 has a life span of 10 years. However the satellite had to be abandoned because of some technical snag. Only INSAT-ID launched in June 1990 is presently operational.

INSAT–I series is now replaced by the INSAT-2 series with five satellites. Out of these INSAT-2A and INSAT-2B were launched in 1992 and 1993.

The second generation INSATS have enhanced capabilities for telecommunication, TV, Radio, broadcasting and meteorology from land and sea. They provide half-hourly observations of weather system over Indian territory and adjoining land and sea areas.

Remote Sensing (IRS): Three Remote Sensing satellites (IRSs) have been operationalised IRS-1A IRS–1B and IRS–P2 launched in 1988, 1991 and 1994 respectively by indigeneous polar satellite launch vehicle. Indigeneously developed and designed these satellites provide data which has major applications in varied areas like agriculture, water resources, land use forest, environment, ocean resources mapping, volcanic activity and geosphere biosphere studies.

India's space programme has generated interest in Indian Space Technology and services among a number of countries. In September 1992 Antrix Corporation Ltd. was established to market Indian space capabilities to other countries. It is a commercial venture of DOS to market wide variety of space products and services. If DOS realises its goals in this decade India is likely to emerge as a major space power in the 21st century and can provide necessary space deterrent capability for its National Security.

Table 18
Space Expenditure

(In Rupees Crores)

Year	*At Current Prices*	*At 1980-81 Prices*
1970-71	—	—
1971-72	—	—
1972-73	—	—
1973-74	18.99	34.83
1974-75	30.73	45.01
1975-76	36.84	54.55
1976-77	39.19	56.85
1977-78	37.37	51.53
1978-79	51.45	70.95
1979-80	57.00	67.12
1980-81	82.11	82.11
1981-82	109.07	99.33
1982-83	94.89	82.38
1983-84	163.37	131.90
1984-85	181.61	137.72
1985-86	229.10	166.72
1986-87	309.99	212.74
1987-88	347.09	220.12
1988-89	422.27	267.80
1989-90	398.56	249.23
1990-91	391.11	219.06
1991-92	482.60	211.50
1992-93	490.92	195.50
1993-94	718.60	264.10
1994-95	774.99	260.43

Sources:

(1) Government of India, *India Budget* (Expenditure Budget and demand for grants for various years (1970-95)) for Department of Space, Ministry of Finance, New Delhi.

(2) Government of India, *Comptroller and Auditor General of India Report:* India Appropriation Account, for various years (1971-95) Ministry of Finance, New Delhi.

Graph 4

Space Exp. Current Prices and Constant Prices

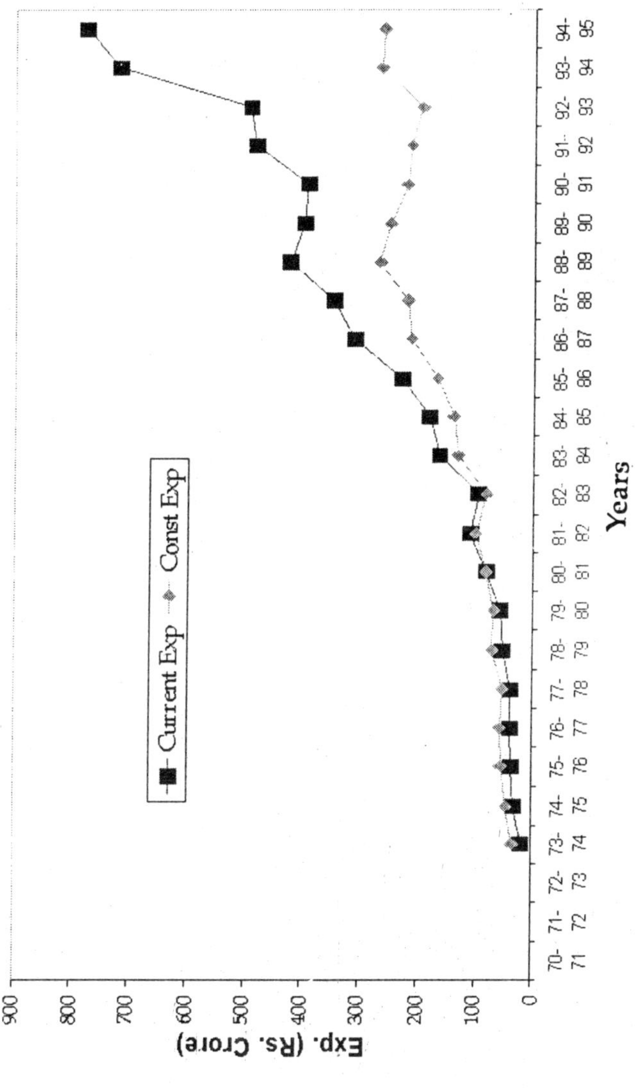

Table 19
Space Expenditure Breakup

(In Rupees Crores)

Year	Total exp On space	Roket Dev.	Satellite Dev.	National Remote	Insat
1972-73	18.23				
1973-74	19.09				
1974-75	18.28				
1975-76	37.15				
1976-77	41.14		NOTE: Separate allocation for these programmes started since 1986-87		
1977-78	44.42				
1978-79	51.45				
1979-80	65.39				
1980-81	96.81				
1981-82	107.13				
1982-83	108.82				
1983-84	99.89				
1984-85	128.02				
1985-86	182.75				
1986-87	310.29	75.42	58.09	2.22	70.47
1987-88	347.83	139.66	88.26	10.15	57.54
1988-89	431.74	166.14	135.30	13.35	71.07
1989-90	303.85	151.60	138.63	11.00	15.69
1990-91	391.11	170.28	121.52	13.40	24.98
1991-92	482.61	222.42	140.93	15.10	40.82
1992-93	510.00	301.74	79.92	12.60	50.56
1993-94	718.06	343.72	80.40	14.00	197.01
1994-95	744.99	367.82	75.08	15.00	230.94
1995-96	911.20	386.54	89.37	13.75	336.25

Dev. = Development

Sources::

(1) Government of India, *India Budget* (Expenditure Budget and demand for grants for various years (1970-95)) for Department of Space, Ministry of Finance, New Delhi.

(2) Government of India, Comptroller & Auditor General of India Report : India Appropriation Account, for various years (1971-95) Ministry of Finance, New Delhi.

Note: Only important items are taken in the break-up table so it will not tally with total space expenditure.

The Department of Space started working separately since 1972. Before this the resources were allocated through the Department of Atomic Energy. On the basis of graph and expenditure table one finds that the space expediture has three distinct phases: (1) 1973-74 to 1982-83, (2) 1982-83 to 1988-89, (3) 1988-89 to 1994-95.

I Phase (1972-73 to 1982-83)

In this phase the space expenditure had exponential growth rate of 19.06 per cent per annum at current prices and 10.28 per cent per annum at (1980-81) prices. In this period the Space programme was directed towards infrastructure build up and training sufficient scientific personnel. In July 1975 a Soviet Rocket launched India's first research satellite, the 'Aryabhatta' followed by Bhaskara projects and Satellite Launch Vehicle Project (SLV), The APPLE, BHASKARA and SLV projects initiated the indigeneous design, development and geostationary satellites for telecommunication and other functions.[35] India had some failures in 1979 and 1981 in SLV–3 projects but space programme continued to get political and adequate economic support.[36]

II Phase (1982-1983 to 1988-89)

In this phase Space expenditure had exponential growth rate of 26.21 per cent per annum at current prices and 19.53 per cent per annum at (1980-81) prices. This period marks the highest growth rate in space expenditure in the period under study. In 1982-83 the total space expenditure was at 94.89 crores of rupees and in 1988-89 it rose to 422.27 crores of rupees at current prices.

The year 1982-83 was very important from the point of view development of Space capability. In April 1983 India completed its (SLV-3) programme which gave competence in the sphere of satellite launchers to India. India was the first developing country to launch a satellite into an orbit with its own launch vehicles.

The infrastructure development of the 1970s were now put to actual application during this period. The SLV-3 programme has potential military use of acquiring Intermediate Range Ballistic Missile (IRBM) capability.[37]

In 1983 India also started its Integrated Guided Missile Development Programme (IGMDP). At the same time ASLV, PSLV and SPSLV programmes, INSAT programmes were on progress, and the Indian Space Expenditure has shown remarkable increase during this period. The fruits of IGMDP could be realised by 1988 in the form of successful tests of TRISHUL, NAG, AKASH, PRITHVI, AGNI and other missiles.[38]

The threats of advancement of space/missiles by development from China and acquisition of sophisticated missiles by Pakistan forced India to spend more during this period. The Afghan crisis in this period was at the peak of super power rivalry and so Pakistan continued to get huge amount of sophisticated military aid from the USA under the pretext of this crisis and this also has contributed to rise in India's space expenditure.

This phase marked the highest growth rate of space expenditure in India during (1972 to 1994-95) period. One of the important reasons was that in this period Rajiv Gandhi gave more attention to the development of those areas which were comparatively lagging behind and which were essential for modernisation of the country.

III Phase (1988-89 to 1994-95)

In this phase space expenditure had exponential growth rate of 12.20 per cent per annum at current prices and (-0.29) per cent per annum at (1980-81) prices. The space expenditure in 1988-89 was Rs. 422.27 crores and in 1994-95 it rose to 774.99 at current prices.

The space expenditure had minimum exponential growth rate in this period in the total duration of this study. After 1988-89 the nagative exponential growth rate is seen at (1980-81) prices. This period can be considered as a period of upgradation and sophistication of space technology along with expansion phase in India. It requires large amount of resources but it seems that due to domestic economic crisis and political instability/lack of political will since 1989 India could not keep pace with it. Since 1988-89 India is facing various economic problems like double digit inflation, stagflation, mounting internal and external debt, increasing fiscal deficit, scanty foreign exchange, slow economic growth rate etc. Hence in real terms the resources for space expenditure are decreasing.

The disintegration of USSR in 1989-90 also has contributed in reducing the Soviet aid in terms of technology to Indian space programme. The USA and other Western countries are apprehensive of Indian space capability and trying to create obstacles by denying technology and other aid to India. The Technology Control Regimes (1986) are becoming powerful and India is suffering although it has developmental intentions for space programmes. The USA tried to stop the second test of the AGNI (i.e. The IRBM surface to surface Missile) in 1992. But in spite of such pressures the second test took place in May 1992. As a reaction to this USA and other developed countries may not give technological support to India in future.

All such factors have contributed in slowing down of the pace of space programme. To resolve the problem of resource crunch to some extent it seems that India has established Antrix Corporation in 1992 which will export market space technology and space services from India to other countries.[39]

Electronics Technology Programme

Electronic technology and Industry have a tremendous potential for improving the standard of living and quality of life of people because of its versatility and easy adaptability. Electronics also play a dominant role in improving productivity industry and socio-economic development

Electronic Technology has a wide-spread applications not only in the commercial world but is also the key to modern warfare so it is an important dual purpose technology. The Gulf war (February 1991) demonstrated a new era of contemporary technology in electronic warfare. The Gulf war has also proved that electronic technology can significantly affect the manner and the mode of war. The sophisticated weaponry can bring qualitative advantages in a war/conflict and therefore these sources of technological strength and their potentials must be developed for national security. Ravindra Pal Sing brings out this point to the forefront in his writing by stating that, "The Gulf war diverted our attention towards the emerging defence arsenal of stealthy microprocessed thermal imaged laser guided satellite vectored electro-magnetically manoeuvred and lethal weaponry.[40]

One understands that the electronic technology and Industry is the source of the above mentioned emerging technologies and therefore it is strategically a very important area. Once the civilian technology is available, it may be possible either to use it directly or by upgrading the same for strategic purposes or vice versa.

Department of Electronics and its Agencies

In order to keep pace with developments in the international scene and considering the increasing importance of electronics for diversified applications the department of electronics was set up by the Government of India in 1971. Since then the Department of Electronics has adopted the policies to bring the benefits of electronic to all walks of life and it is playing a catalystic role in making the Indian Electronics Industry a global player.

The 8th plan (1992-1997) aims at creating an environment in which high level growth of electronics production is maintained and the production levels are achieved almost upto international costs and prices. By 1996-97 the gross output of the industry is estimated to reach a level of Rs.

36,000 crores. Promotion of software development its export and development of micro-electronics and materials industry have also been taken as thrust areas.[41]

The overall production of electronics in India is very widely diffused. There are at present over 3500 units comprising 11 central public sector units. There are 71 units in state public sector, over 500 units in organised private sector, and more than 2000 units in small sector. The public sector units and small sector units each contribute about 28% of electronic production. The organised private sector accounts for 44% production.

The Electronics export increased from Rs. 930 crores to Rs. 2200 crores in 1994. India welcomes and encourages foreign direct investments (FDI) in almost all sectors of electronics since 1991. The department of electronics supports and funds technology development through its councils set up in various fields, namely the Technology Development Council (TDC) for areas like components, computer communication instrumentation etc., the National Radar Council for radars, navigational aids, solars, lasers, Infra red detection etc. National Micro Electronic Council (NMEC) has designed and produced micro electronic items Electronic terial development council developed special ceramics high purity metals and the National Photonic Council (NPC) develops photonic related items.

The computer industry has witnessed a growth of about 50% in the software development and production in late eighties. A separate agency has been established by DOE for computer software. The software required for data collection updating and maintenance is being developed by the National Informatics Centre (NIC) of the DOE on indigeneous computers. NIC NET is established in 1990 for star type computer network.[42]

The department has 3 PSU and it works closely with BEL, ECIL, ITI, BHEL etc.

CMC Ltd.: Was set up in 1976 and is committed to the creative use of computers, Information and technology tools in core sector of economy to improve productivity and quality of life. CMC has executed turn key projects in many important sectors like power, coal, transport, oil etc.

Electronic Trade and Technology Development Corporation (ET & T) ET & T and set up with the objective of expanding foreign trade in electronics and undertaking development in technique in key areas.

Semiconductor Complex Ltd. (SCL) – set up primarily to design develop and manufacture LSI /VLSI circuits. It commenced its growth in April 1984. DOE also has set up time bound R & D projects in some areas like Center for development of Advanced Computing (C-DAC) which has developed, designed and delivered parallel supercomputer with peak computer power. Other projects are fibre optic systems development computer net working etc. The DOE has launched a Standardisation Testing Quality Control (STQC) programme for healthy growth of electronics Industry.[43]

DOE covers areas of strategic electronics like radar project, naval aid and other allied fields. It has achieved reasonable growth in these fields. Some of the equipments like X band radar, surveillance tracking system, fire detection etc. are manufactured and used as important substitutions. It also has developoed electronic control systems for indigenous satellites and launch vehicles.[*44]

The infrastructure and production capabilities in electronics provide India potential military use capability.

Phase in Electronics Expenditure

On the basis of graph and expenditure Table one finds that electronic expenditure has three distinct phases.

(1) First Phase — 1972-73 to 1982-83
(2) Second Phase — 1982-83 to 1988-89
(3) Third Phase - 1988-89 to 1994-95.

Table 20
Electronic Expenditure

(In Rupees Crores)

Year	*At Current prices*	*At 1980-81 prices*
1970-71	-	-
1971-72	3.63	8.80
1972-73	1.11	2.45
1973-74	1.58	2.90
1974-75	5.07	7.43
1975-76	4.78	7.08
1976-77	6.48	9.40
1977-78	9.39	12.95
1978-79	15.41	21.25
1979-80	13.94	16.42
1980-81	14.78	14.78
1981-82	21.25	19.35
1982-83	47.25	41.01
1983-84	37.55	30.32
1984-85	98.70	74.85
1985-86	110.91	80.28
1986-87	104.88	71.98
1987-88	127.61	80.93
1988-89	151.98	89.70
1989-90	104.91	57.56
1990-91	109.12	54.39
1991-92	121.44	53.22
1992-93	87.12	34.70
1993-94	178.00	65.42
1994-95	156.80	52.72

Sources:

(1) Government of India, *India Budget* (Expenditure Budget and Demand for grants for various years (1970-95) for Department of Electronics.

(2) Government of India, Comptroller & Auditor Genral of India Report: India Appropriation Account, for various years (1971-95) Ministry of Finance, New Delhi.

Note: Only important items are taken in the break-up table so it will not tally with total nuclear expenditure. Due to changes in Budgeting method, Department of Atomic Energy is not shown separately since 1987-88.

Graph 5

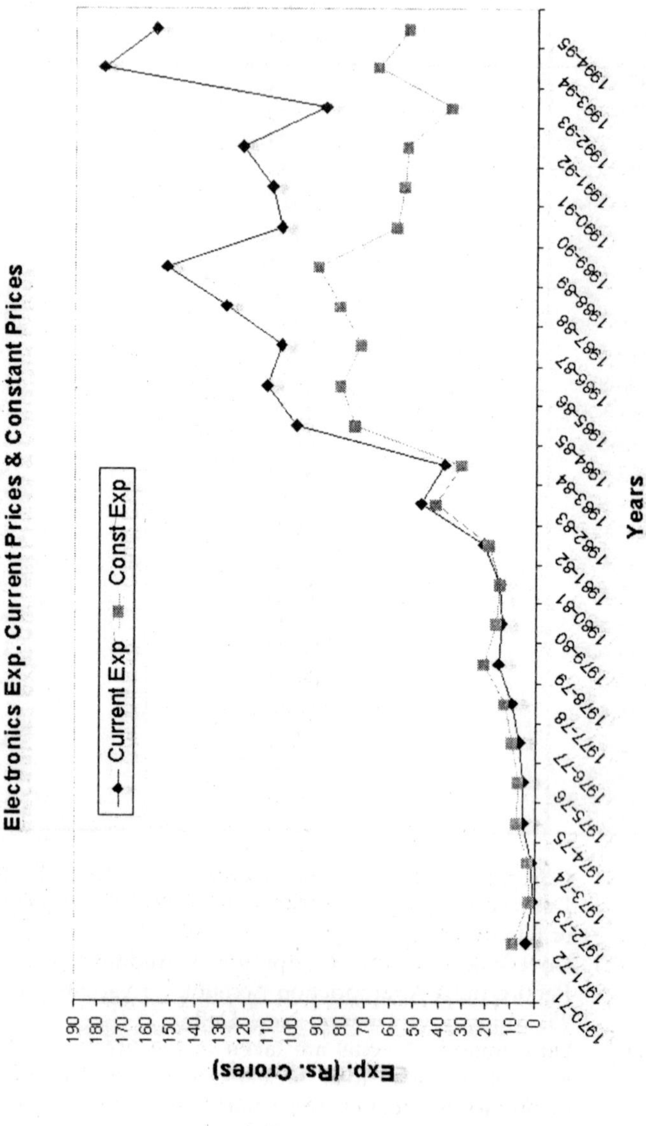
Electronics Exp. Current Prices & Constant Prices
Current Exp
Const Exp
Exp. (Rs. Crores)
190
180
170
160
150
140
130
120
110
100
90
80
70
60
50
40
30
20
10
0
1970-71
1971-72
1972-73
1973-74
1974-75
1975-76
1976-77
1977-78
1978-79
1979-80
1980-81
1981-82
1982-83
1983-84
1984-85
1985-86
1986-87
1987-88
1988-89
1989-90
1990-91
1991-92
1992-93
1993-94
1994-95
Years

I First Phase–1972-73 to 1982-83

In the First Phase electronics expenditure had exponential growth rate of 87.85 per cent per annum at current prices and 26.93 per cent per annum at (1980-81) prices. The electronics expenditure has the maximum exponential growth rate in this phase in the total period of the study. In 1972-73 total electronics expenditure was Rs. 1.58 crores and it rose to Rs. 47.25 crores in 1982-83 at current prices. This period can be called as infrastructure development period for electronics industry in India.

Hence the Government of India invested more in it. In 1978-79 National Radar Council Project (NRC), Centre for Development of Advance Computing (c-DAC) and other projects were undertaken by electronics department. This Department has established three public sector units CMC Ltd., ET&T Ltd., and Semi Conductor Complex Ltd., (1984) for developing the use of electronics in core sectors of economy.[45]

One finds consistency in the policy of development of electronics sector in India in this period. It seems that Indian policy makers had realised that the advances in electronics would have an impact on all walks of life for development purposes and defence purposes and so created large potential base by investing more resources in this field during this period.

II Phase – 1982-83 to 1988-89

Second Phase started in 1982-83 to 1988-89. In this period electronics expenditure had exponential growth rate of 15.60 per cent per annum at current prices and 8.53 per cent per annum at (1980-81) prices. In this period the electronics industry had diversified its applications to almost each and every field of life. The super power project (1984-85) and Technology Development Council (TDC) for areas like electronic component, computer communication, instrumentation were undertaken in this period. The Government information sources state that, "In this period

Indian electronic industry succeeded in getting export orders and entered as a competitor in international markest."[45]

Table 21
Electronics Expenditure Breakup

(In Rupees Crores)

Year	*Total E. Exp.*	*National Radar Council*	*C-DAC & other Programs*
1970-71	1.27		
1971-72	3.68		
1972-73	1.40		
1973-74	1.80		
1974-75	6.98		
1975-76	6.28		
1976-77	8.58		
1977-78	12.72		
1978-79	15.41	1.80	0.96
1979-80	17.83	4.60	0.50
1980-81	18.47	3.90	0.76
1981-82	20.25	3.50	1.34
1982-83	47.35	3.50	0.77
1983-84	37.40	3.70	1.34
1984-85	99.46	3.20	1.50
1985-86	109.60	1.50	2.00
1986-87	108.88	1.90	2.00
1987-88	124.54	2.00	5.24
1988-89	97.73	3.00	4.40
1989-90	106.20	2.50	11.50
1990-91	109.12	2.00	10.75
1991-92	121.44	2.10	7.10
1992-93	88.50	0.70	13.50
1993-94	177.90	1.00	15.00
1994-95	156.80	1.35	11.00
1995-96	161.35	0.84	10.50

Source:

(1) Government of India, *India Budget* (Expenditure Budget and demand for grants for various years (1970-95) for Department of Electronics.

(2) Government of India, Comptroller & Auditor General of India Report: India Appropriation Account, for various years (1971-95) Ministry of Finance, New Delhi.

Note: Only important items are taken in the break-up table so it will not tally with total electronics expenditure. Due to changes in Budgeting method breakup started since 1978-79.

One can easily see that, the electronics industry got advantage of Rajiv Gandhi's policy of modernisation and it upgraded its technology. The revolutionary advance in the field of electronics e.g. sophistication of Telecommunication Systems, Data processing, automation of weapon system, precision guidance, force multiplication effects etc. have enhanced the inherent military/defence potential in electronics. Hence during this phase India tried to consolidate and realise the developed electronics capability of early phase in diversified fields. Rajiv Gandhi focused on Hi-tech areas other than nuclear field which were comparatively lagging behind.

Till this phase India had already developed essential infrastructural base. The private sector electronic industries started playing supportive role for the advancement of technology in electronics area.[47]

So India's expenditure on electronics declined as compared to the first phase.

III Phase – 1988-89 to 1994-95

In the Third Phase (1988-89 to 1994-95) electronics expenditure had exponential growth of 9.39 per cent per annum at current prices and (-99.00) per cent per annum at (1980-81) prices. It means in real terms the electronics expenditure declined in this phase. It was due to the deteriorating economic condition of the country. Since 1987 the growth rate of Gross Domestic Product all over the world started declining and so the developing countries like India faced several problems of foreign aid and foreign exchange.

This certainly affected the growth of electronics industry which is considered as a crucial input of economic and military capability in the present era. V.K. Mdhok has criticised the attitude of Developed Countries in technology transfers and he felt that, "The 1991 Gulf war has demonstrated the use of sophisticated electronic technology in weapon systems and therefore USA and other developed countries tried to deny the Hi-technology in all spheres including electronics through Technology Control Regimes to developing countries like India."[48]

The acquisition of design skills and hi-technology from the developed countries has become high cost exercise and all this has contributed to the slowing down of growth of electronics industry.

In 1989-91 India suffered from political instability and lacked concrete policy decision-making. Even after 1991-95 Narsimha Rao government could not do much for the development of electronics area because of resource crunch and economic crisis pressure. This has led to decline in electronics expenditure in real terms in this phase.

DEPARTMENT OF SCIENCE AND TECHNOLOGY (S&T)

Science and Technology Capability

Technology can play a very vital role in the development of society. It has also great impact on war and defence capability of a nation. India was fortunate in having national leaders like Nehru who fully comprehended the necessity of science and technology for the benefit of Indian people and accordingly created infrastructure for the development of S&T in the country since independence. This type of scientific outlook was instrumental in the formulation of scientific policy resolutions on similar lines in 1983. Technology policy statement (TPS) was formulated which has the basic objective of developing indigenous technology and ensuring efficient absorption and adoption of imported technique appropriate to national priorities according to the availability of resources. It is aimed at attaining technical competence and self-reliance reducing dependence particularly in strategic areas and making maximum use of indigenous resources and skills.[49]

One does not have unlimited resources to develop specialised technologies for specific uses. Due to the resource constraints the dual use technologies are developing and becoming important and so science and technology infrastructure of a country becomes an internal part of defence capability of that country.

It is generally found that military equipment normally has a technical design life closer to 20 years and average operational life of around same period. Technological progress infact intending to stretch the technical life of military equipment closer to 30 years. This requires conscious efforts at planning and allotting appropriate and adequate resources for S&T.

Department of S&T and other Institutions Working Under IT

From the beginning of the first five year plan, the Indian Government has supported S&T by allocating appropriative resources. The Government has adopted 3 level policy for development of S&T development. At the first level it has established various Scientific Departments like Department of S&T, in 1971 Department of Space, Department of Ocean Development, Atomic Energy etc., and various national laboratories under these Departments. At the 2nd level the Government attempted to develop various scientific and socio-economic research organisations under various ministers like Indian Council of Medical Research, DRDO, Indian Council of Agricultural Research. At the third level the State and Union territories Government also established and supported S&T sector development. These steps have built a strong S & T foundation in India. The main contributors to R&D in Indian S&T sector comes from Central Government, state government, higher educational Institutions and universities, public and private sector industries and non-profit research institutions and associations.

As a part of technology promotion programmes the Department of S&T helped in the institution of specific missions which involve the development of product system/ sub-systems. The Department has set up an autonomous body—Technology Information, Forecasting and Assessment Council (TIFAC) with the objective of Technology forecasting and technology assessment. The council also makes technology information nationally accessible and the DST extends financial and administrative support to various research institutions, professional bodies and academics.

It also provides grants-in-aid to 13 autonomous scientific research institutions which are engaged in frontier areas of research in basic and applied sciences.[50]

The Survey of India (SOI) is another premier organisation under the DST. It is responsible for the production of topographical maps for providing services to defence forces and also to other users for various developmental activities. These services are being modernised by the way of introduction of sophisticated equipment aid upgradation technologies. The National Thematic Mapping Organisation under the SOI meets the national needs in cartography and specialised thematic maps. The India Meteorological Deptartment is the principal Government agency working for all matters related to Meteorology, Seismology, and allied subjects and their R&D.

CSIR

The Council of Scientific and Industrial Research (CSIR) is an autonomous body registered under the Societies Act, 1860. It was established in 1942 and works with DST. CSIR has a network of 40 laboratories and 81 field stations/ extension centres/regional centres all over the country to undertake R&D in various areas/disciplines. The CSIR continues to contribute significantly to the industrial and socio-economic development and promoting S&T manpower in the country. Several initiatives have been taken during the initial period of the 8th plan to reorient the R&D programmes and realign priorities to meet the needs of the industries vis-a-vis policies of the liberalisation of GOI.

The Department of Biotechnology (DBT) also works under DST. The DBT since its inception has focused on the promotion of this field for creation of strong, indigeneous, selft-reliant base of modern biology. Areas where biotechnology, can find direct application are agriculture, health, environment, industry and defence departments.

Phases in Science and Technology Department Expenditure Explanation

On the basis of graph and expenditure table 22 one finds that S&T Expenditure had three phases:

(1) First Phase – 1972-73 to 1982-83
(2) Second Phase – 1983-84 to 1989-90
(3) Third Phase – 1989-90 to 1994-95.

I First Phase – 1972-73 to 1982-83

In the First phase (1972 to 1982-83) Science and Technology expenditure had an exponential growth rate of 17.23 per cent per annum at current prices and 7.92 per cent per annum at 1980-81 prices.

In this period Science and Technology Department has established various scientific departments research organisations, Laboratories and specific technology development promotion programmes to create Science and Technology infrastructures.[51]

II Phase – 1983-84 to 1989-90

In Second Phase (1983-84 to 1989-90) Science and Technology expenditure had an exponential growth rate of 18.92 per cent per annum at current prices and 11.73 per cent per annum at (1980-81) prices. This period marks the highest growth rate in current and at (1980-81) prices. The Annual report of the Department of S&T takes a review of Government technology policy statement of 1983, and accordingly the S&T Department has set up an autonomous body – Technology Information Forecasting and Assessment Council (TIFAC).[52]

In this period India concentrated on developing absorption and adoption of imported technology appropriate to national priorities and availability of resources.

Table 22
Science and Technology Expenditure

Year	*At Current prices*	*At 1980-81 prices*
1970-71	-	-
1971-72	29.88	72.49
1972-73	36.15	79.73
1973-74	36.34	66.65
1974-75	51.40	75.30
1975-76	64.86	96.05
1976-77	76.97	111.66
1977-78	86.58	119.39
1978-79	89.61	123.57
1979-80	97.04	114.26
1980-81	108.37	108.37
1981-82	141.26	128.65
1982-83	213.79	185.60
1983-84	171.21	134.23
1984-85	208.10	157.81
1985-86	294.56	151.62
1986-87	328.01	225.11
1987-88	337.81	214.23
1988-89	444.10	216.11
1989-90	497.79	273.60
1990-91	500.00	249.23
1991-92	537.00	235.35
1992-93	640.68	255.50
1993-94	770.00	282.99
1994-95	853.16	286.70

Source:

(1) Government of India, *India Budget* (Expenditure Budget and demand for grants for various years (1970-95) for Department of Science and Technology, Ministry of Finance, New Delhi.

(2) Government of India, Comptroller & Auditor General of India Report: India Appropriation Account, for various years (1971-95) Ministry of Finance, New Delhi.

Graph 6

S & T Exp. Current Prices & Constant Prices

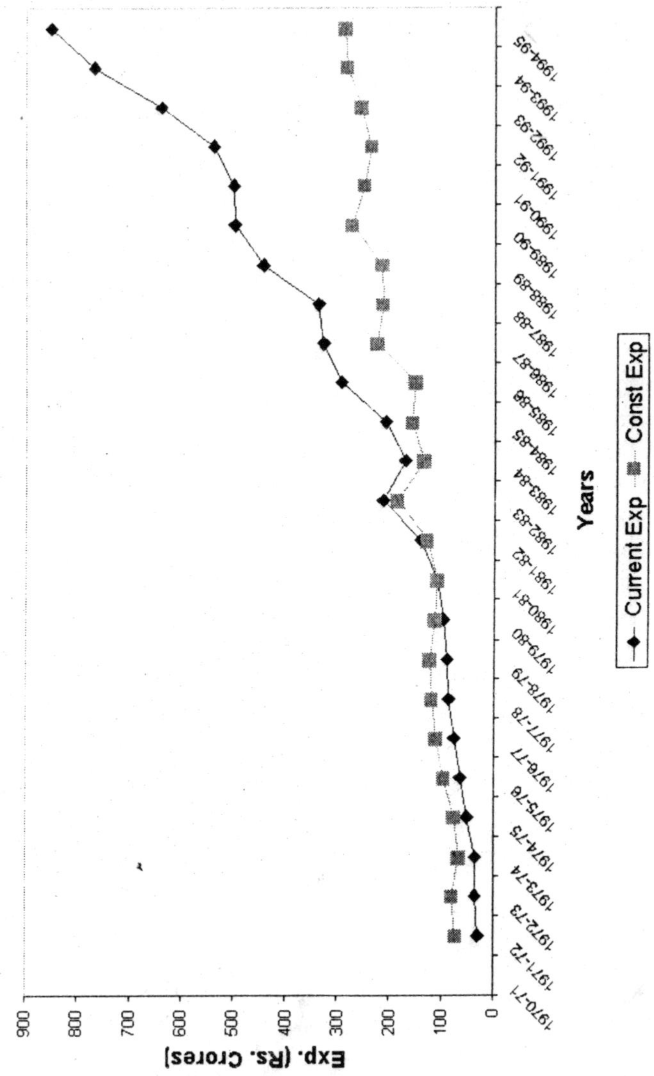

Table 23
Science and Technology Expenditure Breakup

Year	*Total S&T*	*Dept of S&T*	*Dept of Biotech*	*CSIR*
1970-71	25.08	1.75	18.90	5.90
1971-72	30.92	2.20	21.47	6.60
1972-73	35.68	2.90	24.66	8.04
1973-74	38.70	4.03	25.00	9.65
1974-75	51.85	6.13	32.11	13.60
1975-76	63.23	10.13	37.49	15.60
1976-77	76.97	15.63	43.49	17.84
1977-78	86.58	21.78	46.71	18.68
1978-79	89.60	25.84	44.33	19.43
1979-80	100.10	28.14	50.16	21.80
1980-81	112.63	32.21	54.48	25.29
1981-82	122.26	40.69	77.65	39.21
1982-83	155.28	32.53	94.40	28.34
1983-84	168.53	39.38	97.49	31.65
1984-85	325.74	45.58	124.00	35.69
1985-86	408.00	77.37	160.88	41.40
1986-87	329.67	144.08	168.02	17.57
1987-88	368.81	153.82	182.65	32.34
1988-89	444.87	197.70	205.57	41.60
1989-90	499.71	212.38	233.48	53.85
1990-91	536.78	237.96	239.17	59.65
1991-92	581.61	256.58	258.37	66.66
1992-93	638.03	282.46	277.60	77.97
1993-94	769.99	338.95	342.94	88.10
1994-95	866.66	379.83	396.63	90.23
1995-96		418.80	411.03	96.52

Source:

(1) Government of India, *India Budget* (Expenditure Budget and demand for grants for various years (1970-95) for Department of Science and Technology, Ministry of Finance, New Delhi.

(2) Government of India, Comptroller & Auditor General of India Report: India Appropriation Account, for various years (1971-95) Ministry of Finance, New Delhi.

Note: Only important items are taken in the break-up table so it not tally with total S & T expenditure.

III Phase – 1989-90 to 1994-95

In the Third Phase (1989-90 to 1994-95) Science and Technology expenditure had an exponential growth rate of 12.63 per cent per annum at current prices and only 2.00 per cent per annum at (1980-81) prices. This clearly indicates that resources crunch had affected the allocation for Science and Technology Department in real terms.

Department of Ocean Development

Ocean Development Programme

India has more than 7500 km. coastline and has more than 1256 island territories. Its exclusive economic zone (EEZ) (for 200 km) i.e. covers about an area of 20 lakh sq. km. and the continental shelf extends upto 350 nautical miles from the coast. India needs to protect its coastline, island territory, oceanic resources and marine environment. In the view of this the Government of India has set up the Department of Ocean Development in 1981.[53]

It promotes and coordinates the multifaceted endeavours needed for the above and also develops the new emerging area of Antarctic research and deep seabed mining.

Objectives

The eighth plan objectives of the department were (i) to modernise basic and underpinning required for an efficient approach to exploration, exploitation surveillance, and management of marine resources and environment, (ii) effectively safeguard national interest in deep sea bed mining in the central part of Indian Ocean and Antarctica (iii) develop viable marine infrastructure and expertise in this high S&T area.[54]

Antractic Research Programme

India has been participating in Antarctic research programme since 1981. The scientific research expeditions are sent every year to Antarctic region from India. India has established permanent station "Maitri" in 1984-85 which is indigeneously designed. This helps in understanding key global processes that continue to go on our global environment. India has a consultative status in the Antarctic Treaty system. Various government departments, more than 20 research institutes and universities contribute to the Antarctic research programme. The Army, Navy, Airforce and DRDO have provided invaluable logistic support to these research expeditions.

India has done pioneering work in the area of deep sea bed exploration. A mine site of 1,50,000 sq. km. in the central Indian ocean was allotted by the preparatory commission of the International Seabed Authority in August 1987. India was the first country in the world to get pioneer inventor status in 1987.[55]

This has helped India to develop high tech marine technology and exploration of living and non-living resources in EEZ and continental shelf of India. The National Institute of Oceanography was established in India in 1966 under ICSR.

The main objective of this institute is to develop adequate knowledge related to physical, chemical, biological, geological and engineering aspects of seas around India and explore them. The National Institute of Ocean Technology (NIOT) was established in 1993 under Department of Ocean Development (DOD).

It will help in application of knowledge and expertise gained through oceanic research. OD has research vessel OVR 'Sagar Kanya' for R&D and Oceanographic data collection etc.[56]

Table 24
Ocean Development Expenditure

(In Rupees Crores)

Year	*At Current prices*	*An 1980-81 prices*
1970-71	- - -	- - -
1971-72	- - -	- - -
1972-73	- - -	- - -
1973-74	- - -	- - -
1974-75	- - -	- - -
1975-76	- - -	- - -
1976-77	- - -	- - -
1977-78	- - -	- - -
1978-79	- - -	- - -
1979-80	- - -	- - -
1980-81	- - -	- - -
1981-82	- - -	- - -
1982-83	49.28	42.78
1983-84	19.08	15.41
1984-85	18.27	13.86
1985-86	14.12	10.29
1986-87	16.29	11.18
1987-88	16.24	10.30
1988-89	25.09	14.81
1989-90	31.21	17.15
1990-91	39.58	19.73
1991-92	41.37	18.13
1992-93	45.53	18.13
1993-94	56.41	20.73
1994-95	59.00	19.82

Source:

(1) Government of India, *India Budget* (Expenditure Budget and demand for grants for various years (1970-95) for Department of Ocean Development, Ministry of Finance, New Delhi.

(2) Government of India, Comptroller & Auditor General of India Report: India Appropriation Account, for various years (1971-95) Ministry of Finance, New Delhi.

Graph 7

O.D. Exp. Currenent Prices & Constant Prices

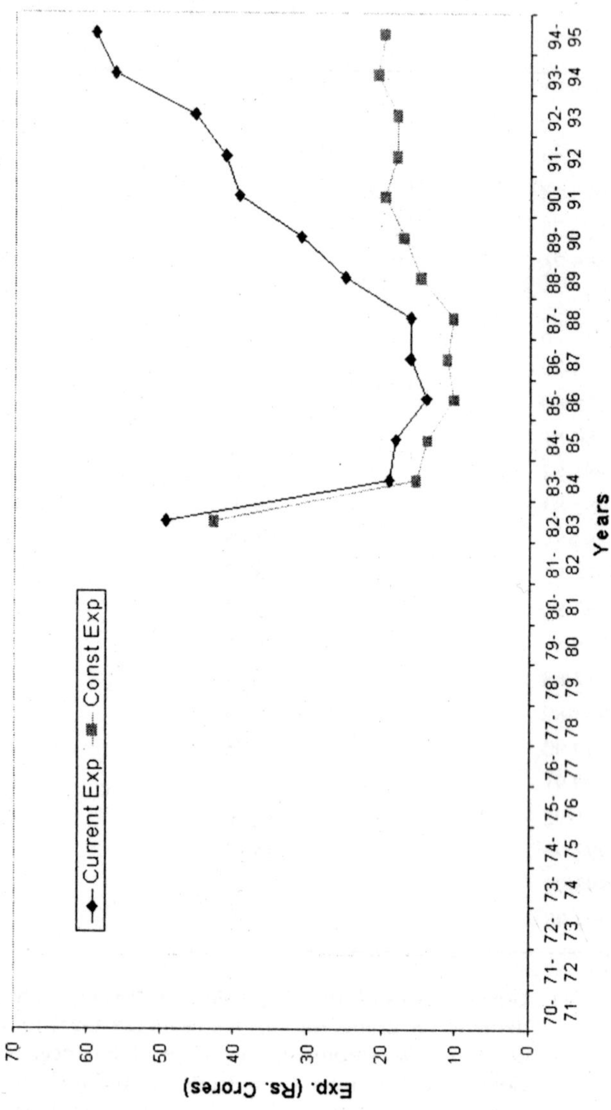

All this infrastructure is important for India from the point of view of Indian National security especially naval capability. India is one of the most important littoral states of the Indian Ocean region. The Indian Ocean has vast amount of ocean resources. India has economic, political, strategic and miliary interests in this region. India's foreign trade also carried out in Indian ocean trade routes. Sardar K.M. Pannikkar and rightly pointed out that the India's security had other interests lie in the Indian Ocean therefore India must have ability to control and influence this region. The Indian government has realised this fact and in 1981 separate department of ocean development has been established. This would help India in developing its economic power and also it provide supportive base for Indian naval power to protect our vital interests.

Table 25
Ocean Development Expenditure Break-UP

Year	*Total exp O.D.*	*Exp. On An. R.*
1983-84	32.36	2.75
1984-85	19.17	3.90
1985-86	28.90	7.00
1986-87	22.28	7.85
1987-88	18.95	6.84
1988-89	29.03	12.75
1989-90	31.36	13.00
1990-91	39.58	15.46
1991-92	41.37	15.38
1992-93	48.17	20.05
1993-94	56.41	21.23
1994-95	59.00	17.30
1995-96	65.94	24.25

Source:

(1) Government of India, *India Budget* (Expenditure Budget and demand for grants for various years (1970-95) for Department of Ocean Development, Ministry of Finance, New Delhi.

(2) Government of India, Comptroller & Auditor General of India Report: India Appropriation Account, for various years (1971-95) Ministry of Finance, New Delhi.

Note: Only important items are taken in the break-up Development expenditure.

Phase in Ocean Development Expenditure

This Department was established in 1982-83. On the basis of graph and expenditure table one finds that this expenditure has three phases in expenditure analysis:-

(1) First Phase – 1983-84 to 1986-87
(2) Second Phase – 1987-88 to 1990-91
(3) Third Phase – 1990-91 to 1994-95

I Phase – 1983-84 to 1986-87

In this First Phase (1983-84 to 1986-87) Ocean Development Expenditure has exponential growth rate (-7.3) per cent per annum at current prices and (-99.0) per cent per annum at 1980-81 prices. This period marked decline, reduction and fluctuations in the Ocean Development Expenditure. In this initial period the Government could not provide required attention/resources to development of this department although its importance was realised.

II Phase – (1987-88 to 1990-91)

In the Second Phase Ocean Development Expenditure had an exponential growth rate of 33.60 per cent per annum at current prices and 23.31 per cent per annum at (1980-81) prices. In this period the Antarctic Research activities, Deep Seabed Exploration, Marine instrumentation programmes, Ocean Thermal Energy conservation programmes were undertaken so that called for increase in expenditure.[57]

III Phase – (1990-91 to 1994-95)

In the Third Phase Ocean Development Expenditure had an exponential growth rate of 11.71 per cent per annum at current prices and 1.44 per cent per annum at (1980-81) prices. This decline was due to worsening of economic situation in the country.

NOTES AND REFERENCES

1. Zuberi H. and Raman S. Kalyan, "Science and Technology for Development; India's space programme" *Strategic Analysis* vol. xvi, No. 11, Feb. 1995 (New Delhi: IDSA publication), pp. 1431 to 1436.
2. Akashi Yasushi, *Disarmament Topical papers 2 Science and Technology and Their Implications for Peace and Security* (New York: United Nations Organisation), 1990, p. 4.
3. Akashi Yasushi, *Ibid,* pp. 4,5.
4. Vitthal, N., "Dual use Technologies: Challenges and Choices," *Strategic Analysis,* Vol. xvi, No. 5, August 1993 (New Delhi: IDSA), p. 589.
5. Quoted in Kapur A., *India's Nuclear Option: Atomic Diplomacy and Decision-Making* (New York: Praeger) 1976 p. 17.
6. Kapur, A., *Ibid,* p. 194.
7. India, Department of Atomic Energy, *Annual Report 1994-95* (New Delhi: Government of India) pp. 145-147.
8. Jain, J.P., *Nuclear India* (New Delhi: Radiant Publication, 1974), p. 158.
9. Kapur A., *op cit.,* p-136.
10. Kaul R. *India's Nuclear Spin Off* (Allahabad: Chanakya Publications, 1974) p. 29.
11. Nanda, R. *National Security: Policy Planning and Perspective* (New Delhi: Lancer Books, 1991), p. 149.
12. Thomas, R.G.C., *Indian Security Policy* (New Jersey: Princetone University Press, 1986), p. 108.
13. Vohra, A.M., "Cover Nuclear Status Suits India," *Times of India,* (Bombay), 14 Jan. 1991.
14. Datta, Savita, "China the Emerging Nuclear Power: A Review," *Strategic Analysis,* Vol. No. 5, August 1993, New Delhi, p. 560.
15. *International Herald Tribune* (17 June 1988) and the *Economist* (5th Sept. 1987, p. 52) as cited in Ron Mathews, *op cit.,* p. 106.

16. India, Department of Atomic Energy, *Annual Report of 1974-75* (New Delhi: Government of India), p. 6

17. Government of India, *India-1995,* Year Book, Ministry of Information and Broadcasting, New Delhi, p. 120.

18. India, Department of Atomic Energy, *Annual Report 1982-83* (New Delhi: Government of India), p. 25.

19. Subramanyam, R.R., "China's Nuclear Postures in the 1990s: Relationship with Pakistan" in *Defence and Nuclear Tangle in South Asia* (New Delhi: ABC Publishing House, 1989), pp. 59-65.

20. Siddiqui, A.R., "Let us keep our Nuclear option open," *Defence Journal,* Vol. XII, No. 8, 1986 pp. 33-34.

21. Spector Leonard, *Nuclear Proliferation Today on basis of Carneige Foundation Report* (USA: Vintage Books, 1994), p. 73-80.

22. Vohra, A.M., Covert Nuclear Status Suits India, *Times of India* (Bombay) 24th Jan. 1991.

23. Cohen S.P., *Nuclear Neighbours in Nuclear Proliferation in South Asia: The prospectus of Arms Control,* London, pp. 1-3.

24. Smith, Chris, *India's Ad-Hoc Arsenal: Direction or Drift in Defence Policy,* Sipri Study (New York: Oxford University Press, 1994), p. 192.

25. Smith, Chris, *Ibid,* p. 194.

26. India, Department of Space, *Annual Report 1972-73* (New Delhi: Government of India), p. 1.

27. Based on the information given in, India, Department of Space, *Annual Report 1991-92* (New Delhi: Government of India), p. 10.

28. N. Raj Gopal, "From Sounding Rockets to Satellites" *Frontline,* (Madras) vol. 3, No. 21 Oct. 3, 1986 p. 81.

29. Smith, Chris, *op cit.,* p. 201.

30. This is based on information given in, *Sipri Year book 1993,* (Oxford: Sipri) p. 245-249.

31. Bhatia, A, "India's Space Programme – cause for concern?", *Asian Survey,* Vol. 15, No. 10, Oct 1985, p. 1017.

32. *India - 1995,* Year Book, *op. cit.,* p. 154.

33. *Military Year Book 1991-92,* Guide Publications, New Delhi, p. 227.

34. This is based on information given in India, Department of Space, *Annual Report 1983-84* (New Delhi: Government of India), p. 9 to 11 .

35. India, Department of Space, *Annual Report of 1976-17* (New Delhi: Government of India), pp. 17.

36. India, Department of Space, *Annual Report 1980-81,* (New Delhi: Government of India), pp. 12-14.

37. Smith, Chris, *op. cit.,* p. 201.

38. *India Military Year Book 1988-89,* New Delhi, p. 125.

39. This is based on information given in, India, Department of Space, *Annual Report 1992-93* (New Delhi: Government of India), pp. 27-30.

40. Singh, Ravindra Pal, "Trans Century Technologies," *Strategic Analysis,* Vol. XIV, No. 4, New Delhi, July 1991, p. 441.

41. This is based on information given in, India, Department of Electronics, *Annual Report 1993-94* (New Delhi: Government of India), p. 7.

42. This is based on information given in, India, Department of Electronics, *Annual Report 1990-91* (New Delhi: Government of India), p. 27.R.R.

43. This is based on information given in, India, Department of Electronics, *Annual Report 1992-93* (New Delhi: Government of India), p. 17.

44. This is based on information given in, *India-1994,* a Reference Annual, Ministry of Information & Broadcasting, Publication Division, New Delhi.

45. India, Department of Electronics, *Annual Report 1984-85* (New Delhi: Government of India) pp. 11-13.

46. India, Department of Electronics, *Anual Report 1985-86* (New Delhi: Government of India), pp. 5-6.

47. *India - 1988,* a Reference Annual, Published by Ministry of Information and Broadcasting, New Delhi, p.

48. Madhok, V. K., "Gulf War and Indian Armed Forces," *USA Journal,* Jan-March 1991 (New Delhi), pp. 65-70.

49. This is based on information given in, *India-1995,* a Reference Annual, Ministry of Information and Broadcasting, New Delhi, p. 143.

51. As stated in the aims and objectives of S&T Department reports for various years and *India–1984,* Year Book, Ministry of Information of Broadcasting, Publication Division, New Delhi, p. 133.

52. India, Department of Science and Technology, *Annual Report 1983-84* (New Delhi: Government of India), p. 17.

53. *India 1981,* Year Book, Ministry of Information and Broadcasting, New Delhi.

54. This is based on information given in, India, Department of Ocean Development, *Annual Report 1992-93* (New Delhi: Government of India), p. 3.

55. This is based on information given in, *India-1994,* Year Book, Ministry of Information & Broadcasting, Publication Division, New Delhi.

56. India, Department of Ocean Development, *Annual Report 1993-94* (New Delhi: Government of India).

57. India, Department of Ocean Development, *Annual Report 1990-91* (New Delhi: Government of India), pp. 13-14.

CHAPTER 9

Defence Expenditure – Further Explanation

(Regression Analysis and Other Statistical Results)

Introduction

In the earlier chapters three determinants of defence budget in India and also dual purpose technology factors have been analysed. The analysis of defence expenditure in India based on the broader definition of defence expenditure for the period 1970-71 to 1994-95 has been presented in chapter 4. The phasewise expenditure analysis of various constituents of defence expenditure has been given in this chapter. This chapter tries to integrate all these results together. It also gives us a comprehensive picture of phasewise expenditure analysis results of defence, police (internal security), nuclear, space, electronics, science and technology and ocean development.

This chapter presents structural changes in the defence expenditure patterns in India during the period of study. It also presents servicewise and itemwise analysis of defence expenditure which can lead us to the better understanding of defence expenditure in India.

A comprehensive definition of defence expenditure has been accepted and on its basis expenditures are analysed. Table 3 in Chapter 4 shows linear regression results for the whole study period (1970-95) for defence, police, nuclear, space, electronics, science and technology, and ocean development expenditure.

Table 26
Phasewise Exponential Growth Rate in Percentage per Annum

Phases	*Current Prices*			*(1980-81) Prices*		
Name of the Ministry/Deptt. and time period	*Growth Rate % p.a.*	*Std. Error*	R^2	*Growth Rate % p.a.*	*Std. Error*	R^2
Defence Expenditure						
P1D (73-74 to 79-80)	10.30	0.0131	0.9172	4.95	0.0090	0.8236
P2D (79-80 to 84-85)	15.48	0.0092	0.9837	6.35	0.0099	0.9052
P3D (84-85 to 87-88)	22.49	0.0178	0.9847	15.40	0.212	0.9580
P4D (87-88 to 94-95)	11.76	0.0105	0.0567	4.19	0.0130	0.1898
Police/Int. Sec. Expenditure						
P1P (73-74 to 79-80)	11.66	0.0071	0.9795	5.74	0.0093	0.8784
P2P (79-80 to 84-85)	17.17	0.0052	0.9958	8.43	0.0056	0.9811
P3P (84-85 to 88-89)	17.58	0.0040	0.9987	10.78	0.0044	0.9962
P4P(88-89 to 94-95)	16.00	0.0044	0.9956	5.37	0.0043	0.9656
Nuclear Expenditure						
P1N (72-73 to 79-80)	13.75	0.0151	0.9235	5.88	0.0181	0.6228
P2N (80-81 to 86 -87)	26.49	0.0240	0.9507	19.10	0.0266	0.9223
P3N (86-87 to 94-95)	2.40	0.0128	0.3286	(-99.06)	0.0126	0.8048
Space Expenditure						
P1SP (73-74 to 82-83)	19.06	0.0163	0.9343	10.28	0.0128	0.8790
P2SP (82-83 to 88-89)	26.21	0.0211	0.9604	19.53	0.0199	0.9411
P3SP (88-89 to 94-95)	12.20	0.0256	0.8021	(-0.29)	0.0259	0.0025
Electronics Expenditure						
P1E (72-73 to 82-83)	37.85	0.0305	0.9248	26.93	0.0299	0.8758
P2E (82-83 to 88-89)	15.60	0.0660	0.4939	8.53	0.0678	0.2286
P3E (88-89 to 94-95)	9.39	0.0551	0.3989	(-99.00)	0.0570	0.0068
Science & Technology Expenditure						
P1ST (72-73 to 82-83)	17.23	0.0120	0.9506	7.92	0.0134	0.7807
P2ST (83-84 to 89-90)	18.92	0.0159	0.9594	11.73	0.0194	0.8667
P3ST (89-90 to 94-95)	12.63	0.0156	0.9353	2.00	0.0183	0.2280

Ocean Development Expenditure						
P1OD (83-84 to 86-87)	(-7.3)	0.0525	0.4926	(-99.12)	0.0503	0.7883
P2OD (87-88 to 90-91)	33.50	0.0353	0.9708	23.31	0.0382	0.9375
P3OD (90-91 to 94-95)	11.71	0.0160	0.9409	1.44	0.0200	0.1450

P1 = Phase 1; P2 = Phase 2; P3 = Phase 3; P4 = Phase 4.
D = Defence; P = Police/Internal Security; N = Nuclear; SP = Space
E = Electronics; ST = Science & Technology; OD = Ocean Development.

Note: Here only defence expenditure is net defence expenditure. Nuclear, Space, Internal Security, Electronics, S&T, OD expenditures are gross expenditures. The recoveries and receipts are not adjusted.

In that table one finds that, in the period (1970-95) the highest exponential growth rate is seen in the electronics expenditure 13.95 per cent per annum (at 198-81 prices) followed by space expenditure 10.39 per cent per annum (at 1980-81 prices), Science and Technology expenditure 6.60 per cent per annum (at 1980-81 prices), police or internal security expenditure 6.57 per cent per annum (1980-81 prices), Ocean Development expenditure 5.32 per cent per annum (at 1980-81 prices) and defence expenditure 4.56 per cent per annum (at 1980-81 prices).

It means in this period all the other supportive expenditures (dual purpose and internal security expenditures) increased alongwith actual defence expenditure. The internal security expenditure had higher growth rate than defence expenditure due to the fact that internal security threats became more dominant than external threats in 1980s and 1990s.

The phasewise explanation of all expenditures have been given in Chapters 6, 7, 8. Each constituent of defence expenditure had three to four phases. The regression analysis results of each phase can be summarised in the table.

Explanation of Phasewise Exponential Growth Rate in Percentage per Annum

The table of Phasewise exponential growth rate in percentage per annum reveals comprehensive picture of phase wise expenditure regression analysis results of defence, police, nuclear space, electronics, science and technology and ocean development expenditures.

It can be seen from the table that in the phase period 84-85 to 1987-1988/1988-89 the defence expenditure has the highest exponential growth rate and police/internal security expenditure also has the highest exponential growth rate at 1980-81 prices. The each expenditure has different time phases but one can observe that more or less in the same time period (82-83 to 88-89 nuclear expenditure, space expenditure science and technology expenditure have the highest exponential growth rate at 1980-81 prices.

Expenditure		*Time period*	*Growth rate % p.a (1980-81 Prices)*
1.	Defence expenditure	84-85 to 87-88	15.40
2.	Police/Internal Security expenditure	84-85 to 88-89	10.78
3.	Nuclear expenditure	80-81 to 86-87	19.10
4.	Space expenditure.	82-83 to 88-89	19.53
5.	Science and Technology expenditure	83-84 to 89-90	11.73

This clearly indicates that India has consolidated its defence and dual technology purpose capabilities in 1980s. The electronics expenditure has the highest exponential growth rate in the period 72-73 to 82-83 which was 26.93 per cent per annum to 1980-81 prices. In 1982-83 to 88-89 time phase electronics expenditure had an exponential growth rate of 8.53 per cent per annum.

This denotes that in 1970s and in early 1980s India has developed basic infrastructural base and in the latter phases utilised and diversified this capability. One observes this especially in case of electronics that private sector also responded well and supported this effort in India.

In Table 26 one observes that approximately after 86-87 the nuclear expenditure, space expenditure, electronics expenditure have negative exponential growth rate. The Ocean Development expenditure has also negative exponential growth rate in the phase 83-84 to 86-87. This clearly indicates that after 1987-88 the expenditure on defence and these other dual areas in real terms has more or less remained frozen. The nominal increase incurrent prices in their expenses has been able to absorb only inflation. The most important reason for this can be seen in the economic crisis which India started facing in this period.

This table and bar diagram gives the distribution of total defence expenditure in the revenue and capital account in percentage terms. It reveals that large share was spent of Revenue account which was around 90 per cent of total defence expenditure for the period 1970-71 to 1983-84. Since 1984-85 the share of revenue expenditure in total defence expenditure started declining. The year 1987-88 marks the drastic decline in the share of revenue expenditure. The revenue expenditure declined by 13.60 per cent than the previous year consequently the declining trend was continued till 1993-94. The year 1994-95 marks the marginal increase of about two per cent in the revenue expenditure share.

The decrease in revenue expenditure was mainly because of increasing share of capital expenditure and to some extent due to changes in the method of defence budgeting.

The declining trend in the revenue expenditure was seen partly due to the decline in revenue expenditure of Army and Air Force the table gives item-wise breakup of defence expenditure. There we find that the share of stores in total defence expenditure declined and the share of pay and allowances also declined marginally. Those two items of revenue expenditure side declined with caused the above trend.

The Structural Changes in Defence Expenditure Pattern in India During (1970-95)

Table 27
Defence Expenditure of India — Revenue & Capital Breakup

Year	*Revenue Def. Exp. As % of TDE*	*Capital Def. Exp. As % of TDE*
1970-71	87.70	12.30
1971-72	88.30	11.70
1972-73	87.10	12.90
1973-74	88.10	11.90
1974-75	90.90	9.10
1975-76	91.10	8.90
1976-77	91.60	8.40
1977-78	90.60	9.40
1978-79	91.20	8.80
1979-80	92.20	7.80
1980-81	91.60	8.40
1981-82	89.60	10.40
1982-83	90.30	9.70
1983-84	89.80	10.20
1984-85	88.90	11.10
1985-86	87.90	12.11
1986-87	87.60	12.40
1987-88	74.00	26.00
1988-89	71.64	28.36
1989-90	70.71	29.30
1990-91	70.49	29.51
1991-92	69.99	30.01
1992-93	68.86	31.14
1993-94	68.57	31.43
1994-95	70.66	29.33

Source: Defence Service Estimates of various years.

Graph 8

Total Defence Exp. Rev. Cap. Breakup

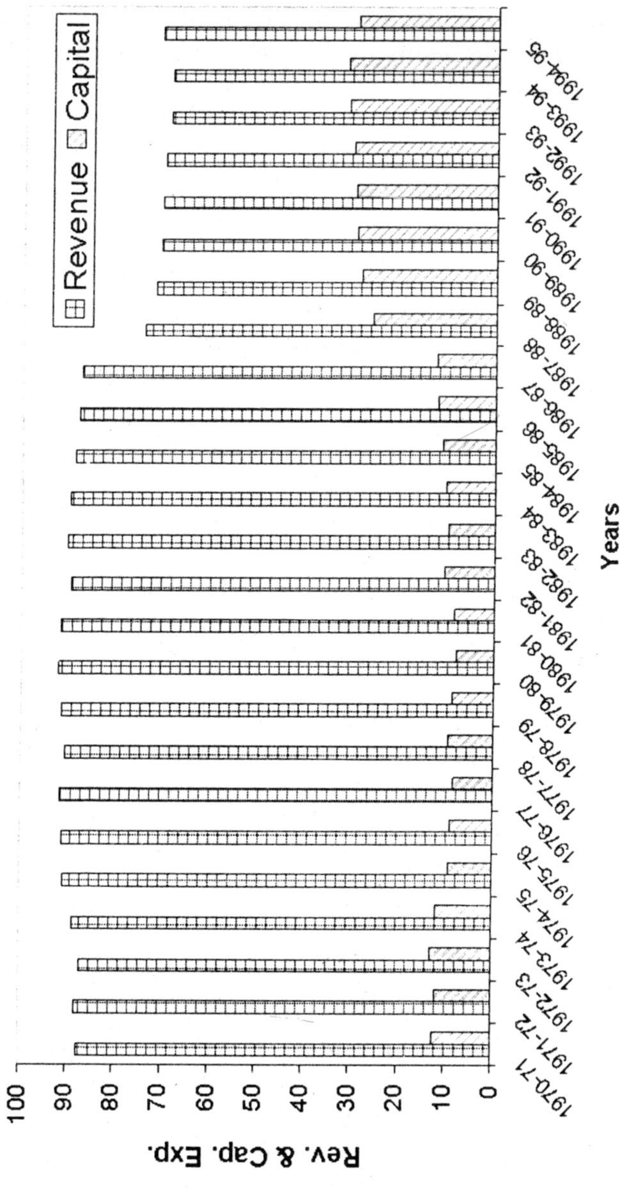

Since 1984-85 there is a continuous increase in the percentage of capital expenditure till 1993-94. the year 1987-88 marks the landmark point. In this year the percentage share of capital expenditure in total defence expenditure doubled as compared to its previous year. In 1986-87 the percentage share of capital expenditure was 12.40 percent which rose to 26.00 per cent in 1987-88. Then it increased progressively to 31.43 per cent in 1993-94. In the period 1970-71 to 1983-84 the percentage share of capital expenditure was around 10 percent of the total defence expenditure which almost tripled in 1994-95.

This increase in the share of capital expenditure can be attributed to the purchase of new and modern equipments especially for Navy and Air Force, upgradation and self reliance programmes for military technology, increasing important to Research and Development and Rajiv Gahdi's new political dynamism.

The Table 28 and bar diagram gives services wise distribution of total defance expenditure in percentage terms. The glace at the table shows that the defence expenditure is unequally distributed in three services i.e. Army, Navy, Air Force.

The major share has always been that at the Army which accounts nearly for about 60 percent of the total defence expenditure, followed by the Air Force which accounts nearly for about 20 per cent and the Navy gets minimum which accounts nearly for about 8 to 13 per cent.

One finds that the share of Army was about 72.70 per cent in 1970-71 it came down to 57.31 per cent in 1983-84. It again rose in the year 1984-85 to 63.24 per cent and started declining in the future period except 1986-87 and came to 57.43 per cent in 1994-95. But overall the share of Army in total defence expenditure has gone down. The increase in the share of Army in total defence expenditure during 1998-85 to 1986-87 can be explained on the basis of new weapon acquisitions of Army, impact of modernisation drive of Rajiv Gandhi and increase in capital expenditure of the army.

Table 28
Servicewise Distribution of Defence Expenditure

Year	*% of Def. Exp. on Army*	*% of Def. Exp. on Navy*	*% of Def. Exp. on Airforce*
1970-71	72.70	7.80	19.50
1971-72	73.50	7.30	19.20
1972-73	63.18	8.40	21.00
1973-74	63.71	8.84	21.02
1974-75	65.03	8.03	20.66
1975-76	64.86	8.70	20.05
1976-77	64.13	8.33	20.48
1977-78	63.14	9.52	20.31
1978-79	60.92	9.14	22.44
1979-80	58.18	9.75	25.81
1980-81	57.81	8.87	24.67
1981-82	57.98	1.42	22.64
1982-83	57.42	0.47	23.65
1983-84	57.31	1.89	21.55
1984-85	63.24	2.21	22.65
1985-86	61.01	2.53	23.30
1986-87	62.46	2.51	21.43
1987-88	60.93	2.85	23.11
1988-89	60.45	3.48	22.51
1989-90	59.63	3.55	23.06
1990-91	56.30	2.70	24.10
1991-92	59.28	2.80	24.80
1992-93	55.22	1.50	29.40
1993-94	57.90	2.30	27.70
1994-95	57.43	2.62	28.38

Source: Defence Service Estimates of various years.

Note: Figures don't tally because there are some other heads of defence expenditure. Figures don't tally because many expenditure items remain unclassified and also due to changes in basic definitions, accounting methods etc. in defence budget.

There is increase in the share of the Navy and the Air Force which can be partly explained by the decline in the share of the Army. The share of defence expenditure on the Navy has maintained progressive increase from 1971-72 to 1989-90 except few years marginal difference.

The share of naval expenditure was less than 10 per cent and total defence expenditure till 1980-81. In the year 1988-89 it has crossed the figure of 13 per cent and reached to 13.55 per cent in 1989-90. After this again it started declining reached to 12.62 per cent in the year 1994.95. The share of Defence Expenditure on Air Force Defence Expenditure on Air Force has increased during this period. But this increase is gradual as compared to the Navy. In 1970-71 the share of Air Force expenditure was 19.50 per cent of total defence expenditure which increased to the level of 25.81 per cent in 1979-80. Then it marginally declined till 1991-92. In 1992-93 it again increased to 29.4 per cent of total defence expenditure. This denotes the gradual shift of the thrust from the Army to the Air Force.

The Table 29 and bar diagram gives service wise percentage of total defence expenditure.

One finds that in case of the Army the revenue expenditure as percentage of total defence expenditure has gone down appreciably from 60.90 per cent in 1970-71 to 48.52 per cent in 1994-95.

In case of the Navy the revenue expenditure shows slow increase from 1971-73 to 1995-96 and then onwords there is a gradual decline in the share of the Navy's revenue expenditure as a percentage of total defence expenditure.

There are marginal upward and downward fluctuations in the revenue expenditure as percentage of total defence expenditure of the Air Force. The Air Force has the highest store in the year 1979-80 which was 24.99 per cent then onwards it started declining and it was the lowest in the year 1988-89 i.e. 13.01 per cent. Again gradually there was increase in the Air Force expenditure and it became 15.90 per cent in the year 1994-95.

Table 29
Table of Servicewise Distribution of Defence Revenue Expenditure % of Total Defence Expenditure

(In Crores of Rs. At Current Prices)

Year	*Army Rev. Exp. as % of TDE*	*Navy Rev. Exp. as % of TDE*	*Airforce Rev. Exp. as % of TDE*
1970-71	60.90	4.60	18.60
1971-72	62.90	4.40	17.80
1972-73	62.10	4.10	17.90
1973-74	60.23	4.80	19.47
1974-75	62.82	4.70	19.20
1975-76	62.35	5.34	19.00
1976-77	61.72	5.73	19.67
1977-78	60.62	5.73	19.35
1978-79	58.49	5.77	21.50
1979-80	55.58	5.98	24.99
1980-81	58.59	5.93	23.78
1981-82	55.03	6.62	21.62
1982-83	54.36	6.16	22.67
1983-84	53.72	7.99	20.52
1984-85	59.69	7.66	21.58
1985-86	57.69	7.36	22.18
1986-87	59.12	6.95	20.43
1987-88	54.40	5.93	13.31
1988-89	52.52	5.79	13.01
1989-90	51.25	5.65	13.03
1990-91	51.34	5.42	13.47
1991-92	49.70	5.72	14.27
1992-93	45.90	5.68	15.69
1993-94	47.57	5.50	15.40
1994-95	48.52	6.21	15.90

Source: Defence Service Estimates - various years.

TDE = Total Defence Expenditure REV. EXP. = Revenue Expenditure

Note: Figure don't tally because there are some other heads of defence expenditure. Figures don't tally because many expenditure items remain unclassified and also due to changes in basic definitions, accounting methods etc. in defence budget.

Graph 9

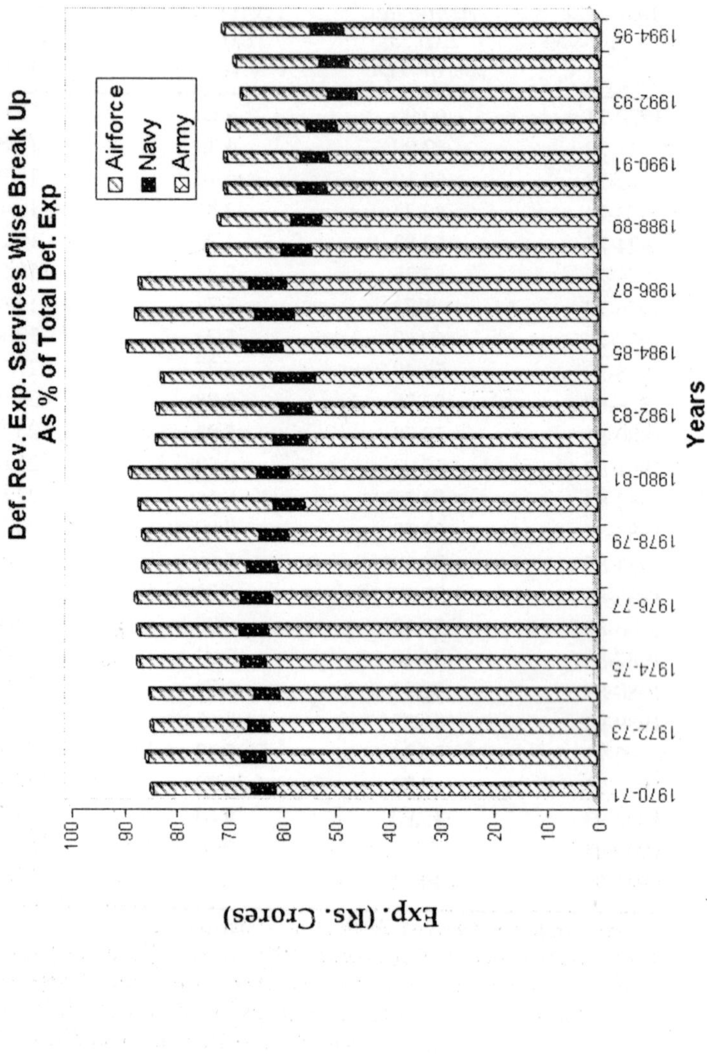
Def. Rev. Exp. Services Wise Break Up
As % of Total Def. Exp
Airforce
Navy
Army
Exp. (Rs. Crores)
0
10
20
30
40
50
60
70
80
90
100
1970-71
1972-73
1974-75
1976-77
1978-79
1980-81
1982-83
1984-85
1986-87
1988-89
1990-91
1992-93
1994-95
Years

The table 30 and bar diagram indicates servicewise capital distribution as percentage of total defence expenditure overall an upward trend is observed for the three services in the capital expenditure during the period of the study (There is marginal decline in case of the Army for some period) The capital expenditure for the Army remained negligible/very small only round 3 per cent from 1973-74 to 1982-83. The year 1986-87 the capital expenditure was 6.55 per cent of TDE which was almost the double of previous years percentage share. Since 1986-87 it has increased continuously due to continuation of modernisation drive for the Army. In the year 1993-94 the capital expenditure share of the Army was the highest i.e. 10.39 per cent of the total defence expenditure (TDE).

The share of the Navy in capital expenditure has been remained large and significant in the total period of the study. It was the highest in the year 1989-91 i.e. 7.87 per cent of the T.D.E. From the year 1981-82 one finds continuously increasing trend of capital expenditure for the Navy (except the year 1983-84) till 1989-90. This was mainly because of modernisation of the Navy equipment purchases, and naval capability expansion programme.

The capital expenditure of the Air Force has shown gradual increase till 1986-87. In the period 1970-71 to 1986-87 the capital expenditure remained low only amount 1 to 1.5 per cent on the average. But year 1987-88 marks the drastic change. In this year the capital expenditure of the Air Force became 9.78 per cent of the T.D.E. and then it continued to increase up to 13.74 per cent in the year 1992-93. Then marginally declined and settled around 12 per cent of the total defence expenditure till 1994-95.

This spectacular upward shift was mainly due to the purchase of aeroplane and Aeroengines, modernisation programmes etc.

This table 31 indicates itemwise breakup of defence expenditure for the period 1970-71 to 1994-95. It has taken into account only main items of defence expenditure of three services.

Table 30
Servicewise Distribution of Defence Capital Expenditure % of Total Defence Expenditure

(In Crores of Rs. at Current Prices)

Year	*Army Rev. Exp. as % of TDE*	*Navy Rev. Exp. as % of TDE*	*Airforce Rev. Exp. as % of TDE*
1970-71	5.00	3.40	1.40
1971-72	4.60	2.90	1.60
1972-73	5.20	3.70	1.69
1973-74	3.46	4.03	1.56
1974-75	2.18	3.34	1.45
1975-76	2.48	3.35	1.07
1976-77	2.43	3.11	0.83
1977-78	2.70	3.80	0.95
1978-79	2.43	3.38	0.94
1979-80	2.62	2.26	0.83
1980-81	2.80	2.94	0.88
1981-82	2.93	4.80	1.03
1982-83	3.05	4.30	0.99
1983-84	3.59	3.91	1.03
1984-85	3.55	4.56	1.80
1985-86	3.31	5.15	1.13
1986-87	3.33	5.58	1.98
1987-88	6.55	6.93	9.78
1988-89	7.90	7.69	9.48
1989-90	8.37	7.87	10.10
1990-91	8.88	7.30	10.58
1991-92	8.39	7.06	10.54
1992-93	9.31	5.90	13.74
1993-94	0.39	6.37	12.05
1994-95	8.91	6.68	11.77

Source: Defence Service Estimates - various years.

CAP. Exp. = Capital Expenditure

Note: Figure don't tally because there are some other heads of defence expenditure. Figures don't tally because many expenditure items remain unclassified and also due to changes in basic definitions, accounting methods etc. in defence budget.

Graph 10

Def. Cap. Exp. Services Breakup As % of Total Defence Exp.

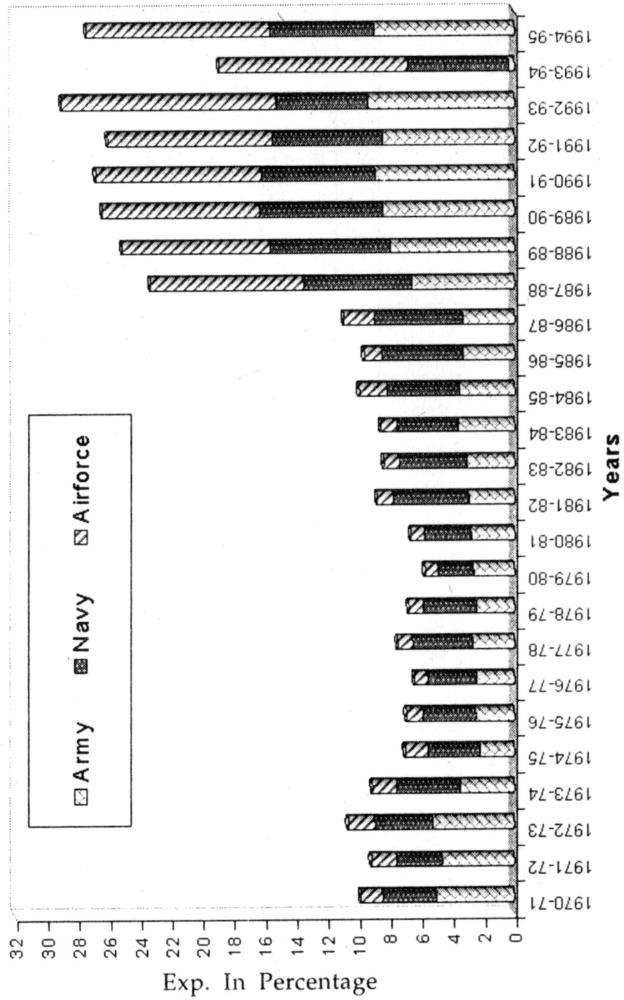

Table 31
Interwise Breakup of Defence Expenditure

(Rs. Crores in Current Price)

Year	Pay & Allow.	Pay & Allow. as % of TDE.	Store	Store As % of TDE.	Trans Port	Trans. as % of TDE.	Ordi-Nance Pacto RIES	O.F. as of TDE.	R & D	R & D % of TDE
1	2	3	4	5	6	7	8	9	10	11
1970-71	423.90	35.30	352.50	29.40	39.70	3.30	130.70	10.90	16.20	1.40
1971-72	441.80	29.00	541.40	35.50	60.50	4.00	194.80	12.80	18.80	1.20
1972-73	478.20	28.90	531.60	32.20	55.50	3.40	250.30	15.10	23.80	1.40
1973-74	573.70	31.20	543.30	32.60	50.00	3.30	235.70	14.00	30.00	1.80
1974-75	789.10	37.40	658.20	31.20	48.90	2.30	261.80	12.40	36.10	1.70
1975-76	869.00	35.10	746.80	30.20	61.10	2.50	368.30	14.90	48.30	2.00
1976-77	875.60	34.20	732.90	30.60	70.70	2.80	418.80	16.30	46.40	1.80
1977-78	885.80	33.60	785.90	29.80	72.90	2.80	395.50	15.00	47.60	1.80
1978-79	927.80	32.30	383.40	31.80	63.20	2.20	448.60	15.60	61.50	2.10
1979-80	947.90	29.10	1160.30	34.60	61.70	1.80	517.70	15.40	92.10	2.70
1980-81	1103.90	28.50	1304.60	33.70	58.30	1.50	614.90	15.90	74.20	1.90
1981-82	1231.50	26.50	1563.10	33.60	71.70	1.50	724.80	15.60	95.10	2.00
1982-83	1440.30	26.60	1902.90	35.20	86.90	1.60	749.00	13.80	113.80	2.10

1983-84	1704.00	27.00	2157.10	34.20	104.10	1.60	797.40	12.60	148.70	2.40
1984-85	2028.00	30.40	2374.00	35.60	125.00	1.90	853.00	12.80	188.00	2.80
1985-86	2347.00	29.90	2860.50	36.40	128.20	1.60	955.00	12.10	256.00	3.30
1986-87	2920.00	27.70	3507.20	40.20	133.00	1.30	1183.00	13.30	368.00	4.20
1987-88	3112.30	26.06	4658.50	38.92	259.20	2.50	383.00	3.20	464.80	5.50
1988-89	3851.10	28.96	4178.20	31.42	283.60	2.80	452.20	3.20	577.78	4.33
1989-90	3886.40	26.80	4280.70	29.52	280.30	2.60	538.00	3.70	607.67	4.19
1990-91	4273.00	27.70	5163.57	33.47	191.23	2.50	523.42	3.40	670.23	4.34
1991-92	4573.80	27.98	4964.00	30.37	254.71	1.60	307.12	1.90	682.86	4.17
1992-93	4732.46	26.92	5435.05	30.92	309.18	1.80	571.06	3.30	788.26	4.48
1993-94	5130.08	23.95	6654.90	30.47	554.83	2.60	471.18	3.40	1046.00	4.86
1994-95	5520.95	23.75	6358.75	27.36	599.15	2.30	621.36	2.70	1175.00	5.10

Source: Defence Service Estimates - various years.

Note: Figure don't tally because there are some other heads of defence expenditure. Figures don't tally because many expenditure items remain unclassified and also due to changes in basic definitions, accounting methods etc. in defence budget.

The store takes the maximum share in TDE followed by the pay and allowances, ordnance factories, Research and Development and Transport. The percentage share of pay and allowances is on decreasing trend. This may be due to the rationalisation measures of the Army. The store indicates the highest percentage share in the year 1986-87 which was 40.20 per cent. The store has shown gradual increase in its share during the period under study. This can be attributed to the purchase of new equipments and maintenance of them. The transport expenditure has more or less remained around 2 per cent of the total defence expenditure. There are no drastic changes in it. The share of ordnance factories remained constant around 13-15 per cent for the period 1970-71 to 1986-87. Since 1986-87 there is domestic decline to 3.20 per cent of total defence expenditure. This was mainly due to the reason that since 1987-88 a separate demand for ordnance factories has been opened in the defence service estimates/ budget. The Research and Development expenditure was around 1.5 to 2 per cent of total defence expenditure till 1986-87. Since 1987-88 it has remained above 4 per cent of total defence expenditure. This was mainly due to the fact that Indian Government gave more weightage to this area and self-reliance programme.

CHAPTER 10

Conclusion

This book Defence/service in India sought to introduce relatively new perspective to the understanding of defence expenditures in the analysis of defence expenditures with special reference to India.

Traditionally defence expenditure analysis has to date to restrict itself to expenditure on military *per se* which would imply that analysis of defence budget would provide an adequate amount of data for the understanding problems of resource allocations for defence in any country by and large.

It begins with the realisation that it is necessary to redefine the approach to defence expenditure. This redefinition would be based on two important considerations. One is the nature of threat perceptions that has changed over the period and secondly the approach to tackling these threats also has changed over the same period of time.

The argument made in this book has been over the years the critical threats to internal security have shifted from problems of border wars/traditional conflicts or conventional wars. This shift indicates that approaches to tackling the problems of security have also to be modified, implicitly the modification would include the ways and means of tackling these threats. Another dimension of change in the threat perception is the overall modernisation especially in the area of science and technology. These are taking place in the nature or approaches. Weapon systems are becoming increasingly more and more sophisticated, technologically. Therefore, the ways and means of tackling problems of threats would not only include change in the policy perceptions but that would also include the change in hardware of tackling these threats.

Therefore the book starts with redefinition of defence expenditure. This redefinition seeks to include expenditures related to internal security and expenditures resulted to science and technology in the understanding or the comprehension of defence expenditure. The central argument here is:

(a) given the growth of problem of internal security, the forces/means used to tackle the problems of internal security must be accounted. In the Indian case the forces would include paramilitary, police, intelligence etc.

(b) Given the technological changes and increasing incorporation of new technologies in defence, it is necessary to identify such areas of technology which relate to defence and which at the same time have basically been civilian technologies. It is in that context this redefinition of defence expenditure incorporates dual purpose technologies specifically nuclear, space, telecommunication, electronics etc. And the consideration of this expenditure was made to comprehend the problem of defence resource allocations. Given this central argument the book presents following main points:

(i) India's defence expenditure would be dependent upon nature of Internal and External Security threats on the one hand and economic capability on the other hand. In the Indian context it is seen that in 1980s internal security threats become more dominant and important. The thrust of modernisation so begins in 1980s in the areas of Science & Technology and these both are reflected in the expenditure patterns in these two sectors. The growth in the expenditures on internal security and also the growth in the expenditures in dual purpose technology areas need to be understood in this changing security environment of 1980s. The rate of growth of internal security expenditure was 6.57 per cent per annum at (1980-81) prices and in the dual purpose technology areas it ranges from 5.32 per cent per annum to 13.96 per cent per annum at (1980-81) prices. The growth rate in these areas has in chapter 8. India has developed dual purpose technology areas especially from 1980s.

(ii) The study of the expenditure charts in the chapter 9 show that the share of Army in total defence expenditure declined continuously, the share of Navy and Air Force are increasing during the period of study. This can be understood in the context of two things:

(a) The shift from external threat to internal threats made it necessary for security expenditure to divert more towards internal security and the role of Army remained almost constant without any new problems of conventional war/border war.

(b) The Navy and Air Force on the other hand were traditionally not given the due share in defence expenditure. Further both these saw rapid change in technology and in corporation of new technologies in these areas required additional expenditures and therefore they started getting more share than before in defence expenditure.

(iii) India's defence expenditure in current prices started rising at a faster rate from 1982-83 onwards. The higher rate of growth was in the year 1986-87 when defence expenditure grew by a record 31.17 per cent in one year as compared to previous year. Then onwards, the annual rate of growth in defence expenditure has been coming down.

(iv) Analysis of itemwise defence expenditure indicates that 'stores gets the maximum share, followed by 'pay and allowances'.

(v) In the period 1984-85 to 1988-89 defence expenditure showed the highest exponential growth rate. Simultaneously the nuclear, space, science and technology as dual purpose technology areas marked the highest exponential growth rate at constant prices, i.e. (1980-81) prices in this period. It shows that India strengthened defence and dual purpose technology areas simultaneously in 1980s. but after 1987-88 it is possibly experiencing a 'resource crunch'.

(vi) One finds that annual defence budget do not sometimes reflect a realistic picture of military operations which take place within the country and across the border, e.g. the IPKF operations expenditure is not reflected in the defence budgets of those years. Therefore, Defence Service Estimates need to be more transparent, more standardised, more realistic and methodological. But of course not sacrificing the secrecy and confidentiality. The confidentiality should not lead to illogic on obscurity.

(vii) Defence expenditure and Interest payments are two main items of non-development expenditure in India. During the study period the interest payments are increasing at the faster rate than the defence expenditure.

(viii) GDP growth rate and defence expenditure have correcation. The increase in defence expenditure seems to have coincided with higher GDP growth rates.

(ix) There is a decline in the share of defence expenditure as a part of this Central Government Expenditure and Total Government Expenditure (Central + States + Union Territories Government expenditure) during the study period. This has been explained with the help of determinants of defence budget especially the indicators of internal and external security parameters.

(x) In the 1990s several changes took place at global level which eventually had impact on India's economic policy. The process of economic liberalisation began in India in 1990s and has had an impact on defence sector. This impact has been seen mainly in the reduction in the real resources for defence which is known as 'resource crunch'. This impact has also been seen mainly in the areas of Science and Technology expenditures and actual defence expenditure. Given the fact that some of the crucial developments in the area of Science and Technology especially in the sectors of nuclear, space and electronics have taken place in the civil sectors/civil laboratories and not in the defence DRDO laboratories, the liberalisation process would have certain impact on this civilian sectors. Over the last few years the defence sector in India is opening up to this facet of liberalisation and seeking to incorporate the developments from the civilian sector in to the defence sector.

Hence an expenditure analysis of resource allocation might be an insufficient indicator to understand this growing interaction. It would suffice to say that changing allocations in this sector do not indicate the growing interaction between defence and civilian sector especially in the context of modernisation of defence forces. It is perhaps be necessary to add in this context that the decisions to open up in the areas of defence export and decision to export weapon and weapon system by India is also indicative of the impact of process of liberalisation. The civil military interactions in near further are bound to increase considerably taking into account private sector in initiative in defence related production industries. India needs a more professional and realistic approach for this.

This book on analyses is threat perceptions, decision-making processes and economics of defence is essentially the beginning in the direction or rethinking on the approaches to defence expenditure. It would definitely be worthily to take up each of dual purpose technology areas especially nuclear, space, electronics and paramilitary and study them individually to find that the degree to which these areas constitute an input into National Security.

This Thesis attempts only a beginning in the Indian context. It attempts to layout a framework for analysis of defence expenditure which is border than traditional framework and as such, it follows some of the new definitions of defence expenditure which are being articulated at the international level especially by international organisations like United Nations Organisation, SIPRI, IMF etc.

Bibliography

Primary Sources

Government Documents and Official Publications

A Kashmir Story, Ministry of Information and Broadcasting (Publication Division), Government of India, New Delhi, 1991.

A Report of Comptroller and Auditor General of India; India Appropriation Accounts, Ministry of Finance, Government of India, New Delhi (1970-71 to 1994-95).

An Unrest in Assam, Ministry of Information and Broadcasting (Publication Division), Government of India, New Delhi, 1986.

Annual Plans, Ministry of Planning, Government of India, New Delhi (1970-71 to 1994-95).

Annual Report, Department of Atomic Energy, Government of India, New Delhi (1970-71 to 1994-95).

Annual Report, Department of Electronics, Government of India, New Delhi (1970-71 to 1994-95).

Annual Report, Department of Ocean Development, Government of India, New Delhi (1970-71 to 1994-95).

Annual Report, Department of Science & Technology, Government of India, New Delhi (1970-71 to 1994-95).

Annual Report, Department of Space, government of India, New Delhi (1970-71 to 1994-95).

Annual Report, Ministry of Defence, Government of India, New Delhi (1970-71 to 1994-95).

Annual Report, Ministry of External Affairs, Government of India, New Delhi (1970-71 to 1994-95).

Annual Report, Ministry of Home Affairs, Government of India, New Delhi (170-71 to 1994-95).

Central Statistical Organisation Reports, Department of Statistics, Government of India, New Delhi (for various years).

Data India Weekly Event Diary, Press Trust of India, Government of India, New Delhi (for various years).

Defence Research and Development - Major Projects, Ministry of Defence, New Delhi, Lok Sabha Secretariat, Government of India, 1986.

Defence Service Estimates, Ministry of Defence, Government of India, New Delhi (1970-71 to 1994-95).

Economic Survey, Ministry of Finance, Government of India, New Delhi (1970-1995).

Estimates Committee 19th Report of 10th Lok Sabha, Ministry of Defence, Lok Sabha Secretariat, New Delhi.

Fifth Report of Standing Committee on Defence 1995-96, Ministry of Defence (New Delhi: Government of India).

Five-year Plans (4th plan to 8th plan), Ministry of Planning, Government of India, New Delhi.

India – Reference Annual (Year Book), Ministry of Information and Broadcasting (Publication Division), Government of India, New Delhi (for various years).

India Budget, Ministry of Finance, Government of India, New Delhi (1970-71 to 1994-95).

National Income Accounts, Statistics Department of Statistics, Government of India, New Delhi (for various years).

Public Accounts Committee Report, Ministry of Finance, Government of India, New Delhi, for various years.

Reserve Bank of India – *Report on Currency and Finance* Ministry of Finance, Government of India, New Delhi (170-71 to 1994-95).

Statistical Outline of India, Ministry of Statistics, Government of India, New Delhi (for various years).

World Military Expenditure and Arms Transfers, U.S. Government, Arms Control and Disarmament Agency, Washington D.C. (for various years).

Institutional Sources and other Sources

Encyclopedia of Economics, New York (1982).

Herrara Remy *Statistics on Military Expenditure in developing countries: concepts, Methodological problems and sources,* OECD Document, Paris, 1991.

Institute for Defence Studies and Analysis (IDSA) *Asian Strategic Review* and other various publications for various years, New Delhi.

International Encyclopedia of *Social Sciences,* New York (1968).

International Institute of Strategic Studies (IISS) various publications including *Military Balance,* London.

Kissing's Contemporary Archives for various years.

Stockholm International Peace and Research Institute, *SIPRI year* book and other publications, Stockholm.

World Bank, *World Development Report* (Annual), New York.

Books

Agarwal, Rajesh K., *Defence Production and Development* (New Delhi: Gulab Vazirani for Arnold-Heinemann Publishers, 1978).

Akashi, Yasashi, *UN Disarmament Topical Papers 2: Science & Technology and their Implications for Peace and Security* (New York: UNO, 1990).

Athawale, Sanhita, *India's Indian Ocean, Islands* (New Delhi: ABC Publication House, 1991).

Ball, Nicole, *The Military in the Development Process* (Claremount, California: Regina Books, 1981).

Baran, Paul A. and Sweezy, Paul A., *Monopoly Capital* (London: Penguin, 1968).

Barnwal, S.P., *Military Year Book (1980-85)* (New Delhi: Guide Publication 1980-85).

Becker, Abrahman, *Military Expenditures Limitations for Arms Control: Problems and Prospects* (Cambridge: Ballinger Publishing Company, 1978).

Benoit, Emile, *Defence and Economic Growth in Developing Countries* (Lexington, 1978).

Braun, D. *Indian Ocean: Region of Peace or Zone of Conflict* (New Delhi: Oxford University Press (1983).

Brown, Herald, *Thinking about National Security* (Colorado: West View Press, 1983).

Clark, J.J., *New Economics of National Defence* (New York: Random House, 1966).

Collins, J.M. *How to Analyse National Security: Conceptual Frame Work of US Defence Planning – A Critique* (New York: West View Press, 1982).

Deger, S. and Sen, S., *Military Expenditure in the Third World Countries: The Economic Effects* (London: Routledge and Kegan Paul, 1986).

Deger, Saadet and West, Robert. (eds.), *Defence Security and Development* (London: Frances (Pinter) Publishers 1987).

Dumas, Llyod J. (ed.), *The Political Economy of Arms Reduction: Reversing Economic Decay* (Colorado: Westview Press, Inc., 1982).

Falk, Richward A., and others (eds.), *Disarmament and Economic Development* (New York: Work Law Fund, 1966).

Frank, Trager and Konnenberg, P.S. (eds.), *National Security and American Society* (Manhatten: Routledge, 1973).

Garnett, John (ed)., *Theories of Peace and Security* (London: MacMillan and St. Martin's Press, 1970).

Ghosh, Ameya, *India's Defence Budget and Expenditure Management in a Wider Context* (New Delhi: Lancer Publishers and Spantech, 1996).

Handa, Rohit *Policy for India's Defence* (New Delhi: Chetana Publications, 1976).

Hefferman, Patrick O. (ed.), *Defence Sense: The Search for a Rational Military Policy* (Cambridge Massachusetts, Ballinger Publishing Company, A Subsidiary of Harper Row, Publishers, Inc., 1983).

Herrera, Remy, *Statistics on Military Expenditure in Developing Countries,* OECD (Organisation for Economic Cooperation and Development), Document, Paris, 1994.

Hitch, Charles J., and McKean, Ronald N., *The Economics of Defence in the Nuclear Age* (Cambridge, Mass: Harvard University Press, 1960).

Jain, J.P., *Nuclear India* (New Delhi: Radiant Publications, 1974).

John, Cullins and Philip Jones, *Public Finance and Public Choice: Analytical Perspective* (London: McGraw-Hill Book Company, 1992).

Kamble, P.R., *Kautilya's Arthasastra* (Delhi: Motilal Banarsidas, 1965).

Kapur, A., *India's Nuclear Option Atomic Diplomacy and Decision Making* (New York: Praeger 1976).

Katz, J.N. (ed), *Arms Production in Developing Countries: An Analysis of Decision-Making,* Lexington: Lexington Books, 1984).

Kaul, R. *India's Nuclear Spin-Off* (Allahabad: Chanakya Publications, 1974).

Kavic, L., *India's Quest for Security Defence Policies 1947-65* (California: University of Calif. Press, 1967).

Kennedy, Gavin, *Defence Economics* (London: Gerald Duckworth & Co. Ltd., 1983).

Kennedy, Gavin, *The Military and the Third World* (London: Gerald Duckworth and Co. Ltd., 1974).

Keynes, J.M., *How to Pay for War* (New York: Harcourt Brace, 1940).

Khanna, D.D. and Mehrotra, P.N., *Defence Versus Development: A Case Study of India,* (New Delhi: Indus Publication Company, 1993).

Khera, S.S., *India's Defence Problems* (Bombay: Orient Longman, 1968).

Knorr, Klaus, *The War Potential of Nations* (New York: Princetone Press, 1956).

Kohali, S.N., *Sea Power and the Indian Ocean* (New Delhi: Tata McGraw Hill, 1978).

Kukreja, Veena, *Civil Military Relations in South Asia: Pakistan, Bangladesh, India* (New Delhi: Sage Publications, 1991).

Lakshmi, Y., *Trends in India's Defence Expenditure* (New Delhi: ABC Publishing House, 1988).

Lipmann, Walter, *US Foreign Policy Shield of the Republic* (Boston: Little, 1943).

Major, Istvan (ed.), *Militarization, Military Conflicts and its Economic Implications* (New Delhi: Hungarian Cultural Centre, 1984).

Mathew, T., *Economics of Public Expenditure* (Bombay: Vora and Company, Publishers Pvt. Ltd., 1972).

Mathews, Ron, *Defence Production in India* (New Delhi: ABC Publishing House, 1989).

Mathur, K.D. and Kamath, P.M., *Conduct of India's Foreign Policy* (New Delhi: South Asian Publishers Pvt. Ltd., 1996).

McKidlay, Robert, *Third World Military Expenditure Determination and Implications* (London: Printer Publishers, 1989).

Musgrave, R. and Musgrave P., *Public Finance in Theory and Practice,* 5th edition (Singapore: McGraw Hill Book Company, 1989).

Nanda, Ravi, *National Security Perspective Policy and Planning* (New Delhi: Lancer Books, 1991).

Nath Rajendra and others (eds.), *India's Security: Threats and Strategies* (Chandigarh: Panchnad Research Institute, 1990).

Olvey, L., Golden, J. and Kelly, Robart, *The Economics of National Security: Weighing the Costs of Defence* (New Jersey: Avery Publishing Group Inc., 1984).

Raghwan, V.R., *India's Need for Strategic Balance* (New Delhi: Delhi Policy Group Publications, 1995).

Rao, PVR, *India's Defence Policy and Organisation Since Independence* (New Delhi: United Service Institute of India Publications, 1976).

Rao, Rama, *Self-Reliance and Security: Role of Defence Production* (New Delhi: Radiant Publishers, 1984).

Schelessinger, James R. *The Political Economy of National Security* (London: Atlantic Books, 1960).

Schmidt, C. and Blackbay, Frank (eds.), *Peace, Defence and Economic Analysis* (New York: St. Martin's Press, 1987).

Steve, Chan and Alex, Mintz (eds.) *Defence, Welfare and Growth: Perspective and Evidence* (New York: Routledge and Kegan, 1992).

Singh, Bhupindar, *Indian Ocean and Regional Security* (Patiala: B.C. Publishers, 1983).

Smith, Chris, *India's Ad-Hoc Arsenal: Direction or Drift in Defence Policy* (New York: Oxford University Press, 1994).

Subramanyam, K., *Defence and Development* (Calcutta: The Minerva Associates, 1973).

Subramanyam, K., *India's Security Perspective, Policy and Planning* (New Delhi: Lancer Books, 1991).

Subrahmanyam, R.R., *Defence and Nuclear Tangle in South Asia* (New Delhi: ABC Publishing House, 1989).

Thomas, Raju, G.C., *Indian Security Policy* (Princeton, New Jersey: University Press, 1986).

Thomas, Raju, G.C., *The Defence* of India: *A Budgetary Perspective of Strategy and Politics* (Meerut: The Macmillan Company of India Limited, 1978).

Tinbergern, J. Fisher, *Warfare and Welfare: Integrating Security Policy into Socio-Economic Policy* (New York: Brighton and St. Martins Press, 1987).

Tuomi and others (eds.), *Militarization and Arms Production* (New York: St. Martins Press, 1983).

Whynes, David, *The Economics of Third World Military Expenditure* (London: The Macmillan Press, 1979).

Wolfers, Arnold, *Discord and Collaboration: Essays on International Politics* (Baltimore, 1962).

Articles and Periodicals

Aneja, Atul, "LCA – A Technological Leap", *The Hindu* (Madras), Jan, 28, 1993.

Balchandran, G., "India's Defence Expenditure in the 1980", *Strategic Analysis,* Vol. 14., Nov. 1991.

Ball, Nicole, "Defence and Development: A Critique of the Benoits Study", *Economic Development and Cultural Change,* 3rd April 1983.

Banerjee, D., "Arms Self-Sufficiency: An Indian Perspective", *Strategic Analysis* (New Delhi), Vol. XIII, No. 6, Sept. 1990.

Banerjee, D., "The Asia-Pacific Region in 1990s" *Strategic Analysis,* Vol. XIII, No. 5, August 1990.

Bansal, Poonam, "India's Defence Expenditure in Perspective", *Southern Economics,* 15 December 1985.

Basu, Biman, "Kalpakkam: A milestone in India's Nuclear Quest", *India and Foreign Affairs* (New York), Vol. 23, No. 6, 15 January 1986.

Benoit, Emile, "Growth and Defence in Developing Countries", *Economic Development and Cultural Changes,* 26 January 1978.

Beri, Ruchita, "Ballistic Missile proliferation", *Asian Strategic Review 1991-92* (New Delhi: IDSA) 1992.

Bhatia, A., "India's Space Programme — Cause for Concern?", *Asian Survey,* Vol. 15, No. 10, Oct., 1985.

Biswas, B. and Rati, Ram, "Military Expenditure and Economic Growth – An Augmented Model for Future Evidence", *Economic Development and Cultural Changes,* Vol. 34, No. 2, University of Chicago Press, January 1985.

Chaudhary, A.R., "Casual Analysis of Defence Spending and Economic Growth", *Journal of Conflict Resolution,* Vol. 35 No. 1, March 1991.

Chibber, M.L., "The Rationalisation of Paramilitary Forces", *Indian Defence Review* (New Delhi, Lancer In International), Vol. II, - 1, January 1987.

Data, Savita, "China the Emerging Nuclear Power: A Review", *Strategic Analysis,* Vol 5, August 1993, New Delhi.

Deger, S., and Sen, Somnath, "Military Expenditure—Spin Offs and Economic Development", *Journal of Development Economics,* Vol. 13, 1983.

Deger, S., and Smith, Ron, "Military Expenditure and Growth in Less Developed Countries", *Journal of Conflict Resolution,* 1983.

Dunne, P., Symposium on "The Political Economy of Military Expenditure" *Cambridge Journal of Economics,* Vol. 14, No. 4, December 1990.

Fredriksen, P.C. and R.E. Looney, "Defence Expenditure, External Public Debt and Growth in Developing Countries", *Journal of Peace Research,* Vol. 23, No. 1, 1986.

Fredriksen, P.C. and R.E. Looney, "Defence Expenditure and Economic Growth in Developing Countries", *Armed Forces and Society,* No. 9, Summer, 1983.

Gandhi, Ved, "India's Self-Inflicted Burden", *Economic and Political Weekly,* 31 August, 1974.

Gopalraj, N., "From Sounding Rockets to Satellites" *Front Line* (Madras, Vol. 3, No. 21, October 1986).

Grant, N.B., "Military Budgeting and National Security", *Indian Defence Review,* Vol., 1, January 1987.

Gupta, S., "The Indian Army: Asking for More", *India Today,* Vol. 10, No. 2, 31 January 1985.

Hazari, K.K., "The Resource Crunch and Defence Management: Sustaining and Modernising the Army in keeping with Security Commitments", *Indian Defence Review* (New Delhi, Lancer International), January 1992.

Hewitt, Daniel, "I.M.F. Study Examines Costs of Military Spending" *Southern Economist,* Vol. 30, No. 6, July 15, 1991.

Hewitt, Daniel, "Military Expenditures in the Developing World", *Finance and Development* (New York), September 1991.

Jacob, G., "India's Army", *Asian Defence Journal* (New York), No. 9, Sept. 1985.

Joerding, W., "Economic Growth and Defence Expenditure", *Economic Development and Cultural Change,* Vol. 35, No. 1, October 1986.

Joshi, Manoj, "Defence Demands: A Close Look at the Outlay", *Frontline* (Madras, M/s. Kasturi and Sons Ltd.,) Vol. 8, No. 16, August 1991.

Kaldor, M., "The Military in Development", *World Development,* Vol. 4, No. 6, June 1976.

Kamath, P.V. "Concept of Human Rights and National Security Constraints: Post-War Experience". *Strategic Analysis,* Vol. XIV, No. 9, Dec.. 1991.

Kapoor, B.D., "Economy in Defence Finance through Better Management", *Indian Defence Review* (New Delhi, Lancer International), January 1992.

Katoch, C.G., "Defence Expenditure: Some Issues," *Indian Defence Review* (New Delhi, Lancer International), January 1992.

Kumar, Rajiv, "Defence Production in the Private Sector", *U.S.I. Journal* (New Delhi, USI), Vol. CXXXI, No. 503, Jan.-March 1991.

Lakshmi, Y., "Defence and Development: An Empirical Study of India" *Strategic Analysis,* Vol. 9, No. 11, February 1986.

Lim, David, "Another look at Growth and Defence in less Developed Countries", *Economic Development and Cultural Change,* No. 31, 1983.

Looney, Robert, "Defence Expenditure: External Public Debt and Growth in Developing Countries", *Journal of Peace Research,* Vol. 26, No. 1, 1989.

Looney, Robert, "Impact of Arms Production on Income Distribution and Growth in the Third World", *Journal Economic Development and Cultural Change,* Vol. 38, No. 1, Oct 1989.

Looney, Robert, "Internal and External Factors Affecting Third World Military Expenditure", *Journal of Peace Research,* January 1989.

Madhok, V.K., "Gulf War and Indian Armed Forces", *USI Journal,* Jan-March 1991 (New Delhi).

Mahapatra, Chintamani, "Indo-US Defence Co-operation: Problems and Prospectus", *Strategic Analysis.* Vol. XIII, No. I, April 1990.

Malik, V.P., "Defence Planning System in India" *Strategic Analysis* Vol. XIII, No. I, April 1990.

Mathew, Thomas (ed), "Internal Affairs — IDR Comments, "*Indian Defence Review* (New Delhi: Lancer International), Vol. 1, Alpha, January 1988.

Mathew, Thomas (ed), "Terrorism IDR Comment", *Indian Defence Review,* Vol. I, 2 July 1986.

Mohan, Raja, "India's Nuclear Diplomacy: The Need for Clarity", *Strategic Analysis,* Vol. 10, No. 3, June 1986.

Nagratnam, A., "Professor Daulat Singh Kothari: A Profile", *Defence Science Journal,* Vol. 44, No. 3 (New Delhi, July 1994).

Naik, M.B., "The Defence Budget", *Janata,* Vol. 45, No. 13, Bombay, May 13, 1990.

Namboodri, P.K.S., "China-Pakistan Nuclear Axis, *Strategic Analysis,* Vol. No. 7, October 1982.

Namboodri, P.K.S., "Pakistan and Nuclear Weapons", *Strategic Digest* (New Delhi, IDSA), Vol. 19, No. 1, January 1989.

Narain, Veer, "Military Expenditure and the Poor" *Indian Defence Review* (New Delhi, Lancer International) January 1992.

Paranjape, H.K., "How Much Defence Can India Afford?", *Mainstream,* Vol. XXVIII, No. 28, May 5, 1990.

Paranjpe, S.B., "India's Defence Policy: New Perspectives", *Journal of Strategic Studies,* Vol. XVII, Allahabad, University of Allahabad, 1992.

Paranjpe, Shrikant, "Beyond the Defence and Development Debate: A Framework for Analysis of Indian Defence Expenditure", *Mondes en Development — Economics, politics and Statistics Quarterly* (ISMEA, Paris), Vol. 21, No. 3, 1993.

Paranjpe, Shrikant, "Deference Expenditure in India: Some Explorations in the Context of Changing Perceptions about Security", *Mainstream,* Vol. XXIX, No. 51, Oct. 12, 1991.

Pende, K.S., "India's Defence and Development" *Indian Journal of Strategic Studies* (Allahabad, Allahabad University), Vol. XVIII, 1993.

Pendse, K.S., "India's Defence Budget — A Case for Better Planning", *India Defence Review,* Vol. XV, No. 6, New Delhi, Lancer International), July 1989.

Pradhan, Pradyot, "Indian Security Environment in the 1990s –External Dimension", *Strategic Analysis,* Vol. XII, No. 6, Sept. 1989.

Prasad, B.A., "Restructuring Forces to Combat Threats to Internal Security", *Strategic Analysis,* Vol. XIV No. 9, Dec. 1991.

Raja, Mohan C., "India's Strategic Environment in 1990s", *Strategic Analysis,* Vol. XIII, No. I, April 1990.'

Rajeev, P.V., "The New Economic Environment and India's Defence Strategy", *Strategic Analysis,* Vol. XIV, No. 8, Nov. 1991.

Rane, A.M., "Dismal Aspects of Military Expenditure", *The Radical Humanist,* Vol. 51, No. 12. March 1988.

Rao, B.N., "Defence Production in the Private Sector", *USI Journal* (New Delhi, USI), Vol. CXXXI, No. 504, April-June, 1991.

Roy, Chaudhari Rahul Roy, "Defence Production in India" *Asian Strategic Review, 94-95* (New Delhi: IDS), 1995.

Samuelson, P.A., "Aspects of Public Expenditure Theories", *The Review of Economics and Statistics,* Vol. XL, No. 4, November 1958.

Samuelson, P.A., "Diagrammatic Exposition of a Theory of Public Expenditure" *The Review of Economics and Statistics,* Vol. 37, No. 4, Nov. 1995.

Satish, M. "Defence Spending: Why It Must be Increased?" *Economic Times* (Bombay), 11 April 1992.

Sharma, G.S. (ed), *R & D. Special Digest* (New Delhi), Jan. 1984.

Shrivastav, H.K., Vital Factors in India's Strategic Planning. *Indian Journal of Strategic Studies,* Vol. XVIII, Allahabad: University of Allahabad).

Siddiqui, A.R., "Let Us keep our Nuclear Option Open", *Defence Journal,* Vol. XII, No. 8, 1986.

Singh, Jasjit, "Defending India in the 21st Century Issues of Affordability and Credibility," *Strategic Analysis,* Vol. XIX, No. 7, Oct. 1996.

Singh, Jasjit, "India's Strategic and Security Perspectives", *Strategic Analysis* (New Delhi, IDSA), Vol. XIII, No. 5, August 1990.

Singh, Jasjit, "Trends in Defence Expenditure", *Asian Strategic Review 1991-92* (New Delhi, IDSA).

Singh, N., "Indian Security Perspectives", *Strategic Analysis,* Vol. 21 No. 5, August 1987.

Singh, N., "South Asian Security: The China, Pakistan—Indian Tangle", *Strategic Analysis,* October 1988.

Singh, Ravinder Pal, "Post-Cold War Dual Use Technology Transfer Order: Policy implications for India", *Strategic Analysis* (New Delhi, IDSA), Vol. XIV, No. 10, Jan, 1982.

Singh, Ravinder Pal, "Trans Century Technologies", *Strategic Analysis,* Vol. XIV, No. 4, New Delhi, July 1991.

Singh, Ravinder Pal, "Politics of Technology Transfers and Industrial Development", Vol. XVI, No. 5, August 1993.

Sinha, "Higher Defence Organisation" *U.S.I. Journal,* Vol. CXI, No. 503 (New Delhi, U.S.I.,) Jan. March 1991.

Smith, R.P., "Military Expenditure and Capitalism", *Cambridge Journal of Economics,* No. 1977.

Sreedhar, "Defence and Development: India's Dilemma for the 1990s", *Strategic Analysis* (New Delhi, IDSA) Vol. 14, No.11, Feb. 1991.

Sreedhar, "Defence Expenditure During the Rajiv Gandhi's Years" *Strategic Analysis,* Vol. XIII, No. II, June 1990.

Stoban, P., "Kashmir Key Issues" *Strategic Analysis* Vol. XVII, No. 1, April 1996.

Tehral, P., "Guns or Grain: Macro Economic Cost of Indian Defence, 1960-70", *Economic and Political Weekly,* No. 49 (December 5, 1981).

US Government, Arms Control and Disarmament Agency, *World Military Expenditures and Arms Transfers: 1989* (Washington DC, 1990).

Verghese, B.G., "Forward Look for Defence", *Monthly Commentary on Indian Economic Condition,* April 1986, Vol. 27, no .9.

Vittal, N., "Dual Use Technologies: Challenges and Choices", *Strategic Analysis,* Vol. CVI, No. 5, August 1993.

Whisker, Sandeep "National Security Council – The Decisive Edge', *Illustrated Weekly of India,* 30th Sept. 1990.

Zuberi, H., and S. Kalyan Raman, "Science and Technology for Development: India's Space Programme" *Strategic Analysis,* Vol. XVII, No. 11, February 1995 (New Delhi: IDSA Publication).

Newspapers

Hindustan Times (New Delhi), 15 October, 1978.

International Herald Tribune (London), 17 June, 1988.

Tarun Bharat (Pune), 29 May, 1996.

The Hindu (The) (Madras), 28 January, 1993.

Times of India (Bombay), 1 January, 1996.

Times of India (Bombay), 24 January 1991.

Index

❑❑❑